365 Amazing Chicken Breast Recipes

(365 Amazing Chicken Breast Recipes - Volume 1)

Eva Rabe

Content

365 Awesome Chicken Breast Recipes

***

1. 001 Chicken And Rice Recipe

Serving: 4 | Prep: | Cook: 60mins | Ready in:

Ingredients

- 4 chicken breast (boneless)
- 1 1/2 cup of rice
- 1 can of cream of mushroom soup
- 3 3/4 cups of water
- 1 chopped onion
- 3 tablespoons of paprika
- salt & pepper to your specs

Direction

- Combine ingredients put chicken breasts on side for final step
- In a 13 x 9 baking pan coated with nonstick pam
- Mix above ingredients and finally place chicken breast on top
- Cover w/ foil
- 350 degree oven for a hr. Give or take
- Until fully cooked time may vary a little

2. 30 Minute Chicken Pomodoro Recipe

Serving: 4 | Prep: | Cook: 30mins | Ready in:

Ingredients

- 4 bone/skin less chicken breasts
- S&p to taste
- 3 T evoo
- 1 onion chopped finely
- 4 garlic cloves, minced
- 1 t dried oregano
- 1/4 t red pepper flakes
- 1 14.5 oz can diced tomatoes
- 1/3 c heavy cream
- 1/4 c chopped basil

Direction

- 1. Pat chicken dry w paper towels & season w salt & pepper. Heat one tablespoon oil in large skillet over med-high heat until just smoking. Cook chicken until golden, about 3 mins per side. Transfer to a plate.
- 2. Heat remaining oil in empty skillet over med-high heat until shimmering. Cook onion until soft about 5 mins. Add garlic, oregano, & pepper flakes & cook until fragrant, about 30 secs. Stir in tomatoes, cream, salt & bring to boil. Return chicken & any accumulated juices to skillet. Simmer, covered, until chicken is cooked through about 10 mins.
- 3. Transfer chicken to platter & tent with foil. Summer sauce, uncovered, until slightly thickened, about 5 mins. Off heat, stir in basil & season w salt & pepper. Pour sauce over chicken & serve. (Over orzo, pasta or rice)

3. ARTICHOKE SAUCE COVERED CHICKEN PASTA Recipe

Serving: 6 | Prep: | Cook: 16mins | Ready in:

Ingredients

- 2 tbsp olive oil

- 1 pound chicken breasts or tenders, cut in bite sized pieces
- 2 cloves garlic, minced
- 1/4 cup white wine
- salt and pepper to taste
- 1 15-oz can artichoke quarters, rinsed, drained, and chopped
- 1/4 cup grated Parmesan
- 1/4 cup fresh basil, chopped
- 1 box corkscrew pasta

Direction

- Cook the pasta according to directions.
- Heat the oil in a large skillet on medium-high.
- Add the chicken and cook 2-3 minutes, until browned.
- Add the garlic and cook another minute.
- Add wine, salt, pepper, and artichokes.
- Reduce the heat to a simmer and cook about 10-12 minutes, until the chicken is cooked through.
- The sauce will thicken a bit as it cooks.
- Turn the heat off and stir in the cheese and basil.
- Serve over the cooked pasta

4. ASIAGO CRUSTED CHICKEN TENDERS Recipe

Serving: 68 | Prep: | Cook: 7mins | Ready in:

Ingredients

- 6 6 oz. single lobe boneless, skinless chicken breasts cut into strips
- 1 cup panko, ground fine
- 1 cup asiago cheese, grated
- 2 tsp. dried oregano
- 2 tsp. dried parsley
- salt and pepper
- 1 cup flour
- 2 eggs
- ½ cup milk

- vegetable oil for frying
-

Direction

- Serves 6 to 8
- Heat the vegetable oil in a large frying pan to 350 F. Combine the cheese, panko, oregano, parsley and salt and pepper in a food processor and process to combine. Place the flour in a small sheet pan and the cheese mixture in another small sheet pan. Beat the eggs and milk and place in a shallow dish. Dredge each tender in the flour, shaking off any excess, then dip in the egg mixture and roll in the cheese mixture. Fry the tenders until just golden on each side, about 4 minutes. Serve with garlic basil aioli or Chipotle aioli.

5. After A Hard Day Chicken Recipe

Serving: 6 | Prep: | Cook: 15mins | Ready in:

Ingredients

- 1 pkg. boneless,skinless chicken breasts cut in 1/2" slices
- 2 Tbs olive oil
- 1/4 c balsamic vinegar
- 1 tsp chicken bouillon dissolved in 1/4 c hot water
- 1Tbs flour

Direction

- Brown chicken in oil until meat is no longer pink. Remove chicken to serving dish. Deglaze pan with vinegar. Add bouillon and bring to boil.
- Whisk in flour and cook to thicken slightly. Drizzle hot mixture over chicken and serve.
- Variation: Add mushrooms, capers, olives or anchovies

6. Ala Creama Recipe

Serving: 4 | Prep: | Cook: 20mins | Ready in:

Ingredients

- half a chicken breast per person cut into cubes or about a cup of shrimp per person
- minced garlic to taste
- one big onion
- mushrooms
- jalapino peppers minced to taste
- red, yellow and green bellpeppers
- and any veggies you desire
- 8oz brick of cream cheese
- 8oz of sour cream
- one medium sized tomatoe
- garlic salt
- seasoning salt

Direction

- Begin cooking pasta or rice
- Fry chicken or shrimp, garlic and veggies in a pan with seasoning salt
- Boil the tomatoes until the skin splits
- In a blender put the tomatoes, cream cheese, sour cream and garlic salt to make the "cream sauce". Blend together until well creamed.
- When meat and veggies are cooked add the "cream sauce" to the pan and heat through
- Serve over pasta or rice

7. Alfredo Chicken With Cinnamon Recipe

Serving: 8 | Prep: | Cook: 20mins | Ready in:

Ingredients

- 2 lbs. chicken breast (I use tenders)
- 1 lb. box rotini
- 2 jars alfredo sauce (I use Classico)

- cinnamon
- parmesan
- pepper
- seasoning salt
- garlic salt

Direction

- Prepare pasta as directed on box, drain & set aside.
- Meanwhile season one side of chicken breast with seasoning salt & pepper.
- Place chicken in lightly oiled skillet seasoned side down and grill.
- Season top side with garlic salt.
- Grill until cooked. You may have to cook in batches. Keep warm in oven.
- Chop chicken into bite sized pieces.
- Warm sauce in large pot.
- Add pasta stirring well to coat.
- Stir in chicken.
- Season with cinnamon to taste. A few shakes. Stir well.
- Top with parmesan.
- Enjoy!

8. Alfredo Sauce Stuffed Chicken Recipe

Serving: 4 | Prep: | Cook: 30mins | Ready in:

Ingredients

- 4 bonless chicken breast (sliced thin like a cutlet)
- 1 Cup shredded part- skim or whole Mozzarella
- 5 slices of bacon (if desired) crisp cooked and crumbled
- 1 egg beaten
- 1/3 cup seasoned bread crumbs
- 2 Tbsp olive oil
- 2 cups alfredo sauce
- 1/4 cup chicken broth

- -------------------------------------
- alfredo sauce Ingredients
- -------------------------------------
- -1 pint of heavy cream
- 1 stick of butter
- 2 Tbsp cream cheese
- 1/2 - 3/4 C parmesan cheese
- 1 tsp. garlic powder
- 1/2 tsp of salt (if desired)
- 1/2 tsp black pepper (if desired)

Direction

- Top each chicken breast with cheese and bacon, roll up and secure with toothpicks.
- Dip chicken in egg then bread crumbs
- In 12 -inch or so skillet heat olive oil over medium-high heat and brown chicken, turning occasionally.
- Stir in Alfredo sauce and broth, bring to boil over high heat.
- Reduce heat to low and simmer, covered for 10 minutes or until chicken is cooked
- Directions for Alfredo Sauce

9. Alfredo Stuffed Chicken Breasts Recipe

Serving: 5 | Prep: | Cook: 45mins | Ready in:

Ingredients

- 5 Boneless, skinless chicken Breasts
- 6 Slices turkey bacon (Or your favorite Bacon)
- 10 ozs fresh spinach
- 4 cloves garlic, minced
- Half of Large onion
- 2 cans rotel diced tomatoes
- 1 jar premade alfredo sauce
- 12 oz cheese (I used mozzarella and Parmesan)
- salt an pepper, to taste
- red pepper flakes, to taste
- italian seasoning, to taste
- 2 tbs of olive oil

Direction

- Preheat oven to 375.
- Sautee garlic and onion in pan in olive oil over medium heat.
- When garlic and onion start to get soft and become fragrant, add in spinach. Let the Spinach sauté for 2-3 minutes.
- Meanwhile, begin cooking your bacon to desired doneness. When bacon is finished, drain on paper towel and let cool.
- When spinach starts to cook down, add in the rotel, season to taste with salt and pepper and cook till spinach is just about done (5-10 mins).
- Drain mixture in colander and let cool.
- Pound Chicken Breasts till they are flat. Be careful not to tear them.
- Season with salt, pepper an Italian seasoning to taste on both sides. Set aside.
- Once mixture is cool, mix in bacon and cheese.
- Lay a nice amount of mixture on top of the chicken breast. Roll and secure with toothpicks.
- Top each stuffed chicken breast with Alfredo sauce.
- Bake in the oven on 375 degrees for 45 mins or until done.
- Serve with a salad, broccoli or green beans.

10. Aneheim Chicken Recipe

Serving: 6 | Prep: | Cook: 60mins | Ready in:

Ingredients

- 2 lbs of chicken breast (boneless skinless breast strips)
- 2 yellow onions cut in thin round slices
- 1 bell pepper (green or red)- cut in thin strips, remove seeds
- 2 aneheim peppers- cut in thin strips, remove seeds
- 3/4 cup butter-melted
- Lawreys seasoning salt

Direction

- Preheat oven at 350 degrees.
- Cut up onion is thin circular slices.
- Cut up peppers in thin long slices.
- Melt your butter and add 1 teaspoon of lawreys seasoning salt to butter.
- In 9x13 pan put layer of onions down.
- Then put a layer of bell peppers and then a layer of aneheim peppers. Placing the peppers here and there onto of the onions.
- Pour 1/2 of the melted butter on top of your onion and peppers.
- Shake a thin sprinkle of Lawreys (maybe a 1 teaspoon) over the butter and onions and peppers.
- Place Chicken side by side on top of the onions and peppers.
- Put another layer of sliced onions, and peppers on top of chicken.
- Pour the remaining melted butter on top of everything.
- Sprinkle another 1 teaspoon of Lawreys on top.
- Cover with foil and cook for 1 hour. May need just an extra 10-15 min.
- It's done when the onions and peppers are very softly cooked.
- Enjoy.

11. Angel Hair Pasta With Chicken Recipe

Serving: 4 | Prep: | Cook: 20mins | Ready in:

Ingredients

- 2 T olive oil divided
- 2 chicken breasts, cubed(EASY BUTTON-left over chicken)
- 1 carrot sliced (EASY BUTTON 1/2-1 cup frozen carrot)
- 1 (10 oz) package frozen broccoli, thawed
- 2 garlic cloves minced
- 12 oz angel hair pasta
- 2/3 cup chicken broth
- 1 tsp dried basil
- 1/4 cup grated parmesan
- Shredded parmesan for garnish

Direction

- In one T olive oil, brown chicken until no longer pink.
- Drain and set aside.
- In skillet cook broccoli and carrot in olive oil, add garlic.
- Start cooking pasta according to package.
- Add chicken broth, basil and parmesan to chicken. Simmer 4 minutes.
- Drain pasta and serve with the chicken veggie mixture.
- Garnish with Shredded Parmesan

12. Apple Kissed Chicken Recipe

Serving: 4 | Prep: | Cook: 30mins | Ready in:

Ingredients

- 1/2 cup apple juice
- 3 tablespoons apple butter
- 2 tablespoons lemon juice
- 4 skinless boneless chicken breast halves
- 1/2 teaspoon adobo seasoning
- vegetable cooking spray
- 1 small white onion thinly sliced
- 1 small apple cored and cut into wedges
- 1 tablespoon corn starch
- 2 tablespoons water

Direction

- Combine first 3 ingredients in a small bowl then stir well and set aside.
- Sprinkle chicken with Adobo.
- Coat large nonstick skillet with cooking spray then place over medium high heat until hot.

- Add chicken and cook 4 minutes on each side then pour apple juice mixture over chicken.
- Top with onion slices then cover and reduce heat then simmer 10 minutes and apple wedges.
- Cover and simmer 12 minutes then transfer chicken and apple wedges to serving platter.
- Dissolve cornstarch in water in a small bowl then add to apple juice mixture stirring constantly.
- Cook over medium heat stirring constantly until mixture thickens then spoon sauce over chicken.

13. Apple And Orange Chicken Recipe

Serving: 4 | Prep: | Cook: 90mins | Ready in:

Ingredients

- 1 ounce package dry onion soup mix
- 4 chicken breasts
- 1 ounce envelope dry cream of chicken soup mix
- 2 tablespoons soy sauce
- 2 cloves crushed garlic
- 1 cup apple juice
- 1 cup orange juice
- 1/2 teaspoon salt
- 1/2 teaspoon freshly ground black pepper

Direction

- Preheat oven to 350.
- Place chicken pieces in a lightly greased rectangular baking dish.
- In medium bowl combine soup mixes, soy sauce, garlic, apple and orange juice, salt and pepper.
- Mix together and pour mixture over chicken then cover and bake 1 hour.
- Remove cover and bake 30 minutes longer to brown the chicken.

14. Artichoke Chicken Recipe

Serving: 4 | Prep: | Cook: 39mins | Ready in:

Ingredients

- 1 (15 oz) can of artichoke hearts
- 2 garlic cloves, finely chopped
- 1 cup grated parmesan cheese
- 1 cup mayonnaise (I use Hellman's)
- 4 boneless, skinless chicken breast halves

Direction

- Preheat oven to 375 degrees
- Mix together artichoke hearts, parmesan cheese, mayonnaise and garlic.
- Place chicken in a greased baking dish and cover evenly with artichoke/cheese mixture.
- Bake uncovered for 30 minutes or until chicken is cooked through.
- ENJOY!

15. Artichoke Chicken Stroganoff Recipe

Serving: 8 | Prep: | Cook: 15mins | Ready in:

Ingredients

- 4 (6 ounce) jars marinated artichoke hearts, drained
- 8 chicken breast halves, skinned, boned and cut into strips.
- 1 cup chopped onion
- 2 cloves garlic, minced
- 4 chicken-flavored bouillon cubes
- 1 1/2 cups boiling waters
- 1/4 cup all-purpose flour
- 1 teaspoon dry mustard
- 1 teaspoon dried whole dillweed
- 1 (8 ounce) carton sour cream
- 1/4 teaspoon salt

- Hot cooked rice or noodles

Direction

- Drain artichokes, reserving marinade. Set artichoke hearts and marinade aside.
- Sauté chicken, onion, and garlic in 1/4 cup reserved marinade in a large skillet until chicken is lightly browned and onion is tender.
- Dissolve bouillon cubes in boiling water: pour over chicken.
- Combine flour, dry mustard, and dill weed in a small bowl: stir well. Add flour mixture to remaining artichoke marinade: stir until smooth. Pour over chicken. Bring mixture to a boil; cover, reduce heat and simmer 4 to 5 minutes or until chicken is done. Remove from heat.
- Stir in reserved artichoke hearts, sour cream, and salt. Serve over rice or noodles.

16. Asian Grilled Chicken Recipe

Serving: 6 | Prep: | Cook: 45mins | Ready in:

Ingredients

- 1/4 cup honey
- 3 tbls red wine vinegar
- 1/4 cup soy sauce
- 1 clove garlic, minced
- 2 tbsp fresh parsley, minced
- 2 tsp fresh ginger, grated
- 1/2 tsp pepper
- 6 chicken breasts, rinsed, patted dry and cut into chunks

Direction

- Combine all ingredients and mix well.
- Add chicken. Cover. Refrigerate for 2-3 hours.
- String chicken on skewers alone or with onion and green peppers.

- Grill until chicken is cooked, approximately 20 minutes.

17. Aunt Nancys Chicken Recipe

Serving: 4 | Prep: | Cook: 180mins | Ready in:

Ingredients

- Armour dried beef
- 1c sour cream
- 1 can cream of chcken or mushroom
- 4 boneless chicken breasts
- 8 slices slightly cooked bacon

Direction

- Place beef on the bottom of casserole dish
- Wrap chicken with partially cooked bacon
- Mix sour cream and soup together, pour over chicken
- Baked uncovered at 275 degree for 3 hours.

18. Avocado & Tomato Stuffed Chicken Recipe

Serving: 2 | Prep: | Cook: 30mins | Ready in:

Ingredients

- 1/2 cup - flour
- 1/2 tsp - garlic powder
- 3 big dashes - Simply Tasteful's "Dried tomato and garlic Pesto" mix
- 2 - chicken breasts pounded out thin
- 2 - slices of onion
- 2 - grapevine tomatoes (sliced
- 1 -avocado (pealed and sliced)
- olive oil
- parmesan cheese (shredded bag kind)
- salt and pepper

Direction

- Coating:
- Put flour, garlic powder, pesto mix, and pepper (to taste) in a mixing bowl.
- Put 1 of the pounded out chicken breast on a plate, Sprinkle salt on inside of chicken. In the center of the chicken, sprinkle cheese. Layer with avocado, tomato then onion on one end of the chicken. Fold other end over the top of the fixings. Place toothpicks inside chicken to keep contents from falling out. Roll chicken carefully in bowl to coat the outside with mixture. It's okay if the coating gets inside the chicken. Repeat with other chicken breast.
- In a non-stick skillet, heat up a little olive oil in pan. Place chicken in skillet, cover, and cook on medium high heat. 2 minutes on each side.
- While chicken is cooking, heat oven to 350 degrees. Place cooked chicken in baking pan. Sprinkle chicken with Parmesan cheese. Cook chicken for 20 minutes.
- I served mine with rice.... oh and don't forget to remove the TOOTHPICKS!

19. BBQ Chicken Penne Al Gitano Recipe

Serving: 4 | Prep: | Cook: 25mins | Ready in:

Ingredients

- 2 Boneless, Skinned chicken breasts (seasoned with BBQ spices), Barbecued and cut into cubes
- 3 Cups dry penne pasta
- 1 1/2 Cups pasta sauce (spaghetti sauce-bottled or homemade)
- 1 Cup Shredded Mozza-Cheddar Mix cheese
- 1/4 Cup Grated parmesan cheese
- 1 Diced jalapeno pepper OR 1 Tsp. hot pepper flakes
- Fresh Grated pepper
- Pinch salt

Direction

- Grill chicken, cool and cut into bite sized pieces
- Cook Pasta until al dente, drain
- Place Pasta, cut up chicken, sauce and pepper flakes/diced jalapeno pepper and salt and pepper, mix well.
- Spray a large casserole dish with Cooking Spray
- Place pasta chicken mix in casserole dish and spread shredded cheese and grated parmesan on top
- Bake at 350F for about 25 minutes until bubbly
- Enjoy!

20. BBQ Crockpot Chicken Recipe

Serving: 8 | Prep: | Cook: 480mins | Ready in:

Ingredients

- 3 large chicken breasts (I use frozen)
- 1 bottle barbecue sauce
- 2 cans of tomatoes (oregano basil garlic flavor)
- 1 large onion chopped
- 1 tsp garlic powder
- 1 tsp cayenne pepper
- chicken broth to cover chicken

Direction

- Put all ingredients in crockpot on low and cook for 8 hours
- Uncover for last hour to let sauce reduce and thicken

21. Bacon BBQ Chicken Sandwich Recipe

Serving: 4 | Prep: | Cook: 25mins | Ready in:

Ingredients

- 4 Boneless skinless chicken Breast

- 1/2 Lb bacon
- 4 Sliced cheddar cheese
- 1/2 Cups your favorite bbq sauce
- 4 T. butter
- salt & pepper
- 4 rolls or buns
- lettuce-sliced
- tomato-sliced
- onion-sliced

Direction

- Salt and Pepper your chicken and place into pan with butter and cook through until golden brown. In separate pan fry bacon until done and set aside. Do not overcook it you want your bacon soft.
- Once chicken is done remove from heat and place some bacon and cheddar cheese slices on top of each piece of chicken and cover with lid to melt the cheese for a about 2 minutes.
- Place a piece of chicken on each bun and top with bbq sauce, lettuce, tomato and onion.
- Enjoy

---

22. Baked Chicken Breasts And Potatoes Recipe

Serving: 2 | Prep: | Cook: 45mins | Ready in:

Ingredients

- chicken breasts (1 or 2 pieces per person depending on their size)
- 4-6 bigger potatoes, preferably a sweeter type
- milk
- creamy, spreadable cheese, not very salty (one of those you can spread on bread easily)
- pepper and paprika spice (sweet, not chilli) or a mix of spices for grilling

Direction

- Set the oven to 250°C and let it heat up while you work. Wash the chicken breasts, if they are too big, slice them in halves. Gather your spices and rub them onto the chicken breasts. Peel the potatoes and wash them thoroughly. Chop the potatoes into 4-6 parts (depends on their size). Try to have them chopped into somewhat even pieces, that'll make the baking easier to keep an eye on.
- Put a layer of aluminium foil on a cooking pan or a cookie sheet with raised edges. I suggest using two, one for the chicken and one for the potatoes, because the chicken will leak juices and that could ruin the potatoes. You should bend the edges of the aluminium foil upwards so no juices from the chicken will run off the foil on the pan/sheet.
- Note: For this recipe, it is crucial that you can blow hot air on the chicken and potatoes intensively. A convection type oven has a fan for this. It's very useful if you don't want to add any oil yet you want to make the potatoes slightly crispy. If you don't have it, it might not matter much, but you may need to bake the potatoes a bit longer to have them somewhat crispy.
- If the oven is heated up to 250°C, put in the potatoes (into the middle) and the chicken pan/sheet above the potatoes. Turn on the fan for about 8-10 minutes. After that, turn off the fan and set the oven to 200°C, it should be near this temperature by now anyway.
- Get the potato sheet out, turn the potatoes over and put that sheet back into the oven.
- Let it bake for about 10-15 minutes, after this, check whether the potatoes or the chicken need to be turned around. It's a good idea to do that for the potatoes, it's usually not necessary for the chicken, but you've better off safe than sorry. After this, put them in for another 10-15 minutes.
- Now we can start making a cheese 'sauce'. It's basically milk, molten cheese (non-spreadable cheese often doesn't completely melt, which is what I like to avoid here). Get a small pot and put a bit of milk in it. There should be a layer of milk, about 1 cm thick. Start heating the milk up. When it starts boiling or it's close to boiling, add some cheese. Not all of it, as you'll

probably want to go slow on this and if it's the first time you're making this, you'll need to decide how thick the cheese sauce should be. I like it when it's a thick liquid, so I add a bit more milk sometimes. If you have spreadable cheese triangles, start with 4 of them and the amount of milk I mentioned before. When the cheese melts, you can decide how much more and how thick you want it to be.

- The sauce, chicken and potatoes should be all done in about the same time. You can serve them immediately.
- Note: you probably don't want to add any spices on the potatoes. Salt is not necessary in this recipe, as there's lots of it in the cheese. This way, you can enjoy the true taste of baked sweetish potatoes and have a nice piece of meat to it. If you go with a different sauce, you can have a pretty low fat meal. You can use a marinade for the chicken if you don't want a sauce or anything else to go with it.

23. Baked Chicken Breasts Supreme Recipe

Serving: 8 | Prep: | Cook: 45mins | Ready in:

Ingredients

- 1-1/2 cups sour cream
- 1/4 cup lemon juice
- 1/2 teaspoon worcestershire sauce
- 1/2 teaspoon celery seed
- 1/2 teaspoon Hungarian sweet paprika
- 1 clove garlic minced
- 1/2 teaspoon salt
- 1/4 teaspoon freshly ground black pepper
- 8 boneless skinless chicken breast halves
- 2 cups fine dry bread crumbs

Direction

- In large bowl combine first eight ingredients then place chicken in mixture and turn to coat.

- Cover and marinate overnight in the refrigerator.
- Remove chicken from marinade then coat each piece with crumbs.
- Arrange in a shallow baking pan then bake uncovered at 350 for 45 minutes.

24. Baked Chicken In Poblano Cream Sauce Recipe

Serving: 6 | Prep: | Cook: 40mins | Ready in:

Ingredients

- 3 Boneless skinless chicken breast halves
- 2 Tbsp olive oil
- salt and pepper (to taste)
- 1 1/2 Cup monterey jack cheese (shredded)
- *****Poblano Cream Sauce*****
- 1 Fresh Poblano chili
- 1/2 white onion
- 3 cloves garlic
- Drizzle of olive oil
- 1/4 Bunch cilantro
- 1/4 cup milk
- 1/2 tsp salt
- 2 Tbsp butter
- 1 Tbsp all-purpose flour
- 1/4 cup heavy cream
- juice of half a lime

Direction

- Preheat oven to 425 degrees (F)
- Cut the poblano pepper in half, stem and seed
- Cut the cleaned and skinned half white onion into large wedges
- Peel the garlic
- Place these above items in an 8 x 8 (or whatever you have) baking dish and drizzle with olive oil, turn to coat completely
- Place in the oven and roast for approx. 20 minutes until the skin starts to separate from the chilies

- In the meantime cut your chicken breast halves in half again to make something more like a scallopini. (i.e.: with the breast flat on the cutting board use your knife to cut parallel to the board to divide it into two equal pieces that look like the original breast, just thinner)
- Salt and pepper the chicken on both sides
- Heat the 2 Tbsp. of olive oil in a skillet until just short of smoking
- Sauté the chicken breast pieces in the skillet for about 2 minutes a side until they have a little color on them
- Remove the chicken to a plate (or if you time this step right with the roasting and the creation of the sauce you can move them straight to the baking dish you used to roast the veggies and save yourself a plate to wash)
- Remove the roasted veggies from the oven and lower the temperature to 350 degrees (F) DON'T forget this step!
- Peal the separated skin off the poblanos (a fork can help as they are hot)
- Place the roasted veggies in a blender
- Add the cilantro, salt and milk
- Puree the mixture
- In a small saucepan over medium heat melt the butter
- When the butter is melted add the flour and stir for a minute until fully incorporated and slightly cooked
- Add the poblano puree to the sauce pan and stir
- Add the Heavy cream to the sauce pan and stir constantly for a couple of minutes until fully incorporated and thickened a bit
- Remove from the heat and add the juice of the half lime, stir to incorporate
- If you have not already, place the chicken breasts in a single layer to fill the baking dish used to roast the veggies
- Pour the Poblano Cream Sauce over the chicken
- Top the breasts with the cheese
- Bake in the oven for 20 minutes until the cheese is melted and bubbly and the chicken is cooked through
- ENJOY!

25. Baked Chicken Salad Pie Recipe

Serving: 6 | Prep: | Cook: 55mins | Ready in:

Ingredients

- 2 cups cooked chicken breast, shredded
- 1/2 cup light cheddar cheese, shredded
- 2 eggs
- 1/2 cup finely diced celery
- 1/4 cup finely chopped sweet videlia onion
- 1/2 cup cream of chicken soup
- 1/2 cup light sour cream
- 1/2 cup light mayo
- 2 tablespoons unbleached flour
- 2 tablespoons champagne mustard (I prefer Cherchies brand) Dijon will also work
- 1 deep dish ready-made 9" pie crust

Direction

- Preheat oven to 350
- Prepare your pie crust by poking gently with fork and baking slightly, about 7 minutes
- In mixing bowl, slightly beat the two eggs
- Add all remaining ingredients and mix well
- Pour mixture into pie crust
- Bake at 350 for 45-50 minutes (until slightly browned)

26. Baked Parmesan Chicken Recipe

Serving: 6 | Prep: | Cook: 1hours | Ready in:

Ingredients

- 1 tablespoon olive oil
- 2 cups seasoned bread crumbs
- ¾ cup Grated parmesan cheese

- 1 teaspoon paprika
- 1 teaspoon Each salt and freshly grated black pepper
- ½ cup (1 stick) butter
- 4-6 Boneless, skinless chicken breasts or thighs

Direction

- Preheat the oven to 350°.
- Line a 13 x 9 x 2" baking dish with foil and spread the olive oil over the foil.
- Combine the bread crumbs, parmesan cheese, paprika, salt and pepper in a shallow pie plate.
- Place the butter in another shallow pie plate and melt in the microwave.
- Taking one piece of chicken at a time, dip both sides of the chicken in the butter, then in the breadcrumbs.
- Lay the chicken on the foiled lined baking dish.
- Pour any remaining butter on top of the chicken.
- Bake 45-60 minutes depending on the thickness of the chicken or until done.

27. Baked Pineapple Chicken Recipe

Serving: 2 | Prep: | Cook: 45mins | Ready in:

Ingredients

- 1/4 cup chicken broth
- 3 Tbsp. reduced sodium soy sauce
- 1 tsp. ground ginger, divided
- 2 bone in chicken breast halves, skin removed
- 1 can (8-oz.) unsweetened crushed pineapple, undrained
- 1 tsp. cornstarch
- 2 tsp. orange marmalade
- 1 tsp. lemon juice

Direction

- In a large plastic bag, combine the broth, soy sauce and 1/2 tsp. ginger, add chicken. Seal bag and turn to coat, refrigerate for 2 hours, turning occasionally.
- Preheat oven to 350*F.
- Drain pineapple, reserving 1/2 cup juice, set aside 1/4 cup pineapple.
- Refrigerate remaining pineapple and juice for another use.
- In a saucepan, combine cornstarch and reserved pineapple juice until smooth. Stir in the pineapple, orange marmalade, lemon juice and remaining ginger.
- Bring to boil, cook and stir 1-2 minutes or until thickened.
- Drain and discard marinade. Place chicken in a 9" square baking dish coated with cooking spray. Top with pineapple mixture.
- Bake uncovered for 45 minutes or until juices run clear.
- Nutritional Facts:
- One serving
- Cal.   207
- Fat   3 g
- Sat. fat.   1 g
- Chol.   68 mg
- Sodium   330 mg
- Carbs.   18 g
- Fiber   1 g
- Protein   26 g
- Diabetic Exchange: 3 lean meat, 1 fruit

28. Balsamic Oregano Chicken Recipe

Serving: 0 | Prep: | Cook: 1hours | Ready in:

Ingredients

- 4 large bone-in chicken breasts, skin removed
- 1/4 cup balsamic vinegar
- 1 Tblsp olive oil
- 1 tsp dried oregano
- salt & freshly ground black pepper to taste

Direction

- Clean chicken and place in lightly greased baking dish (bone side down).
- Mix the balsamic vinegar and olive oil, evenly pour over the chicken.
- Sprinkle with oregano, salt, and pepper.
- *crushing the oregano (or any dried herb used in cooking) between your fingers before using will release additional flavor*
- Tightly cover with aluminum foil and bake 20 mins.
- Baste with juices; continue baking uncovered for about 20-30 more minutes (depending on the size and type of chicken you use).
- Most recipes say to cook until juices run clear, but it's safer to check it with a meat thermometer. My thermometer says to cook poultry to 180 degrees, I usually take it out of the oven at 175 and let it rest, covered, for about 5 minutes and it continues to cook internally.

29. Barbecued Chicken Burritos Recipe

Serving: 4 | Prep: | Cook: 180mins | Ready in:

Ingredients

- 3 chicken breasts, poached and shredded
- olive oil
- 1 green bell pepper, julienned
- 1 green pepper, julienned
- 1 onion, julienned
- Tony Chacherie's seasoning
- barbecue sauce
- shredded mexican cheese
- flour tortillas (10-")

Direction

- I poached the chicken breasts in the crockpot with salt and pepper for 3 hours on high.
- (I was at work while this part was going.)
- I drained off the chicken and shredded it.
- Put the veggies in a skillet and cooked down until limp in the olive oil.
- Add the seasoning as the veggies were cooking.
- Mixed the barbecue sauce in with the chicken by hand until it reached the consistency I liked.
- Warmed up the tortillas in the microwave and served up the chicken with the veggies and cheese.
- Some nachos finished off a meal that was easy after a day at work and the family enjoyed.
- (The kids thought it was FUN.)
- -Susana

30. Basil Chicken Recipe

Serving: 4 | Prep: | Cook: 15mins | Ready in:

Ingredients

- vegetable oil
- 4 skinless, boneless chicken breasts OR 8 skinless, boneless chicken thighs
- 1/2 small red onion
- 1/2 cup orange or mango juice
- 1 tsp each dried basil leaves and ground cumin
- 1/2 tsp salt
- 1/2 lime
- 1/4 cup coarsely chopped fresh basil

Direction

- Lightly oil a large frying pan and set over medium heat.
- When hot, add chicken and cook until lightly golden, 3 to 4 minutes per side.
- Meanwhile, thinly slice red onion.
- When chicken is golden, scatter onion around chicken.
- Pour in orange juice.
- Sprinkle with dried basil, cumin and salt.

- Using a wooden spoon, scrape up and stir in any brown bits from pan bottom.
- Bring to a boil, then reduce heat to medium-low.
- Cover and simmer, turning chicken halfway through, until chicken is springy when pressed, 6 to 8 minutes.
- Squeeze juice from lime overtop.
- Remove chicken and place on dinner plates.
- Increase heat to high.
- Boil pan juices, stirring often, until slightly thickened, about 2 minutes.
- Stir in fresh basil.
- Drizzle over chicken.
- Great with jasmine rice and slices of mango.

31. Basil Rathbone Less Chicken With Triple Pesti Recipe

Serving: 4 | Prep: | Cook: 20mins |Ready in:

Ingredients

- 4 large boneless chicken breasts
- flour
- 2 eggs + ¼ cup of milk
- Medium grained bread crumbs
- ---CLASSIC PESTO---
- 1 ½ cup of loosely packed fresh basil
- Half a cup of toasted pine nuts
- About ¾ cup of olive oil
- Half a cup of grated parmesan cheese
- salt, pepper
- ---SUNDRIED tomato "PESTO"----
- 1 cup of sundried tomatoes
- Half a cup of light, toasted walnuts
- Half a cup of olive oil
- Half a cup of flat leafed parsley
- Half a cup of very, very finely chopped scallions
- 1 cup of sweet red wine
- Half a cinnamon stick
- 4 tbls. of thyme honey
- ---garlic PESTO—
- 12-16 large cloves of fresh garlic
- ¾ cup of toasted skinless almonds
- Half a cup of olive oil
- The juice of a big fat lemon
- Half a cup of very firm dry feta cheese.

Direction

- CHICKEN: Cut the breasts in half and then pound them till they are about half an inch thick. Dredge them well in flour, next into egg wash and then coat them completely in the breadcrumbs which could have some salt and pepper in them. Pan fry them in olive oil until golden brown and fully cooked.
- PESTO I: this is the neutral one so I left out some of the normal ingredients. Combine everything but the cheese and oil into a food processor and in short spurts, begin to add the oil and chop. Do NOT purée. You should still be able to discern some texture. It will start to separate, but that ok just stir it well before serving. Finish with the cheese and season with salt and pepper.
- PESTO II: the sweet. Fully rehydrate the tomatoes and drain well. Put the honey, cinnamon and the wine into a small pan and reduce it until thick and syrup-like. It should be about 1/3 of a cup.
- Put the tomatoes, parsley and the walnuts into a food processor and proceed as before but make this one a little tighter. Mix in the wine/honey and the scallions and season with salt only.
- PESTO III: herein lies the bite. Put the garlic, almonds and lemon juice into a food processor and in the same short pulse and oil method chop them to the point just before a purée. The feta should be crumbled as finely as is humanly possible and mixed in at the very end.
- All these should be made as fresh as possible. If not the tomato one may be made a day in advance, the basil can too but it will de-colour some. The garlic however is the one that must be made and used within 1-2 hours.

- TO SERVE: Set two halves of chicken breast slightly overlapping, on one side of the plate. Start with the basil pesto and spread a thick ring all the way around just shy of the outer edge. Next spread the tomato pesto along the inside of that. Finally add a small bit of the garlic in the very inside of that which should be in the centre. Thus having three separate concentric rings with the naked edges of the fried chicken exposing themselves.
- I did serve this once, and nobody died. When I did so I made some orzo to which I added eggplant, zucchini, summer squash, red bell pepper all of these being grilled and fresh chopped spinach, and spread it out alongside the chicken.

32. Bbq Chicken Pizza Recipe

Serving: 4 | Prep: | Cook: 7mins | Ready in:

Ingredients

- 3 boneless skinless chicken breasts
- 1 yellow onion
- 1/2 cup shredded cheddar cheese blend
- 1/8 cup green onions
- 1 cup of Bbq sauce of your choice
- 1/2 tsp. salt and pepper
- 1/2 tsp. garlic powder
- 2 Tbs. olive oil
- 12" premade thin pizza crust (or make your own)

Direction

- Preheat oven according to directions or your recipe.
- Heat 1 1/2 Tbs. of oil in skillet.
- Slice yellow onion and add to pan.
- Cook until caramelized.
- Add Bbq sauce and cook on low 2 min. (I used 1/2 cup Famous Dave's Devil's Spit and 1/2 cup Famous Dave's Sweet and Zesty)
- Remove onion and Bbq from pan.

- Chop chicken into bite size pieces and add to pan with salt, pepper and garlic powder.
- Cook until no longer pink.
- Brush crust with remaining olive oil.
- Spread onion and bbq mix on crust.
- Add chicken.
- Top with cheese and green onion.
- Bake and Serve!

33. Beer B Q Chicken Sliders Recipe

Serving: 6 | Prep: | Cook: 60mins | Ready in:

Ingredients

- 3-4 skinless, boneless chicken breast halves
- 1 can beer
- 1 cup bbq sauce
- poultry seasoning
- Small hamburger buns

Direction

- Trim and cut chicken breast halves in half.
- Rinse and dry each quartered chicken breast with a paper towel.
- Lightly sprinkle each side with the poultry seasoning and set aside.
- In a 4 quart (or larger) bowl, Using a medium sized whisk, lightly whisk the beer and bbq sauce together.
- Put the chicken in a resealable gallon Ziploc bag with the marinade and refrigerate overnight.
- Preheat grill to 350 deg.
- Oil grill grates with olive oil.
- Grill for about 10 to 12 minutes per side. (Over indirect heat at ~350 deg.)

34. Beer Batter Chicken Strips Recipe

Serving: 4 | Prep: | Cook: 1hours | Ready in:

Ingredients

- 1 large egg
- 3/4 cup of beer
- 1 cup flour
- 1 teaspoon baking soda
- 1 teaspoon salt
- poultry seasoning
- 2 teaspoons smoked paprika
- ground black pepper
- 3 chicken breasts cut into strips

Direction

- Beat the egg slightly with a whisk, then beat in the beer.
- Add the dry ingredients, except poultry seasoning, and whisk until smooth.
- Cover and let stand for 25 to 30 minutes.
- Cut chicken breasts into strips.
- Sprinkle poultry seasoning on the chicken strips, using your hand to spread evenly on both sides.
- Heat oil over medium high heat to approximately 350 degrees. (I use a deep fryer)
- Dip chicken strips in batter, and add to hot oil.
- After about 1 minute, turn strips over.
- Continue cooking, and turning strips until done. About 3 to 6 minutes.
- Drain on paper towels.

35. Big Jims BBQ Chicken Recipe

Serving: 34 | Prep: | Cook: 25mins | Ready in:

Ingredients

- For the spice rub
- 1 tablespoon ground allspice
- 2 tablespoons chopped garlic

- 1/2 jalapeño chili pepper, seeded and chopped
- 2 teaspoons dried thyme
- 1 teaspoon dried basil
- 1 teaspoon dry mustard
- 2 teaspoons ground coriander
- 1/2 teaspoon ground cloves
- 1 teaspoon ground ginger
- 1/4 teaspoon ground cinnamon
- For the chicken
- 4 each bone-in, skin-on chicken breast halves, legs and thighs
- For the barbecue sauce
- 1 tablespoon extra-virgin olive oil
- 1/4 cup diced onion
- 2 tablespoons chopped garlic
- 1/2 jalapeño chili pepper, seeded and chopped
- 2 tablespoons spice Rub
- 1/2 cup mango nectar or *Coca cola
- 3/4 cup ketchup
- 2 tablespoons molasses or *Steen's Pure cane syrup
- 2 teaspoons cider vinegar
- 2 teaspoons lemon juice
- 2 teaspoons creole mustard
- 1 tablespoon hot pepper sauce, such as Tabasco, or to taste
- *1/4 cup Captain Morgan spiced rum

Direction

- For the spice rub: In a small, resealable plastic food container, combine all ingredients and mix well. Refrigerate if not using immediately.
- For the chicken: Pat the chicken pieces dry with paper towels and place in a large baking dish. Set aside 2 tablespoons of the spice rub for the barbecue sauce and spread the remaining rub over the chicken pieces. Let stand at room temperature for 2 to 3 hours, or cover and refrigerate overnight.
- For the barbecue sauce: In a small saucepan over medium-high heat, heat the oil. Add the onion, garlic and jalapeño chili pepper and cook until softened, 3 to 4 minutes. Add the remaining 2 tablespoons spice rub and cook, stirring, for 30 seconds. Add the remaining sauce ingredients, reduce the heat to medium

and cook, with bubbles just breaking the surface, for 15 minutes. If not using right away, let cool, cover and refrigerate.

- When ready to cook, prepare the grill. If using a gas grill, preheat the grill to medium. If using a charcoal grill, start the charcoal or wood briquettes. When the briquettes are ready, distribute them evenly under the cooking area for direct heat. Lightly oil the grate.
- Place the chicken pieces on the grill with the bone side down. Cook for 20 to 25 minutes, turning frequently, until the chicken is cooked through (the breast meat will cook faster than the dark meat). Baste the chicken with some of the barbecue sauce and cook 5 more minutes, turning each piece after basting. Serve hot or warm, with additional sauce at the table.

Serving: 8 | Prep: | Cook: 45mins | Ready in:

Ingredients

- * 1 cup Chicken Breast, Cooked
- * 1 1/2 cups Black Beans, Canned
- * 1/2 cup Organic Quinoa
- * 1/2 cup Corn, Yellow
- * 1 cup Medium Salsa
- * 8 Low Carb Low Fat Tortilla
- * 1 cup Monterey Jack Cheese With Jalapeno Peppers

Direction

- In a large mixing bowl pour in the undrained can of black beans.
- Use a potato masher and mash up the beans.
- Add the salsa and give it another mash.
- Heat a large skillet and pour in the quinoa. Toast the quinoa for about 5 minutes.
- Pour bean mixture over the quinoa add the corn and chopped cooked chicken.

- Mix well, cover and reduce heat. You want to give the quinoa time to absorb the liquid from the beans and salsa.
- Wrap the tortillas in a clean dish towel. Dribble a bit of water on top of the towel and heat in microwave for about 1 minute to soften the tortillas.
- Shred the cheddar cheese and place a small amount in the on the tortilla. Maybe 1 tbsp. to each.
- Preheat oven to 375, spray a glass baking pan with PAM.
- Divide the bean and chicken mixture on each tortilla. Roll up burrito style and put in the pan. Sprinkle remaining shredded cheese on top and put in oven to brown the cheese, maybe 15 minutes.

37. Blackened Chicken Pizza Recipe

Serving: 0 | Prep: | Cook: 4hours | Ready in:

Ingredients

- 1 cup warm water
- 1 tablespoon white sugar
- 1 (.25 ounce) package active dry yeast
- 2 tablespoons vegetable oil
- 3 cups all-purpose flour
- 1 teaspoon salt
- 6 slices bacon (optional)
- 6 tablespoons butter
- 2 cloves garlic, minced
- 1 1/2 cups heavy cream
- 2 egg yolks
- 1/2 cup freshly grated parmesan cheese
- 1/2 cup freshly grated romano cheese
- 1/8 teaspoon ground nutmeg
- 1/2 teaspoon paprika
- 1/4 teaspoon cayenne pepper
- 1/4 teaspoon ground cumin
- 1/4 teaspoon crumbled dried thyme
- 1/8 teaspoon salt

- 1/8 teaspoon ground white pepper
- 1/8 teaspoon onion powder
- 2 skinless, boneless chicken breast halves
- 1 tablespoon vegetable oil
- 1 cup shredded mozzarella cheese, or more if desired
- 1/2 cup baby spinach leaves
- 3 tablespoons freshly grated parmesan cheese
- 1 roma (plum) chopped

Direction

- Mix water, sugar, yeast, and 2 tablespoons of vegetable oil for several seconds on low speed in the work bowl of a large stand mixer fitted with a dough hook. Stop the mixer and add the flour and salt. Start the mixer on low speed and mix until the flour mixture is incorporated with the yeast mixture; turn speed to medium-low and machine-knead the dough until springy and smooth, 10 to 12 minutes. Sprinkle dough with flour occasionally if it sticks to the sides of the bowl.
- Form dough into a ball and place into an oiled bowl; turn the dough over in the bowl several times to oil the surface of the dough. Cover the dough with a towel, set into a warm place, and allow to rise until double, 30 minutes to 1 hour.
- Cook the bacon in a large, deep skillet over medium-high heat until evenly browned, about 10 minutes; drain on a paper towel-lined plate and allow to cool; chop and set aside.
- Melt butter in a saucepan over medium-low heat. Cook the garlic in the melted butter until fragrant, about 1 minute. Stir the cream into the butter mixture. Add the egg yolks and whisk with the butter mixture until smooth. Stir 1/2 cup of Parmesan cheese, the Romano cheese, and nutmeg into the mixture; season to taste with salt. Bring the sauce just barely to a simmer over low heat; cook and stir at a simmer until cheeses have melted and sauce has thickened, 3 to 5 minutes. Remove from heat and set aside.
- Preheat oven to 350 degrees F (175 degrees C).

- Mix the paprika, cayenne pepper, cumin, thyme, 1/8 teaspoon of salt, white pepper, and onion powder together in a bowl. Rub one side of each chicken breast thoroughly with the spice mixture. Heat 1 tablespoon vegetable oil in a skillet over high heat. Sear the chicken breasts, seasoned sides first, in the hot oil until the spices turn almost black, about 1 minute per side; transfer to a baking sheet.
- Bake the chicken breasts in the preheated oven until no longer pink in the center and an instant-read meat thermometer inserted into the thickest part of a breast reads at least 160 degrees F (70 degrees C), 5 to 10 minutes; set aside.
- Punch down pizza dough and roll out onto a floured work surface. Shape pizza crust on a large pizza stone or heavy baking sheet. Poke several holes in the crust with a fork to help it release steam.
- Bake the crust in the oven until top is very lightly cooked, 5 to 7 minutes. Remove from oven and spread a layer of Alfredo sauce over the crust. Spread the mozzarella cheese in an even layer over the sauce. Slice the blackened chicken breasts and arrange over the mozzarella cheese. Sprinkle pizza with spinach leaves and chopped bacon. Top with 3 tablespoons of Parmesan cheese.
- Return pizza to oven and bake until the mozzarella cheese is melted and browned, 15 to 20 minutes. Sprinkle pizza with chopped Roma tomatoes to serve.

38. Boneless Chicken Breasts With Grapes Recipe

Serving: 6 | Prep: | Cook: 30mins | Ready in:

Ingredients

- 3 whole boneless skinless chicken breasts
- salt and freshly grated nutmeg as needed
- 2 tablespoons butter

- 1 tablespoon orange marmalade
- 1/4 teaspoon dried tarragon
- 1 green onion thinly sliced
- 1/3 cup dry white wine
- 1 cup seedless grapes
- 1/4 cup whipping cream

Direction

- Sprinkle chicken breasts with salt and nutmeg.
- In large frying pan heat butter over medium high heat and brown chicken lightly.
- Add marmalade, tarragon, green onion and wine then cover reduce heat and simmer 10 minutes.
- Add grapes then cover again and continue cooking 10 minutes.
- Using a slotted spoon remove chicken and grapes to heated serving dish and keep warm.
- Add cream to liquid in pan then bring to boil stirring constantly.
- Cook until sauce is reduced and slightly thickened then salt to taste and pour over chicken.

39. Bourbon Chicken With Apricots Recipe

Serving: 4 | Prep: | Cook: 30mins | Ready in:

Ingredients

- 4 chicken breast halves
- 1/2 teaspoon salt
- 1/8 teaspoon freshly ground pepper
- 2 tablespoons butter
- 1 large white onion diced
- 1 teaspoon paprika
- 1-1/2 cups chopped green onions
- 1/2 cup orange juice
- 2 tablespoons bourbon
- 1 cup fresh apricots chopped
- 1/8 teaspoon ground nutmeg

Direction

- Sprinkle chicken with salt and pepper then arrange in rectangular baking dish and set aside.
- Melt butter in skillet over medium heat then add diced onion to skillet and sauté 5 minutes.
- Stir in paprika then set aside 1 tablespoon green onions and stir remaining green onions into mix.
- Cook stirring occasionally 4 minutes.
- Spread onion mixture evenly over chicken then drizzle with orange juice and bourbon.
- Bake at 400 for 50 minutes turning and basting occasionally with pan drippings.
- Top with chopped apricots and sprinkle with nutmeg then bake 5 minute more.
- Transfer chicken to a serving dish and drizzle with pan drippings and sprinkle with green onions.

40. Boursin Sun Dried Tomato Stuffed Chicken Breasts Recipe

Serving: 4 | Prep: | Cook: 40mins | Ready in:

Ingredients

- 4 boneless, skinless chicken breasts, pounded flat
- 1 pkg boursin cheese
- 6 sun-dried tomatoes, hydrated and finely chopped
- E.V.O. O.
- about 1/2 tsp dried basil or to taste

Direction

- Spread Boursin on flattened chicken to cover
- Sprinkled chopped Sun-Dried tomatoes over cheese
- Roll up from short side and secure with wooden toothpick or
- Place seam side down in oiled baking dish
- Brush with about 1/2 the E.V.O.O. mixed with basil

- Bake at 350 for 30 - 40 minutes or until juice runs clear basting with Olive oil/basil mixture once during baking
- Serves 4

41. Braised Chicken With Mushrooms And Sun Dried Tomatoes Recipe

Serving: 4 | Prep: | Cook: 30mins | Ready in:

Ingredients

- 1/3 cup thinly sliced drained sun-dried tomatoes packed in oil, reserving 1 1/2 tablespoons of the oil
- 1 large whole chicken breast with skin and bones (about 1 1/4 pounds), halved
- 1 small onion, chopped fine
- 2 large garlic cloves, minced
- 1/2 teaspoon dried basil, crumbled
- 1/4 teaspoon dried hot red pepper flakes, or to taste
- 1/2 pound mushrooms, sliced
- 1/4 cup dry red wine
- 1/4 cup balsamic vinegar
- 1/2 cup chicken broth
- 2 tablespoons tomato paste
- a beurre manié made by kneading together 1 1/2 teaspoons softened unsalted butter and 1 1/2 teaspoons all-purpose flour
- 3 tablespoons minced fresh parsley leaves (preferably flat-leafed)
- cooked rice or noodles

Direction

- In a heavy skillet heat the reserved tomato oil over moderately high heat until it is hot but not smoking, in it, brown the chicken, patted dry and seasoned with salt and pepper, and transfer it to a plate.
- In the fat remaining in the skillet cook the onion, the garlic, the basil, and the red pepper flakes over moderately low heat, stirring, until the onion is softened.
- Add the mushrooms and salt and pepper to taste and cook the mixture over moderate heat, stirring, until the mushrooms are softened.
- Whisk in the wine, balsamic vinegar, the broth, and the tomato paste, add the chicken to the skillet, and bring the liquid to a boil. Simmer the mixture, covered, for 20 to 25 minutes, or until the chicken is cooked through.
- Transfer the chicken to a platter and keep it warm, covered. Whisk the beurre manié into the sauce, whisking until sauce is smooth, add the sun-dried tomatoes, and simmer the sauce, whisking, for 2 to 3 minutes, or until it is thickened.
- Stir in the parsley. Place chicken on the rice or noodles and pour the sauce over.

42. Breaded Chicken With Ham Roasted Peppers And Provolone Recipe

Serving: 46 | Prep: | Cook: 12mins | Ready in:

Ingredients

- 1 1/3 cup seasoned bread crumbs
- 1/2 cup flour
- 3 boneless chicken breasts, filleted so you have 6 pieces
- 2 eggs, beaten
- 2 TB butter
- 2 TB olive oil
- 3/4 cup chicken broth
- 3/4 cup white wine
- sliced ham
- sliced provolone cheese
- roasted red peppers, sliced (for 3 breasts, filleted, I use one whole small jar, about 6-8 oz)
- 2-3 tsp cornstarch

Direction

- In a pie dish or plate, combine the bread crumbs and flour.
- In a bowl, beat the eggs.
- Combine the broth and wine, and dissolve the cornstarch in a small amount of the broth/wine mixture. Set both things aside.
- Dip each piece of chicken, one at a time, into the egg, completely coating them, then dredge each in the breadcrumb/flour mixture, set aside.
- **You've filleted the chicken, right? I hope so! You'll have such juicy chicken! **
- In a large nonstick pan, heat the butter and olive oil over med-med high heat.
- Add the chicken and cook 3 minutes on one side, turn them and cook for 3 more minutes, or until mostly done. It's ok if it's *almost* done, because you'll be putting them back in the pan, anyway.
- Transfer the chicken to a plate and set aside.
- Add the broth/wine mixture to the pan, scraping the bottom to get up all of the good cooked bits of chicken.
- Add the cornstarch that you've dissolved in a bit of the broth and wine, and stir for a couple of minutes, until you see it start to thicken.
- Add the chicken back to the skillet, and top each piece with some ham, sliced peppers, and then the cheese.
- Cover and cook until the cheese is all melty, about 2 minutes.
- Serve with some sauce drizzled over each piece of chicken.
- If you find you want more sauce, increase the broth and wine to about 1 cup each, but you'll also need a bit more cornstarch.

43. Breaded Lemon Chicken Recipe

Serving: 6 | Prep: | Cook: 30mins | Ready in:

Ingredients

- 2 lbs Bonless chicken breast (cut into strips about 3 to 4 inches long and about 1 to 2 inches wide) or buy the chicken breast fillets (already cut into size)
- 2 cups dried or store bought bread crums (if dried crush really fine)
- 4 tbsp lemon pepper seasonings
- 1 tbsp sea salt **NOT seasoned salt**
- 1 lemon
- 1/4 cup veggie oil

Direction

- Mix bread crumbs, salt, and lemon pepper seasoning in bowl.
- In large frying pan put oil and set on stove.
- Cut lemon into squeezable slices
- Bread chicken good on both sides
- Cook on med heat until golden brown AND cooked all the way through.
- While chicken is cooking squeeze lemon slices over the chicken evenly both sides.
- * If the chicken is browning faster than cooking all the way through, turn down the heat** =)
- Recommendation~> be careful how much fresh lemon you use until you know how strong you like it on this dish.

44. Breast Of Chicken In Red Wine Sauce Recipe

Serving: 6 | Prep: | Cook: 20mins | Ready in:

Ingredients

- 3 slices bacon
- 6 pieces chicken breast skinless and boneless
- 1/2 teaspoon salt
- 1 teaspoon freshly ground black pepper
- 1 cup flour
- 2 tablespoons olive oil
- 1-1/2 cups small pearl onions peeled
- 1 cup dry red wine
- 1/2 cup chicken stock

- 1 teaspoon dried thyme

Direction

- Fry bacon until crisp then drain well and break into pieces and reserve. Season breasts with salt and pepper then dip in flour. Heat olive oil in the sauté pan. Add breasts and brown well on both sides. Remove from pan and keep warm. In the same pan add onions, wine, stock and thyme. Cook until onions are soft and sauce thickens. Adjust seasonings. Return meat to pan and continue cooking until done.

45. Breast On A Stick Recipe

Serving: 4 | Prep: | Cook: 20mins | Ready in:

Ingredients

- 2 lbs boneless, skinless chicken breast
- 2 tbsp olive oil.........
- 2 cloves garlic - chopped......
- juice from 1 lemon
- 1/4 tsp cumin......
- 1/4 tsp each salt and pepper.........
- 1/2 tsp cayenne pepper.........

Direction

- Mix the oil, lemon juice, spices and garlic in a large bowl.
- Cut the chicken into cubes.
- Add the chicken to the bowl, stir to coat the chicken with the marinade.
- Cover and place in the refrigerator for 3 hours. Turn occasionally.
- Put the chicken on to skewers and grill over hot charcoal for 10- 15 minutes, turning frequently and basting with marinade.
- Serve with bread and salad.

46. Broccoli Cheese Chicken Recipe

Serving: 4 | Prep: | Cook: 45mins | Ready in:

Ingredients

- 4 boneless chicken breast
- flour
- 4 tbs butter
- frozen bag broccoli cuts
- 1 can broccoli cheese soup
- 1/3 c milk

Direction

- Cover chicken breast in flour.
- Melt butter in skillet.
- Sauté Chicken in butter until golden.
- Spray baking dish and put broccoli cuts in bottom of dish.
- Put chicken on top.
- Mix the can of broccoli cheese soup with milk and pour on top of chicken.
- Put foil over the baking dish.
- Bake at 350 for 45 minutes.
- This dish is great with rice.

47. Buffalo Chicken And Potatoes Recipe

Serving: 6 | Prep: | Cook: 70mins | Ready in:

Ingredients

- 1-1/4 lbs boneless,skinless chicken breasts,cut in 1" strips
- 1/3 c buffalo wing sauce
- 6 c frozen(thawed) southern-style hash brown potatoes
- 1 c ranch or blue cheese dressing
- 1/2 c shredded cheddar cheese
- 1 can (10 oz) cream of celery soup
- 1/2 c cornflake crumbs
- 2 TB butter,melted
- 1/4 c chopped green onions (3-4 med.)

Direction

- Heat oven to 350'.Spray 13x9" baking dish with spray.
- In med. bowl, stir together chicken strips and wing sauce.
- In large bowl, stir together potatoes, dressing, cheese and soup. Spoon into baking dish. Place chicken strips in single layer over potato mixture.
- In small bowl, stir together crumbs and butter. Sprinkle in baking dish.
- Cover with foil. Bake 30 mins; uncover and bake 20-25 mins longer or till potatoes are tender and juice of chicken is no longer pink when centers of thickest pieces are cut.
- Sprinkle with green onions.

48. Butter Baked Chicken Recipe

Serving: 4 | Prep: | Cook: 40mins | Ready in:

Ingredients

- 4 boneless, skinless chicken breasts (use the best quality ones you can, as it really makes a difference)
- 1/2 cup of all purpose flour plus 2 tbsp for butter sauce
- 1/4 tsp salt
- 2 grinds of peppercorns, or a healthy dash of ground pepper
- 1 tbsp of dried parsley
- 1 tsp grated parmesan
- 1 tsp garlic powder
- 1/2 stick of butter
- 1/4 tsp dried thyme
- 2/3 cup chicken broth

Direction

- Put the 1/2 cup of flour in a shallow bowl with all of the seasonings except the thyme and mix through
- Dredge the chicken breasts in the flour

- Dredge them again
- Place them in a glass baking dish and bake them at 375 for approx. 40 minutes
- Start the butter sauce by melting the butter in a heavy sauce pan, letting it color a little bit if you like
- Add the 2 tbsp. of flour and stir over heat until well incorporated
- Add the chicken broth and thyme, and whisk it over medium heat until it comes to a boil and thickens
- Serve over the chicken, or in a gravy boat on the side

49. CRANBERRY CHICKEN MARGARITA Recipe

Serving: 6 | Prep: | Cook: 10mins | Ready in:

Ingredients

- 6 boneless, skinless chicken breast halves
- 2 tablespoons olive oil
- coarse salt
- 1 small garlic clove, minced
- 1 cup Ocean Spray- whole berry cranberry sauce
- 3 tablespoons tequila
- 1 teaspoon lime juice
- 1 1/2 tablespoons chopped cilantro
- lime wedges

Direction

- Slice breasts in half horizontally. Pound with a meat mallet or rolling pin to about 3/8-inch thickness.
- Heat oil in a large skillet over medium heat. Add chicken and cook until lightly browned, about 3 minutes per side. Remove chicken to a warm serving platter and sprinkle lightly with coarse salt. Cover loosely with foil; keep warm until serving time.
- Add garlic to skillet and cook over low heat 1 minute. Stir in cranberry sauce and tequila;

bring to a boil. Reduce heat. Simmer 5 minutes or until sauce is thickened, stirring occasionally. Stir in lime juice and cilantro.

- Spoon some of the sauce over chicken. Sprinkle with additional cilantro, if desired. Serve immediately with remaining sauce, lime wedges and coarse salt.
- Makes 6 servings.

50. Cajun Chicken Pasta Recipe

Serving: 4 | Prep: | Cook: 30mins | Ready in:

Ingredients

- 4 boneless skinless chicken breast halves cut into thin strips
- 2 tablespoons cajun seasoning
- 2 tablespoons butter
- 8 ounces canned mushrooms stems and pieces drained
- 2 cups heavy whipping cream
- 1/4 teaspoon dried basil
- 1/4 teaspoon sea salt
- 1/8 teaspoon garlic powder
- 1/8 teaspoon freshly ground black pepper
- 1 teaspoon Tabasco sauce
- 1 teaspoon all purpose flour
- 1 pound linguine cooked and drained
- 2 teaspoons grated parmesan cheese

Direction

- Place chicken and Cajun seasoning in a bowl or plastic bag then toss to coat.
- In large skillet over medium heat sauté chicken in butter for 7 minutes.
- Add mushrooms then cook and stir 3 minutes then reduce heat.
- Add cream and seasonings to taste then heat through and toss with linguine.
- Sprinkle with parmesan cheese and serve immediately.

51. Cant Tell Its Gluten Free Fried Chicken Recipe

Serving: 6 | Prep: | Cook: 20mins | Ready in:

Ingredients

- 1 quart buttermilk
- 1 tablespoon hot pepper, Hot Shot
- 1 tablespoon seasoned salt, Jane's Crazy Salt
- 1 tablespoon granulated garlic
- 1 cup cornstarch
- 1 cup potato starch
- 1 teaspoon xanthan gum
- 2 teaspoons baking powder
- 1 tablespoon seasoned salt, Jane's again
- 1 tablespoon hot pepper, Hot Shot again
- 1 teaspoon granuated garlic
- 6 chicken breast halves

Direction

- Combine all marinade ingredients and marinate chicken overnight or at least a few hours.
- Mix dry ingredients. When chicken has marinated, place dry ingredients in bag, then chicken and shake well to coat, covering completely. Remove breast from bag and place on rack for 20 minutes to set coating.
- In the meantime, put canola oil in an electric skillet about an inch up the side. Set control to 375 degrees and bring oil to temperature.
- Carefully place each piece of chicken in skillet skin side down. Fry on each side until golden brown. Don't hurry it.

52. Cap N Crunch Chicken Recipe

Serving: 4 | Prep: | Cook: 35mins | Ready in:

Ingredients

- 2c crushed Cap'n Crunch cereal
- 4 boneless, skinless chicken breasts
- 1/2c milk/buttermilk
- enough oil to cover chicken at least 1/2 way in your skillet (or however much it takes in your deep fryer)

Direction

- Trim your chicken
- Spread cereal on plate or pie pan
- Pour milk into wide bowl
- Soak chicken breasts in milk while your oil heats to about 350
- When the oil is ready coat the chicken in crushed cereal and press it in firmly
- Cook chicken 8-10min total - turn once about 3/4 way thru cooking if using a skillet
- Drain on paper towels or paper bags
- Enjoy!

53. Champagne Chicken Recipe

Serving: 4 | Prep: | Cook: 25mins | Ready in:

Ingredients

- 2 tablespoons all-purpose flour
- 1/2 teaspoon salt
- 1/4 teaspoon garlic powder
- Dash of pepper
- 4 skinned and boned chicken breasts halves, flattened
- 2 tablespoons butter or margarine, melted
- 1 tablespoon olive oil
- 3/4 cup champagne or white wine
- 1/4 cup chicken broth
- 1/4 cup sliced fresh mushrooms (optional)
- 1/2 cup heavy whipping cream

Direction

- Combine flour, garlic powder, salt, and pepper; lightly dredge chicken in flour mixture.

- Heat butter and oil in a large skillet; add chicken, and cook about 6 minutes on each side.
- Add champagne and chicken broth; cook over medium heat about 12 minutes or until chicken is tender. Remove chicken and set aside.
- Add mushrooms and whipping cream to skillet; cook over low heat, stirring constantly, just until thickened. Add chicken, and cook until heated.
- Serve with rice or couscous

54. Champagne Chicken And Shrimp Recipe

Serving: 4 | Prep: | Cook: 20mins | Ready in:

Ingredients

- 1 pound large shrimp (16 to 20 count), peeled and deveined
- 3 tablespoons fresh lemon juice
- salt and pepper to taste
- 4 tablespoons butter
- 4 boneless, skinless chicken breast halves
- 1 cup fresh mushrooms, sliced
- 1/2 large sweet onion, chopped
- 1 cup chicken stock or broth
- 1/3 cup all-purpose flour
- 1 1/2 cups half and half or light cream
- 3/4 cup champagne (serve the rest at dinner!)
- 16 ounces angel hair pasta, cooked and drained

Direction

- Combine peeled shrimp, lemon juice, salt and pepper. Set aside.
- In large skillet, melt butter.
- Add chicken breasts and brown on both sides and cook until chicken juices run clear.
- Remove from skillet and keep warm (I put them in a 250 degree oven).

- Add mushrooms and onion to skillet and sauté until mushrooms and onion are softened. (You may need to add more butter.)
- Remove and spoon over chicken. Keep warm.
- Add shrimp and sauté just until shrimp turn pink.
- Divide shrimp over chicken breasts.
- Whisk together chicken stock and flour. Add to skillet.
- Whisk over medium heat until thickened.
- Add half and half and Champagne. Cook until heated through.
- Divide pasta over 4 dinner plates.
- Top with chicken and mushrooms and shrimp.
- Spoon sauce over.
- Garnish with fresh parsley and pass the remaining Champagne.

55. Cheddar Chicken And Potatoes Recipe

Serving: 4 | Prep: | Cook: 22mins | Ready in:

Ingredients

- 4 slices bacon
- 4 boneless,skinless chicken breast halves (1lb)
- 4 c (1 lb) frozen diced potatoes with peppers and onions,thawed
- 4 oz. (1 c) shredded sharp cheddar cheese

Direction

- Cook bacon in large non-stick skillet over med. heat 5 mins. or till crisp. Remove from skillet to paper towel; discard drippings.
- Add chicken to skillet; cook 5 mins on each side or till done. Remove chicken from skillet; cover to keep warm
- Crumble bacon. Add to skillet with potatoes; cook and stir 5 mins.; or till heated through.
- Place chicken over potatoes; top with cheese. Cover; cook 2 mins. or till cheese is melted.

56. Cheesy Chicken And Rice Enchiladas Recipe

Serving: 6 | Prep: | Cook: 1hours30mins | Ready in:

Ingredients

- ½ onion, diced
- 2 Boneless chicken breasts, cut into bite-size pieces
- 2 TBS oil
- 2 cups cooked rice
- ½ cup sliced black olives - I use a whole can
- 20 oz enchilada sauce --This is where I use homemade -- I'm too picky
- 15 oz salsa
- 8 large tortillas
- 4 cups cheese, shredded
- salt and pepper, to taste
- sour cream

Direction

- Preheat oven to 375. Grease a 9×13 baking dish.
- Heat oil in a large skillet and add chicken and onion; season with salt and pepper. Cook until onion is soft and chicken is lightly browned and cooked through.
- Combine the cooked rice, chicken and onion mixture, and olives in a large bowl.
- Dump enchilada sauce and salsa in skillet (I use the same one from the chicken) and warm over low heat until just warm.
- Warm tortillas in oven 10-15 seconds until slightly warmed.
- For assembly -- have everything close at hand!
- Spoon some of your enchilada sauce into your baking dish to coat the bottom. Dip a tortilla in the skillet with your enchilada sauce so that both sides are nice and coated. Place it flat in your baking dish and spoon some of your chicken/rice mixture in. Sprinkle a small pinch of cheese over the mixture and put about a tablespoon of sour cream on top. Roll

up the tortilla and put it seam side down at the end of your pan. Continue with the remaining ingredients until the pan is nice and full. Drizzle remaining sauce over enchiladas and then cover with cheese. (You can add more sliced olives to the top if you'd like!)

- Bake for 30 minutes or until the cheese is nice and melted and bubbly.

57. Cheesy Chicken Enchilada Dinner Recipe

Serving: 5 | Prep: | Cook: 30mins | Ready in:

Ingredients

- 1 pound boneless skinless chicken breast halves cut into small pieces
- 16 ounce jar chunky salsa divided
- 1-1/4 cups shredded cheddar cheese divided
- 10 flour tortillas
- 2-1/2 cups frozen corn cooked

Direction

- Heat large non-stick skillet sprayed with no stick cooking spray on medium high heat.
- Add chicken then cook and stir 6 minutes or until cooked through.
- Stir in 1/2 cup of the salsa and 2/3 cup of the cheese then mix lightly.
- Spread 1 cup salsa onto bottom of rectangular baking dish.
- Spoon 1/4 cup chicken mixture down center of each tortilla then roll up.
- Place tortillas seam sides down on salsa in dish then top with remaining salsa and cheese.
- Bake at 350 for 20 minutes or until heated through then serve with corn.

58. Cheesy Chicken Manicotti Recipe

Serving: 8 | Prep: | Cook: 30mins | Ready in:

Ingredients

- 16 ounces ricotta cheese
- 2 eggs, beaten
- 3 cups shredded mozzarella cheese (leave one cup set aside)
- 1/4 cup fresh parsley
- 1 jar (26-32 oz. size) spaghetti sauce or Marinara
- 1/4 cup grated parmesan cheese, divided
- 1/2 lbs cooked chicken breast, diced finely

Direction

- Prepare manicotti according to package directions.
- Drain.
- In medium bowl, combine chicken, eggs, ricotta, parsley, 2 cups of the mozzarella and half of the parmesan, mix well.
- Spoon chicken mixture into each manicotti shell.
- In 13 x 9-inch baking dish, spread 1 cup spaghetti/marinara sauce.
- Lay manicotti in rows in sauce.
- Spoon remaining sauce over manicotti.
- Top with remaining mozzarella.
- Cover; bake at 375 degrees for 30 minutes or until hot and bubbly. Sprinkle with cheese.

59. Cheesy Chicken N Broccoli Skillet Recipe

Serving: 4 | Prep: | Cook: 25mins | Ready in:

Ingredients

- 4 small boneless skinless chicken breast halves (1 pound)
- 1/4 cup milk

- 1/4 pound Velveeta in 1/2" cubes
- 2 cups frozen broccoli florets
- 1/4 cup parmesan cheese, divided

Direction

- Heat large nonstick skillet over medium-high heat.
- Add chicken to pan.
- Cover.
- Cook chicken 5 to 7 minutes on each side OR until cooked through.
- Remove chicken from skillet.
- Keep warm (the chicken, not you!).
- Add milk, Velveeta, broccoli and 2 tablespoons Parmesan cheese to pan.
- Cook on medium heat, uncovered, for 4 minutes OR broccoli is heated.
- Return chicken to skillet.
- Cook and stir for 1 minute OR until chicken is coated and heated through.
- Sprinkle with remaining Parmesan cheese.

60. Chef Albys Chicken Piccata Recipe

Serving: 4 | Prep: | Cook: 30mins | Ready in:

Ingredients

- 4 skinless/boneless chicken breasts butterflied and cut in half
- sea salt & some freshly ground pepper
- flour for dredging
- 6 tbs butter
- 5-6 tbs olive oil
- 1/3 cup lemon juice
- 1/2 cup chicken stock
- 1/2 jar brined capers
- 1/4 cup dry white wine
- 1 (or more) tbs minced garlic
- Fresh lemon slices
- 1/3 cup fresh parsley chopped

Direction

- Season the chicken with salt and pepper.
- Dredge chicken in flour and shake off any excess.
- In a large skillet melt 2 Tbs butter and 3 TBS olive oil.
- Add chicken and cook for about 3 minutes each side.
- Remove and transfer to a holding plate.
- In the pan add the lemon juice, stock and capers. Bring this to a boil.
- Add the rest of the ingredients-butter/ garlic, NOT THE WINE YET, and stir it vigorously.
- Return the chicken to the pan and add lemon slices.
- Slowly add the wine cover and cook 5-10 minutes until done.
- Serve over rice or pasta and spoon the sauce over the chicken along with the lemon slices and capers. Sprinkle the chopped parsley over chicken and enjoy.
- NOTE: As an extra flavor you can lightly sprinkle some cinnamon on the chicken too.

61. Chevre Stuffed Chicken Breasts Recipe

Serving: 4 | Prep: | Cook: 45mins | Ready in:

Ingredients

- 3 oz. herb coated fresh goat cheese
- /14 C sun –dried tomatoes packed in olive oil, chopped
- 1 love garlic, finely chopped
- 1/8 tsp freshly ground black pepper
- 4 (6-8oz) boneless, skinless chicken breasts
- 1 ½ T olive oil
- ½ tap kosher salt

Direction

- Preheat oven to 375
- Spray a 9 x 13 baking pan with cooking spray

- Using a fork, mix together goat cheese, sun-dried tomatoes, garlic and pepper in a small bowl
- Make a pocket in each chicken breast by cutting a 3 x 1 ½" deep horizontal slit into the smooth part of the breast on the thickest side, taking care not to cut all the way through
- Stuff goat cheese mixture into pockets; use a toothpick inserted diagonally to close pocket
- In a large non-stick skillet, heat oil on medium high
- Sprinkle chicken with salt; place stuffed chicken in skillet with the smooth rounded side down
- Cook 5 minutes or until golden
- Remove from pan and place golden side up into baking pan
- Bake at 375 for 14 to 16 minutes or until cooked through or internal temp is 175F
- Remove toothpicks, slice and serve immediately

62. Chicken & Artichoke Bake Recipe

Serving: 6 | Prep: | Cook: 1hours | Ready in:

Ingredients

- 3 lbs boneless, skinless chicken breasts
- 1 tsp paprika
- 1 tsp dried rosemary
- 1/4 cup plus 2 tbsp butter
- 1 can artichoke hearts, whole, drained
- 1/4 lb mushrooms, sliced
- 2 tbsp flour
- 2/3 cup chicken broth (I use veg broth)
- 3 tbsp dry sherry
- salt & pepper to taste

Direction

- Preheat oven to 375 degrees.
- Mix salt, pepper paprika & rosemary in small bowl. Sprinkle chicken with spice mixture. In a

skillet, melt 1/4 cup butter and brown chicken over low-medium heat. Transfer chicken to a shallow 2 qt. casserole dish, reserving drippings. Place artichoke hearts in dish with chicken. Set aside.
- Add 2 tbsp. butter to pan drippings, melt over low heat. Add mushrooms, cook for 5 minutes. Stir in flour, cook for a couple of minutes, and then gradually add chicken broth and sherry. Cook while whisking over medium heat until thickened. Pour over chicken & artichoke hearts. Cover & bake approximately 50 minutes or until chicken is completely cooked through.

63. Chicken & Black Bean Taco Pizzettas Recipe

Serving: 12 | Prep: | Cook: 2hours | Ready in:

Ingredients

- 1 1/2 recipe of Wolfgang Puck's pizza dough (I used agave instead of honey this time)
- http://www.foodnetwork.com/recipes/wolfgang-puck/pizza-dough-recipe2/index.html
- ~
- 2 cups monterey jack cheese
- 1/2 cup medium cheddar cheese
- homemade fresh salsa (recipe below)
- 1 cup roasted chicken breast, diced, mixed with taco seasoning
- additional taco seasoning, for sprinkling
- 1 can organic cup black beans
- 1/4 cup scallions, diced
- fresh cilantro, chopped, for garnish
- ~
- Fire roasted Tomato Salsa:
- 15 oz organic fire roasted tomatoes
- 1 fresh vine-ripened tomato, halved and seeded
- 1/2 a sweet yellow onion
- 1 clove garlic

- 1 jalapeno pepper, halved (remove or keep seeds for mild or hot)
- 1/8 cup fresh cilantro
- juice of one fresh lime
- sea salt, to taste

Direction

- Make salsa:
- Place all ingredients in food processor and pulse until everything is finely chopped. Drain excess liquid with a strainer and place in container in fridge until ready for use.
- Prepare pizza dough, as instructed.
- To assemble:
- Preheat oven to 450F degrees. On floured work surface, divide dough into 12 balls and roll into circles (as thick or as thin as you like) Place rolled out pizza dough on parchment lined baking sheets (I was able to fit 6 per sheet).
- Sprinkle cheeses across each crust. Top each with a few teaspoons of salsa, sprinkle of green onions and beans over the cheese. Sprinkle lightly with additional taco seasoning.
- Bake pizzettas for 7 minutes, remove from oven, top with chicken (pressing down into the cheese a bit) and bake for another 5-8 minutes, or until the cheese is golden and bubbly. Remove from oven and sprinkle with fresh cilantro before serving.

64. Chicken A La Pablo De Sarasate Damn Good Chicken Recipe

Serving: 4 | Prep: | Cook: 2hours | Ready in:

Ingredients

- 4 large boneless skinless chicken breasts
- 2 cups of coarse fresh bread crumbs
- 2 large eggs
- 1/3 cup of heavy cream
- ½ oz. of fresh oregano

- 6 oz. of dried serrano ham
- ---QUESO AZUL con ALMENDRAS SAUCE----
- 1 cup of crumbled Campos de Toledo
- 1 cup of heavy cream
- ¾ cups of toasted almond (processed to a paste)
- 4 cloves of garlic minced finely
- 4 heaping tbls. of butter
- 1-2 oz of Jerez brandy
- Very coarse cracked mixed peppercorns
- ---PILAF SERASATE ---
- 3 cups of long grained white rice
- 1 quart of chicken stock + 3 cups of water
- 3 bay leaves
- Half a cup of olive oil
- 1 lb. of Chorizo Iberico
- 1 cup of cracked green olives (in mid Eastern store)
- 2 bunches of scallions
- 1 cup of dry white wine
- Fresh chopped flat leafed parsley
- salt, white pepper
- 1 cup of sour cream
- 2 tbls. of high grade chili powder
- 2 tsp. of cumin

Direction

- FOR THE CHICKEN: Self-explanatory. However chop up the ham very small and the oregano too. Mix them into the bread crumbs and make gold both sides in olive oil. Finish in the oven.
- FOR THE SAUCE: In a sauce pan cook the garlic in the butter for a minute then introduce the brandy. When that has cooked out, put in the almonds and the cream. Slowly reduce by half and melt in the cheese. A little lumpiness is OK also a wee bit of fresh rosemary could be added so long as it does not interfere with the oregano in the chicken coat. Season liberally with the pepper.
- FOR THE RICE: Boil the rice in the stock/water to which the bay leaves were added. When done, but firm drain it right at the time they are to go into this below:

- Remove the stones from the olives and chop them and the chorizo to a small size. Chop the scallions roughly. Heat the oil in a sauté pan and cook them all for 2-3 minutes.
- Put in the wine and reduce by half. Dump in the rice and mix well seasoning with the salt and pepper and the parsley. Mix the cumin and chili powder into the sour cream and use it to drizzle over the rice when served with the chicken topped with the bleu cheese sauce and some kind of roasted gourd.

65. Chicken Alfredo Lasagna Recipe

Serving: 4 | Prep: | Cook: 45mins | Ready in:

Ingredients

- 1 Baked chicken breast
- 1/2 a medium onion
- Diced mushrooms
- 1 Jar of premade alfredo sauce
- No pre-cook lasagna noodles(8oz)
- olive or vegetable oil
- 1 cup Parmesean cheese
- 1 cup Mozzarella
- 1 pint of ricotta cheese
- garlic(optional)
- 1 egg

Direction

- This recipe is entirely dependent on the Alfredo sauce you buy. I got an Alfredo sauce made by Classico called "roasted garlic" Alfredo sauce. 1 Jar of that was plenty.
- Bake the chicken first. No seasoning is needed. 1 medium sized chicken breast should be enough to cover the whole meal. I usually bake the chicken for 20 minutes at 450.
- Slice up half of an onion. It doesn't need to be extremely fine, but no big chunks. After you have them sliced, sauté the onions in a pan for a few minutes in oil.

- Dice mushrooms or use pre-sliced mushrooms.
- In a mixing bowl, add the egg, all of the ricotta cheese, all of the onion, and about 1/4 cup of parmesan. Mix it all up.
- On the bottom of your lasagna pan, apply a thin coat of oil and then apply another thin coat of Alfredo sauce over top.
- Layer the noodles over the first layer.
- Cut up the chicken so you have fairly small chunks of chicken and spread it over the first layer. Take the mushrooms and spread them around the same layer. Now take the ricotta cheese mixture and spread it over top of the first layer. Add a very light layer of Alfredo sauce on top of it.
- Repeat this process until you have come to the level of the pan.
- Bake the lasagna for about 45 minutes and then let it cool for about 10 minutes.
- You should never have to add any salt or garlic. Those flavors are definitely represented. I love my food salty and this satisfied that for me.

66. Chicken And Biscuits Recipe

Serving: 20 | Prep: | Cook: 15mins | Ready in:

Ingredients

- 2-3 C mashed potatoes
- 1/2 onion, chopped
- 2-3 skinless, boneless chicken breasts
- 2 C fresh or frozen vegetables
- 1 can chicken broth
- 2/3 C milk
- 1/3 C water
- 3 TBSP corn starch
- 2 C flour
- 2 1/2 tsp baking powder
- 3/4 tsp. salt.
- 5 TBSP shortening
- 3/4 C milk

Direction

- Preheat oven to 450.
- Cook and mash potatoes. You should make enough to get about 2-3 cups of mashed potatoes.
- Spread potatoes over the bottom of a medium sized cake pan or casserole dish.
- Cut chicken into small chunks. (If using frozen chicken, cook until thawed, and then cut into chunks)
- In a skillet or frying pan, cook onion and chicken, until chicken is just slightly pink on the inside.
- Add frozen vegetables to pan, and cook until vegetables are heated through, and chicken is no longer pink.
- Add chicken broth and milk to skillet. Heat to boiling.
- In a small glass, mix together water and corn starch. Add mixture to skillet and stir until chicken broth mixture becomes thick. (If mixture is not thick enough to your liking, repeat this step.)
- Pour mixture over potato layer.
- In a medium bowl, mix together 2 C flour, baking powder and 3/4 tsp salt.
- Cut in shortening until mixture is crumbly.
- Stir in milk just until dough is moistened, then drop by spoonfuls onto chicken mixture.
- Bake at 450 for 12 to 15 minutes, or until biscuits are golden brown, and cooked on the bottom.
- Serve hot.

67. Chicken And Black Bean Stuffed Burritos Recipe

Serving: 4 | Prep: | Cook: 30mins | Ready in:

Ingredients

- 1/4 cup water
- 2 tablespoons fresh lime juice
- 1/2 teaspoon chili powder
- 1/4 teaspoon ground cumin
- 1/4 teaspoon black pepper
- 1/8 teaspoon ground red pepper
- 2 cups shredded rotisserie chicken breast
- 1/4 cup thinly sliced green onions
- 3/4 cup canned black beans, rinsed and drained
- 1/2 cup refrigerated fresh salsa
- 4 (8-inch) flour tortillas
- 1/2 cup shredded monterey jack cheese
- cooking spray

Direction

- Bring first 6 ingredients to a boil in a small saucepan. Stir in shredded chicken and green onions.
- Combine beans and salsa. Spoon 1/4 cup bean mixture and 1/2 cup chicken mixture down center of each tortilla; sprinkle with 2 tablespoons cheese. Roll up.
- Heat a large skillet over medium-high heat. Coat pan with cooking spray. Add 2 burritos. Place a cast-iron or other heavy skillet on top of burritos, and cook for 3 minutes on each side. Remove from pan, and repeat procedure with the remaining 2 burritos.

68. Chicken And Eggplant Alfredo Recipe

Serving: 4 | Prep: | Cook: 45mins | Ready in:

Ingredients

- 5 cups vegetable oil
- 4 eggs, beaten
- 2 cups milk
- 5 cups dry Italian bread crumbs
- 3 large eggplants, sliced into 1/3 inch rounds
- 3 pounds skinless, boneless chicken breasts, cut into strips and pounded to 1/4 inch thick
- 16 ounces mozzarella cheese, grated
- 2 (16 ounce) jars alfredo sauce

- an of course some slap yo mama seasoning.. / or use some of your favorite.. any way use.. about 1/4 teaspoon sprinkle this onto your boneles chicken breast strips..

Direction

- Heat oil in deep-fryer to 375 degrees F (190 degrees C). Preheat oven to 225 degrees F (110 degrees C).
- Blend eggs and milk together in a large bowl. Place bread crumbs in another large bowl. Dip eggplant slices first into egg mixture, then bread crumbs, coating well. Fry in batches in hot oil, turning to brown evenly, then transfer to a paper towel-lined dish to drain. Repeat process for the chicken, lightly browning but not overcooking.
- Generously grease a large, deep baking dish. Working in single layers, arrange eggplant, then chicken, then shredded mozzarella cheese, until all ingredients are gone. Pour Alfredo sauce evenly over the top.
- Bake in the preheated oven for 30 minutes. Increase heat to 350 degrees F (175 degrees C), and continue baking for another 20 minutes. Serve hot.

69. Chicken And Sausage Jambalaya Recipe

Serving: 68 | Prep: | Cook: 75mins | Ready in:

Ingredients

- 2 chicken breasts
- sea salt
- black pepper
- cayenne pepper
- olive oil
- 200g Cooking chorizo, 1cm cubes
- 1 large onion, roughly chopped
- 1 green pepper, roughly chopped
- 1 red pepper, roughly chopped
- 4 sticks of celery, trimmer and roughly chopped
- 3 fresh bay leaves
- 4 sprigs of fresh thyme
- 4 cloves of garlic, peeled & sliced
- 1-2 fresh red chillies, deseeded and finely chopped
- 1 400g tin chopped tomatoes
- 1.5 litres of chicken stock
- 700g long grain rice
- 1tsp parsley

Direction

- Season the chicken with salt, pepper and a pinch of cayenne
- Brown the chicken pieces and sliced sausage over a medium heat
- After 5 minutes, once browned on all sides, add onion, peppers, celery, bay, thyme, and a pinch of salt and pepper
- Stir, then fry on a medium heat for 10 minutes, stirring every now and then
- Once the vegetables have softened, add garlic and chillies.
- Stir for around a minute, then add tinned tomatoes and chicken stock
- Bring to the boil, then turn down the heat, put lid on the pan, and simmer for 30 minutes
- Add rice, give it a stir, and replace lid
- Cook for a further 15-20 minutes, stirring every few minutes
- Add enough water to make it a porridge consistency, replace lid and cook for a further 3-4 minutes
- Stir parsley through and serve

70. Chicken Andouille With Creamy Tomato Sauce Pasta Recipe

Serving: 4 | Prep: | Cook: 15mins | Ready in:

Ingredients

- 1 lb. chicken andouille sausage links

- 1 boneless skinless chicken breast
- 1/2 sweet onion, chopped (or less)
- McCormick roasted garlic and red bell pepper seasoning blend (or omit, not necessary)
- 1 28 oz. can crushed tomatoes
- 1 14 oz. can chicken broth
- 1 Tbls. Dijon mustard
- 1 8 oz. block of cream cheese (I used Philly light)
- 1 Tbls. dried basil (if you use fresh, about 1/4 cup chopped, or more)
- 1 tsp. marjoram
- pasta, Any type you like, I used short wide egg noodles approx. 10 oz. dry (I didn't measure, just dumped in what I thought I needed)

Direction

- Chop onion, set aside
- Cut each Andouille link in half lengthwise and slice in 1/4 inch pieces, set aside
- Cube chicken breast, set aside
- Meanwhile bring water to boil for pasta, add when ready
- Sauté onion in a little olive oil till just about clear, remove
- Add chicken and Andouille and cook till just done
- Return onions to pan
- Add crushed tomatoes and chicken broth and bring to simmer
- Add mustard and seasonings
- Turn off heat (or remove if using electric heat)
- Add cream cheese and slowly incorporate (I use the back of my spoon and press on it gradually pulling away till dissolved)
- Return to heat and add pasta, stir till heated through
- Serve immediately

71. Chicken Asparagus Roll Ups Recipe

Serving: 4 | Prep: | Cook: 30mins |Ready in:

Ingredients

- 1/2 cup mayonnaise
- 3 tablespoons Dijon mustard
- 1 lemon, juiced and zested
- 2 teaspoons dried tarragon
- 1 teaspoon ground black pepper
- 1/2 teaspoon salt
- 16 spears fresh asparagus, trimmed
- 4 skinless boneless chicken breast halves, pounded to about 1/4 inch thickness
- 4 slices provolone cheese
- 1 cup panko bread crumbs

Direction

- Preheat oven to 475
- Grease a baking dish
- In a bowl, mix together the mayo, mustard, lemon juice, zest, tarragon, salt and pepper until the mixture is well combined
- Set aside
- Cook asparagus in the microwave on high until bright green and just tender, 1 to 1 1/2 minutes
- Place one slice cheeses on each prepared chicken breast and top with 4 asparagus spears per breast
- Roll the chicken around the cheese and asparagus, making a tidy package
- Place seam side down in the prepared dish
- With a brush, apply a thin coating of the mayo mixture to each breast and sprinkle each with panko crumbs, pressing the crumbs into the chicken to make a coating
- Bake until the crumbs are browned and the chicken juices run clear, about 25 minutes

72. Chicken Asparagus Mushroom Bake Recipe

Serving: 6 | Prep: | Cook: 35mins | Ready in:

Ingredients

- 1 Tbs. butter
- 1 Tbs. olive oil
- 2 boneless chicken breast {cut into bite size peices
- 2 cloves garlic minced
- 1 cup {Large can mushroom peices}
- 2 cups sliced aspargus
- black pepper to taste
- 1 pkg. cornbread stuffing{^ oz}
- 1/4 cup dry white wine Optional
- 1 can {41 1/2 oz chicken broth
- 1 can {101/2 oz}cream asparagus or cream of chicken soup {Undiluted

Direction

- PREHEAT OVEN 350 heat butter and oil in skillet until butter is melted
- Cook chicken and Garlic 3 minutes over medium high heat until CHICKEN is no longer pink add mushrooms cook and stir 2 minutes Add Asparagus cook stir 5 minutes or until crisp tender season.
- Put in a 2 1/2 Quart casserole top with stuffing mix. Add wine to skillet, cook and stir 1 minute over medium high heat. Scrape up any brown bits from bottom of skillet. Add broth and soup, cook and stir till well blended pour into casserole mix. WELL bake 35 MINUTES OR UNTILL LIGHT BROWN

73. Chicken Bacon And Pasta Recipe

Serving: 4 | Prep: | Cook: 30mins | Ready in:

Ingredients

- 1 boned and skinned chicken breast cut into slices
- 1 pound bacon cubed
- 1 white onion chopped
- 1 pound spiral pasta
- 1/2 cup romano cheese
- 2 cups heavy cream

Direction

- Fry bacon until crisp then remove and drain on paper towels.
- Sauté onions in 2 tablespoons of the bacon drippings then add chicken and cook 10 minutes.
- While chicken cooks prepare pasta according to package directions.
- When pasta is al dente drain then rinse well and return to pan.
- Add onions and chicken then mix well and stir in cheese and cream.
- Put over low heat until mixture is heated through.
- Add drained bacon and mix well then sprinkle with freshly ground black pepper and serve hot.

74. Chicken Biryani Recipe

Serving: 4 | Prep: | Cook: 40mins | Ready in:

Ingredients

- 500 g chicken breast, diced
- 200 ml yoghurt
- 1 tsp ground turmeric
- 1 tsp hot chilli powder
- 1tsp garam masala
- 3 cm knob of ginger, peeled and grated
- 3 garlic cloves, crushed
- 1 tsp vegetable oil
- 2 tbsp ghee or butter
- 2 medium onions, finely sliced
- 1 cinnamon stick
- 5-6 cloves

- 3 cardamom pods

Direction

- Mix the yoghurt with turmeric, chili powder, garam masala and half the ginger and garlic. Add the chicken, stir to coat, and marinate in the fridge for at least 30 minutes.
- Heat the oil and 1 tablespoon of ghee in a heavy-based pan and fry the onions for 8-10 minutes.
- Remove the onions from the pan with a slotted spoon, add the remaining ghee, and fry the cinnamon, cloves and cardamom for 30 seconds.
- Add the chicken and marinade to the pan, and stir well.
- Simmer for about 10 minutes on a medium heat, until the chicken is cooked through.

---

75. Chicken Breasts Stuffed With Perfection

Serving: 0 | Prep: | Cook: | Ready in:

Ingredients

- 6 breast half, bone and skin removed (blank)s skinless, boneless chicken breast halves - pounded thin
- 1 (8 ounce) bottle Italian-style salad dressing
- 8 piece (blank)s slices of stale wheat bread, torn
- ¾ cup grated Parmesan cheese
- 1 teaspoon chopped fresh thyme
- ⅛ teaspoon pepper
- 1 ½ cups feta cheese, crumbled
- ½ cup sour cream
- 1 tablespoon vegetable oil
- 3 cloves garlic, minced
- 4 cups chopped fresh spinach
- 1 bunch green onions, chopped
- 1 cup mushrooms, sliced
- 1 (8 ounce) jar oil-packed sun-dried tomatoes, chopped

Direction

- Place chicken breasts in a large resealable plastic bag. Pour in Italian dressing, seal tightly, and refrigerate at least 1 hour.
- Place the stale bread, Parmesan, thyme, and pepper into a food processor. Pulse until the bread is processed into crumbs. Set aside.
- In a large bowl, stir together the feta and sour cream. Set aside.
- Heat the oil in a large skillet over medium heat. Stir in the garlic. Then add the spinach, and cook until it wilts. Stir in green onions, cook 2 minutes. Remove spinach to a plate, and leave any liquid in the pan. Stir in mushrooms, and sauté until soft. Remove mushrooms to plate with spinach. Allow to cool briefly, then combine spinach and mushrooms with feta and sour cream mixture.
- Stir the sun-dried tomatoes into the mixture, and spread onto a large cookie sheet. Place in the freezer for about 30 minutes.
- Preheat the oven to 400 degrees F (200 degrees C).
- Place chicken breasts on a cookie sheet, and place about 3 tablespoons of the filling mixture in the center of each breast. Roll the breasts, and secure with a toothpick. Transfer chicken breasts to a baking dish, and sprinkle breadcrumb mixture over chicken breasts.
- Bake, uncovered, in a preheated oven for 25 minutes.
- Marinating Footnote
- The nutrition data for this recipe includes information for the full amount of the marinade ingredients. Depending on marinating time, ingredients, cooking method, etc., the actual amount of the marinade consumed will vary.
- Nutrition Facts
- Per Serving:
- 622 calories; protein 43.4g 87% DV; carbohydrates 34.7g 11% DV; fat 35.2g 54% DV; cholesterol 119mg 40% DV; sodium 1516.6mg 61% DV.

76. Chicken Breasts With Garlic And Balsamic Vinegar Recipe

Serving: 4 | Prep: | Cook: 20mins | Ready in:

Ingredients

- 4 skinless, boneless chicken breasts (about 1 1/4 lbs. total)
- salt and freshly ground pepper to taste
- ¾ pound small or medium mushrooms
- 2 tablespoons flour
- 2 tablespoons olive oil
- 6 cloves of garlic, peeled
- ¼ cup balsamic vinegar
- ¾ cup fresh or canned chicken broth
- 1 bay leaf
- ½ teaspoon minced fresh thyme or
- ¼ teaspoon dried thyme or 1 tablespoon fresh thyme
- 1 tablespoon butter

Direction

- Tip 1: Always read a recipe in its entirety before beginning.
- Tip 2: Pound the chicken breasts to desired thickness for even cooking.
- Sprinkle chicken breasts with salt and pepper.
- Rinse mushrooms, drain and pat dry.
- Season flour with salt and pepper and dredge the chicken breasts in mixture.
- Shake off excess.
- Heat oil in heavy skillet over medium-high heat and cook the chicken breasts until nicely browned on one side, about three minutes.
- Add whole garlic cloves.
- Turn chicken breasts and scatter mushrooms over them.
- Continue cooking, shaking the skillet and redistributing the mushrooms so that they cook evenly.
- Cook about 3 minutes and add vinegar, broth, bay leaf and thyme. Cover tightly and cook over medium-low heat for 10 minutes.
- Turn pieces occasionally as they cook.
- Transfer chicken to warm serving platter and cover with foil.
- Cook sauce with mushrooms, uncovered, over medium-high heat for about 7 minutes.
- Swirl in the butter.
- Discard bay leaf. Pour mushrooms and sauce over chicken and serve.
- Yields 4 servings.

77. Chicken Breasts With Herb Stuffing Recipe

Serving: 4 | Prep: | Cook: 25mins | Ready in:

Ingredients

- 1 tbsp chopped garlic
- 2 cups baby spinach
- 1/4 cup chopped fresh parsley
- 1/4 cup chopped fresh
- 2 tbsp chopped fresh tarragon
- 2 tbsp fresh bread crumbs
- 1 tsp orange zest
- 2 tbsp orange juice
- 1 tbsp Dijon mustard
- salt and freshly ground pepper
- 3 tbsp olive oil
- 4 boneless chicken breasts, skin on
- Sauce
- 1/4 cup fresh orange juice
- 1/2 tsp grated orange zest
- 1/4 cup dry vermouth
- 1/2 cup whipping cream.
- herb Fritters
- 1/4 cup all-purpose flour
- 1/4 cup sparkling water
- salt and pepper to taste
- 12 sprigs fresh mint leaves
- 1 1/2 cups vegetable oil
- vegetable Confit:
- 2 tbsp butter
- 1 1/2 cups red potatoes, diced into 1/2-inch cubes

- 6 garlic cloves, peeled and halved
- 2 cups morel mushrooms, sliced in half
- 1/2 cup asparagus tips
- 1 cup peeled blanched fava beans
- salt and freshly ground pepper
- 2 tbsp chopped fresh chervil

Direction

- Preheat oven to 425°F
- In a food processor or by hand, combine garlic, spinach, parsley, chives, tarragon, bread crumbs, orange zest, orange juice, mustard, salt, pepper and 2 tbsp. olive oil.
- Reserve 1 tbsp. oil to fry chicken.
- Insert a sharp knife into the thick end of each chicken breast and cut a lengthwise pocket three quarters of the way across chicken breast.
- Lay breast flat open and spread with about 2 tbsps. Spinach mixture.
- Fold breast back together.
- Season breasts with salt and pepper.
- Reserve any leftover spinach mixture.
- Set ovenproof skillet on medium-high heat and add remaining oil.
- Add chicken, skin-side down and fry until crisp and golden, about 2 minutes.
- Flip breasts over and place skillet in oven.
- Bake for 15 to 20 minutes or until juices run clear.
- Remove chicken from skillet. Skim any fat and add orange juice, orange zest and vermouth.
- Bring to boil scraping up any sticky bits on the base of pan.
- Reduce until syrupy, about 1 minute.
- Add cream and bring to boil.
- Stir in reserved spinach mixture.
- Reduce until slightly thickened.
- Season to taste.
- Serve chicken over vegetable confit and drizzle with sauce.
- Garnish with herb fritters (recipe follows)
- Vegetable Confit
- Morel mushrooms must be well rinsed because they retain grit.
- Put them in a strainer, run cool water over them and shake the strainer as you rinse.
- Pat dry with paper towels and use immediately.
- If morels are unavailable use oyster mushrooms.
- Substitute peas for favas if desired.
- Heat butter in skillet over medium heat.
- Add potatoes and sauté for 1 minute.
- Add garlic, cover and cook 5 minutes or until potatoes are tender.
- Add morel mushrooms and asparagus tips and sauté for 2 minutes or until asparagus is tender crisp.
- Add fava beans.
- Cook 1 minute longer or until favas are heated through.
- Season with salt and pepper
- Divide confit into 4 portions on 4 plates.
- Serve chicken breasts on top of confit.
- Sprinkle with chervil.
- To prepare fava beans, shell the beans from their pods.
- Bring a pot of water to the boil.
- Add beans and return to boil.
- Drain and refresh with cold water.
- Slip blanched beans from tough outer skins.
- Herb Fritters
- In a small bowl, mix flour and sparkling water.
- Season with salt and pepper.
- Dip mint into batter, shaking off excess.
- Heat oil until a cube of bread fried in the oil turns brown in 15 seconds.
- Fry mint leaves in hot oil for 15 seconds, gently turn over and fry another 15 seconds until lightly golden.
- Drain on paper towels.
- These fritters may be made several hours ahead and reheated on a baking sheet in a 350°F oven for 3 minutes.

78. Chicken Breasts With Prosciutto Amp Sage Recipe

Serving: 6 | Prep: | Cook: 20mins | Ready in:

Ingredients

- 6 boneless, skinless, chicken breast halves, pounded to an even thickness
- 24 leaves of fresh sage, stems removed
- 6 slices prosciutto
- 1 1/2 tablespoons olive oil
- 3 tablespoons dry oloroso sherry (or other sherry)

Direction

- Rinse and pat dry the chicken breast halves.
- Place chicken breast halves smooth-side-up on a work surface. Place four sage leaves at an angle atop each half, spacing them evenly for a uniform striped look. Carefully center a prosciutto slice atop the breast and wrap the slice around, securing it with toothpicks.
- In a nonstick skillet, heat the olive oil to medium. Place the chicken breasts sage — side-down in the pan. Cover and cook ten minutes. Turn the chicken breasts and continue cooking, uncovered, until cooked through, about 5-7 minutes depending on the thickness of the breasts. Add the sherry and increase the heat to medium-high. Cook, scraping to loosen any browned bits, for one minute, until a light coating of the syrup pan drippings remains. Remove from heat and serve the chicken with the drippings.

79. Chicken Breasts With Tomatoes And Olives Recipe

Serving: 4 | Prep: | Cook: 15mins | Ready in:

Ingredients

- 4 (6oz) boneless,skinless chicken breast halves
- 1 c multi-colored cherry or gape tomatoes,halved
- 3 Tbs oil and vinegar dressing
- 20 olives (Kalamata and Picholine)olives,halved
- 1/2 c (2oz)crumbled feta cheese

Direction

- Prepare grill to med-high heat. Sprinkle chicken evenly with1/4 tsp salt and 1/4 tsp pepper. Place chicken on grill rack coated with cooking spray, and grill 6 mins each side or till chicken is done. Keep warm.
- Combine tomatoes, 1-1/2 Tb dressing and olives in a med. skillet over med. heat, and cook for 2 mins or till tomatoes soften slightly and mixture is thoroughly heated, stirring occasionally. Brush chicken with remaining 1-1/2 Tb dressing.
- Cut each chicken breast half into 3/4" slices. Top each half with 1/4 c tomato mixture.
- Sprinkle each serving with 2 Tbsp. cheese and torn basil leaves, if desired.

80. Chicken Broccoli Cassorole Recipe

Serving: 5 | Prep: | Cook: 40mins | Ready in:

Ingredients

- 2 Boneless chicken breasts
- 1 can cream of mushroon soup
- 1 lb chopped thawed broccoli
- 1 cup shedded cheddar cheese
- 1/4-1/2 cup milk
- 1/4 cup parmesan cheese
- 1/2 Bisquick

Direction

- In a bowl mix together Parmesan cheese and bisquick--set aside for later

- Broil the chicken breast in a large pot with enough water to cover the breasts.
- Once the chicken is cooked let it cool enough to where you can peel it into small pieces.
- Mix can of cream of mushroom soup, and milk, add pieces of chicken. (The consistency should be creamy)
- In a 9x13 inch baking dish layer the chicken mixture, broccoli and cheese. Start with cheese on bottom
- Take the Parmesan cheese mix and that is your last layer of the casserole
- Bake at 375 degree for 25 minutes
- More cheese can be added once it's out the oven

81. Chicken Cacciatore A Classic Recipe

Serving: 4 | Prep: | Cook: 60mins | Ready in:

Ingredients

- 1 onion, chopped
- 1/4 cup water
- 1 cup whole tomatoes, undrained and chopped
- 1/2 cup tomato puree
- 1 tsp dried whole oregano
- 1/2 tsp garlic powder
- 1/8 tsp pepper
- 4 chicken breast halves (~ 2 lbs) skinned
- 2 cups hot cooked spaghetti

Direction

- In a 10 inch skillet, combine onion and water, cover and cook over medium heat for 3 to 4 minutes or until onion is tender.
- Stir in tomatoes, tomato puree, and seasoning, cover. Reduce heat and simmer for 10 minutes.
- Add chicken to the skillet, spoon tomato mixture over the chicken, cover and simmer for 30 minutes.

- Uncover and simmer an additional 15 minutes.
- Serve over the hot spaghetti.

82. Chicken Cacciatore Recipe

Serving: 0 | Prep: | Cook: 1hours | Ready in:

Ingredients

- 1. 6 chicken thighs
- 2. 2 chicken breasts with skin and backbone, halved crosswise
- 3. 2 teaspoons salt, plus more to taste
- 4. 1 teaspoon freshly ground black pepper, plus more to taste
- 5. 1/2 cup all-purpose flour, for dredging
- 6. 3 tablespoons olive oil
- 7. 1 large red bell pepper, chopped
- 8. 1 onion, chopped
- 9. 5 large white mushrooms sliced.
- 10. 3 garlic cloves, finely chopped
- 11. 3/4 cup dry white wine or rice vinegar or Merin
- 12. 1 (28-ounce) can diced tomatoes with juice
- 13. 3/4 cup reduced-sodium chicken broth
- 14. 3 tablespoons drained capers
- 15. 1 1/2 teaspoons dried oregano leaves
- 16. 1/4 cup coarsely chopped fresh basil leaves

Direction

- 1. Sprinkle the chicken pieces with 1 teaspoon of each salt and pepper. Dredge the chicken pieces in the flour to coat lightly.
- 2. In a large heavy sauté pan, heat the oil over a medium-high flame. Add the chicken pieces to the pan and sauté just until brown, about 5 minutes per side. If all the chicken does not fit in the pan, sauté it in 2 batches.
- 3. Transfer the chicken to a plate and set aside. Add the bell pepper, onion and garlic to the same pan and sauté over medium heat until the onion is tender, about 5 minutes. Season with salt and pepper.

- 4. Add the wine and simmer until reduced by half, about 3 minutes. Add the tomatoes with their juice, broth, capers and oregano. Return the chicken pieces to the pan and turn them to coat in the sauce. Bring the sauce to a simmer.
- 5. Continue simmering over medium-low heat until the chicken is just cooked through, about 30 minutes for the breast pieces, and 20 minutes for the thighs.
- 6. Using tongs, transfer the chicken to a platter. If necessary, boil the sauce until it thickens slightly, about 3 minutes. Spoon off any excess fat from atop the sauce. Spoon the sauce over the chicken, then sprinkle with the basil and serve.

83. Chicken Casserole Recipe

Serving: 6 | Prep: | Cook: 47mins | Ready in:

Ingredients

- 4 boneless chicken breasts
- 4 slices of cheddar cheese--you can use swiss instead
- 1 can of cream of chicken soup
- 1/4 C. white wine
- 3/4 C. Pepperidge Farm stuffing
- 1/4 C. oleo or butter-melted
- parsley

Direction

- Put chicken in a greased pan and top with the cheese, mix soup and wine, pour over the chicken; mix oleo and stuffing and top all. Bake at ~350° for 45-50 minutes.
- Bake uncovered.

84. Chicken Casserole W Bacon And Corn Recipe

Serving: 6 | Prep: | Cook: 1hours20mins | Ready in:

Ingredients

- 1 1/2 cups of long grain, uncooked rice
- 6-8 slices of bacon
- 1/2 large yellow onion, diced
- 2-3 lrg boneless, skinless chicken breasts (or about 2 lbs)
- 1 1/2 cups frozen corn (or frozen mixed vegetables)
- 1 heaping Tablespoon flour
- 3 cups chicken broth
- 1/4 cup sour cream or half and half (dairy free coffee cream works)
- 1/2 tsp garlic powder
- 1/2 tsp dried basil
- 1/2 tsp dried oregano
- 1/4 tsp paprika
- 1/4 tsp freshly ground black pepper
- 1/8 tsp sea salt
- Optional: 1 cup shredded cheddar cheese (Monterey Jack, Provolone or Pepper Jack is great too)
- ~2-3 green onions, sliced; or parsley for optional topping
- *Feel free to use any herbs and spices you like in your corn chowder! If you like it spicy, Cajun spice would go great in this instead of the herbs and spices called for.
- **For extra creaminess try substituting some of the frozen corn for a can of creamed corn.

Direction

- Preheat the oven to 350F. Grease a 9x13" casserole dish
- Using kitchen shears cut the bacon strips into 1/2 inch pieces over a large frying pan. Add enough cold water to the pan just to cover the bottom of the pan. Break up any pieces of bacon that are stuck together and spread evenly in the pan. Place over high heat, stirring often. Once the water is almost

evaporated reduce the heat to medium, stirring frequently until crisp. Place the bacon on paper towels to drain.

- Remove all but 1-2 tablespoons of bacon fat from the pan and sauté the onion over medium heat.
- Meanwhile, use the same kitchen shears and cut the chicken breasts into 1" pieces over the casserole dish. (This saves from cutting board clean up!) Sprinkle the herbs and spices over the chicken breast and toss to coat. Stir in the rice and corn.
- Once the onion is soft, add the tablespoon of flour and stir for one minute (adding more bacon fat or oil if needed) slowly add the chicken broth while stirring constantly and bring to a simmer. Add the simmered broth, bacon and sour cream or half and half to the casserole dish and stir to combine.
- Cover tightly with foil and bake for 35-45 minutes, until the rice is tender. Remove foil and top with cheese, bake for another 10-15 minutes until the rice is fully cooked and cheese is melted.
- Top with sliced green onions or parsley if desired. Enjoy! :)

85. Chicken Casserole With Pasta Tomato And Broccoli Recipe

Serving: 8 | Prep: | Cook: 20mins | Ready in:

Ingredients

- No-Stick cooking spray
- 2 teaspoons vegetable oil
- 2/3 cup chopped onion
- 2 large cloves garlic, minced
- 1 pound boneless, skinless chicken breasts, cut into 1-inch pieces
- 2 (14 1/2 oz.) cans whole tomatoes, drained and coarsely chopped
- 1 (8 oz.) can tomato sauce
- 1/4 cup ketchup

- 1 1/4 teaspoons dried basil leaves
- 3/4 teaspoon dried oregano leaves
- 1/4 teaspoon salt
- 1 (10 oz.) package frozen broccoli cuts, thawed and well drained
- 5 ounces uncooked small macaroni, cooked and well drained
- 1/2 cup grated parmesan cheese, divided

Direction

- HEAT oven to 350°F. Coat 13 x 9 x 2-inch baking dish with no-stick cooking spray.
- HEAT oil in large skillet over medium-high heat. Add onion and garlic. Cook and stir until tender. Add chicken. Cook and stir just until chicken is no longer pink in center. Stir in tomatoes, tomato sauce, ketchup, basil, oregano and salt. Bring to a boil. Reduce heat to low. Simmer 5 minutes, stirring occasionally.
- COMBINE broccoli, macaroni, chicken mixture and 1/4 cup cheese in large bowl. Stir well. Spoon into prepared dish. Sprinkle with remaining 1/4 cup cheese.
- BAKE 20 minutes. Do not overbake. Remove dish to cooling rack. Serve warm.

86. Chicken Cheddar Stuffing Casserole

Serving: 0 | Prep: | Cook: | Ready in:

Ingredients

- 2 packages (6 ounces each) chicken stuffing mix
- 2 cans (10-3/4 ounces each) condensed cream of mushroom soup, undiluted
- 1 cup 2% milk
- 4 cups cubed cooked chicken
- 2 cups frozen corn
- 2 cans (8 ounces each) mushroom stems and pieces, drained
- 4 cups shredded cheddar cheese

Direction

- Prepare stuffing mixes according to package directions. Meanwhile, in a large bowl, combine soup and milk; set aside. Spread the stuffing into two greased 8-in. square baking dishes. Layer with chicken, corn, mushrooms, soup mixture and cheese.
- Cover and freeze one casserole for up to 3 months. Cover and bake the second casserole at 350° for 30-35 minutes or until cheese is melted.
- To use frozen casserole: Remove from the freezer 30 minutes before baking (do not thaw). Bake at 350° for 1-1/2 hours. Uncover; bake 10-15 minutes longer or until heated through.
- Nutrition Facts
- 1 each: 373 calories, 21g fat (12g saturated fat), 96mg cholesterol, 822mg sodium, 21g carbohydrate (3g sugars, 1g fiber), 26g protein.

87. Chicken Cheese Steak Recipe

Serving: 4 | Prep: | Cook: 180mins | Ready in:

Ingredients

- Ingredients
- 4 chicken breasts - boneless
- 2 med onions, sliced
- 2 can sliced mushrooms or fresh in equal amounts
- 3 or 4 tbs butter
- 1 can, cheddar cheese soup
- 5 oz milk
- 1 dash parmesan cheese (1 to 2 tbs)

Direction

- Sauté onions and mushrooms in butter in a small frying pan until onions are translucent. Set aside 1/2 the onion/mushroom mix.
- In a large measuring cup, mix soup and milk and stir to remove any lumps.

- Place chicken in a 5-quart slow cooker and pour other ingredients over chicken.
- Sprinkle with Parmesan cheese and cook on high for 3 hours or on low for 6 hours.
- Shred chicken with 2 forks before serving.
- Serve on a warm hoagie bun and top with 1/2 the sautéed mushrooms and onions
- Be sure to warm the Mushrooms and onion that has been set aside before topping.
- Can also be served over mashed potatoes, rice or on toast.
- Excellent over steamed vegetables such as cauliflower or broccoli.

88. Chicken Chow Mein With Lemon Reduction Sauce Recipe

Serving: 6 | Prep: | Cook: 30mins | Ready in:

Ingredients

- chicken breast, raw
- 3 whole lemons
- 1 lb. fresh bean sprouts
- about 20 snow peas
- soya sauce (KIKKOMAN highly recommended)
- Chinese dry noodles
- 1 can bamboo shoots
- carrot shreds
- 1 small can water chestnuts
- 2 medium sized shallots, thinly sliced
- 4 green onions
- 6 mushrooms, thinly sliced
- salt and pepper to taste
- dry mustard powder
- 1 tsp sugar
- Chinese five-spice herbal blend
- olive oil
- 1 clove garlic

Direction

- Cut the raw chicken breast into bite-sized pieces.
- Parboil these gently for one minute.
- In a wok or deep frying pan, combine:
- 2 tbsp. olive oil
- The chicken
- Bamboo shoots
- Water chestnuts
- Mushrooms
- Shallots
- Carrot shreds
- Soya sauce
- Chinese five-spice blend
- Simmer until the shallots are lightly caramelized, then add:
- Snow peas
- Bean sprouts
- Simmer on low heat until sprouts are translucent, and slightly softened, then turn off the heat.
- In the meantime, prepare the lemon reduction:
- Place the juice of all the lemons into a skillet.
- Add the mustard powder --- 1 tsp.
- Add the sugar
- Cook on medium-high heat, stirring constantly, until the mixture is reduced to one half its original volume.
- Pour into the wok-----
- Plate:
- Top with finely chopped green onions and Chinese dried noodles---
- ENJOY!

89. Chicken Cilantro Soup Recipe

Serving: 6 | Prep: | Cook: 30mins | Ready in:

Ingredients

- cooked chicken carcass
- 3 carrots
- 3 celery stalks
- one whole onion cut into chunks
- 10 black peppercorns
- 3 chicken breast, cooked and chopped
- salt and pepper
- 1 can (28 ounce) Italian plum tomatoes, with juice
- 1 teaspoon dried or 2 tsp. fresh oregano
- cilantro

Direction

- Place carcass in a soup pot and cover with water. Add carrots, celery onion and peppercorns and salt to taste. Heat to boil, then lower heat and simmer 3 hours.
- Strain broth and discard vegies. Refrigerate broth about 4 hours and skim off fat. Return to stove over medium heat.
- Roughly chop tomatoes and add to the broth with their juice. Add oregano, cooked chicken and any additional salt and pepper. Cook over medium heat for 30 minutes them serve with a sprinkle of cilantro.

90. Chicken Clemenceau Recipe Recipe

Serving: 2 | Prep: | Cook: 1hours | Ready in:

Ingredients

- ,chicken Clemenceau Recipe
- 4 Tbsp Unsalted butter, in all
- 2 chicken breasts, lightly pounded
- 2 Cups Mushrooms, thickly sliced
- 1 Small Onion, chopped
- 2 Green Onions, sliced
- 3 Large cloves Garlic, minced
- 1/2 Cup Dry White Wine
- Kosher Salt & black pepper
- 3 Tbsp Vegetable Oil, in all
- 1 Large Russet Potato, 1/2 inch dice
- 2 Tbsp Italian Parsley, minced
- 1 Cup Small Green Peas, canned (Petit Pois)

Direction

- Preheat an oven to 400 degrees F.
- Toss the diced potatoes in 2 Tbsp. of the oil and season liberally with kosher salt and black pepper. Place on a baking sheet, and into the oven for 45 minutes, occasionally turning them with a spatula for even browning.
- When the potatoes are almost golden brown, heat 2 Tbsp. of the butter, and 1 Tbsp. of the oil in an ovenproof skillet. When the fat is bubbling and hot, add the chicken breasts, which have been seasoned with kosher salt & black pepper, brown quickly on both sides, remove to a plate.
- In the same hot pan add the mushrooms, sauté until golden brown. Add the onions and garlic, season with a little salt and pepper, sauté until the onions are almost tender and have some color. Deglaze the pan with the white wine, cook for 2 minutes. Stir in 1 Tbsp. of the parsley.
- Place the chicken back in the pan and cover with some of the "sauce." Place in the oven until the chicken is just cooked through.
- To Assemble:
- Divide the Brabant potatoes between two warmed plates, making a pile in the center, place a chicken breast on each.
- Melt the remaining butter into the sauce, and fold in the Petit Pois until just warmed through. Divide the sauce over the two chicken breasts and garnish with the remaining parsley.
- Serves 2.

91. Chicken Club Sandwich Recipe

Serving: 2 | Prep: | Cook: | Ready in:

Ingredients

- 2 boneless, skinless chicken breast halves, grilled or roasted and thinly sliced
- 8 slices of thick-cut bacon, fried crisp and drained
- 1 cup iceberg lettuce, shredded
- 6 slices of tomato, medium thickness
- 2 Tbsp. mayonnaise
- 4 slices of whole wheat bread, toasted until just lightly browned
- salt and pepper to taste

Direction

- Spread a thin layer of mayonnaise on two pieces of the toast.
- Divide the chicken slices between the two sandwiches and lay atop the mayo.
- Place four slices of bacon on each sandwich, followed by three tomato slices.
- Balance a handful of the shredded iceberg lettuce on top of the tomatoes.
- Spread a thin layer of mayo on the other two pieces of toast, and press the mayo side down to assemble.
- Makes 2 sandwiches.

92. Chicken Coconut Curry Recipe

Serving: 4 | Prep: | Cook: 60mins | Ready in:

Ingredients

- 8 Skinless, Boneless chicken breasts
- 2 tbsp Groundnut or sunflower oil
- 1 tbsp garlic and ginger paste
- 2 Medium Potatotes, peeled
- 1/2 tsp Tumeric
- 2 tbsp Rogan Josht curry paste (Gorimas)
- 1/2 tsp salt
- 1/2 tsp Chilli Powder
- 300ml chicken stock
- rice noodles

Direction

- Chop the Chicken into bite size pieces and marinade in the Garlic, Ginger and Curry Paste for an hour.
- In a blender, blend the chopped onions

93. Chicken Corriander Recipe

Serving: 2 | Prep: | Cook: 20mins | Ready in:

Ingredients

- 2 chicken breasts (skin off) cubed
- 3 - 5 cloves garlic (depending on your taste)
- 1 tablespoon of fresh ginger blended with 1 tbsp of water (the stuff in tubes is good enough)
- 7oz fresh coriander (a large bunch or 3 small packets)
- 1/2 fresh green or red chilli (or more if you like it hot) finely chopped (seeds make it hotter)
- 1/4 teaspoon cayenne pepper
- 1tsp ground cumin
- 1tsp ground coriander
- 1/2 tsp turmeric
- 4 - 5 tablespoon lemon juice (fresh or bottled is fine)
- ¼ to ½ pint water (depending on how much sauce/gravy you like)
- 4 tablespoon vegetable oil

Direction

- Heat the oil in a pan and cook the chicken cubes until white, remove with a slotted spoon and put the chicken to one side.
- Add the fresh ginger to the pan and cook on a low/medium heat for 1 - 2 minutes (stirring all the time so it doesn't burn), until the oil has been absorbed into the ginger, add the garlic into the oil until softened (only a few seconds).
- Add the chopped chilli and all the other spices, stirring well in to make a paste.
- Add the cooked chicken back to the pan and mix well coating all the chicken pieces with the paste. Add chopped coriander leaves (I chop with scissors - makes it much easier)
- Add about 1/4 pint water and the lemon juice, bring to a boil then cover tightly with a tight lid and cook on a low heat/simmer for 15

minutes, then turn all the chicken pieces over and cook for a further 15 mins.
- Serve with spiced Basmati rice.

94. Chicken Cream Casserole Recipe

Serving: 8 | Prep: | Cook: 45mins | Ready in:

Ingredients

- 4 or 5 large chicken breasts or 3 cans chicken
- 1 or 2 cans cream of mushroom soup
- 4 to 8 oz sour cream
- Ritz crackers
- butter

Direction

- Preheat oven to 350
- Cook chicken breasts and cut into bit size pieces or drain canned chicken
- Put in greased 13x9 dish
- Stir together soup and sour cream
- **Sample mixture to get to your desired taste, some like it tangier than others**
- Pour over chicken
- Place in oven
- Melt about 1 stick butter
- Crush about 2 rolls of Ritz crackers
- Add crackers to butter to coat all crackers (add more butter or crackers as needed)
- Remove chicken from oven and sprinkle crackers on top
- Put back in oven about 30-45 minutes
- **NEXT NUMBERS ARE VARIATIONS**
- Use veggies instead of chicken to use as a side dish
- Use BOTH chicken and veggies for a one dish meal

95. Chicken Cutlets Braciole Recipe

Serving: 4 | Prep: | Cook: 45mins | Ready in:

Ingredients

- 1/2 c hot water
- handful of golden raisins
- 1/4 c pine nuts
- 1 c flat-leaf parsley
- 1 TB lemon zest
- 2 cloves garlic,finely chopped
- 3 slices white sandwich bread,torn
- 1/2 c grated parmigiano-Reggiano
- 4 pieces boneless,skinless chicken breast
- salt and fresh ground black pepper
- 2 TB extra virgin olive oil
- 2 TB butter
- 1 c dry white wine
- 2 c tomato sauce
- 2 TB fresh tarragon,a few sprigs,leaves chopped

Direction

- Pour very hot tap water into small bowl. Add raisins and plump 5 mins.
- Lightly toast nuts in small fry pan over med-low heat.
- Drain raisins, pat dry. Place raisins, garlic nuts, parsley, lemon zest, torn bread and cheese into processor pulsing into a stuffing.
- Butterfly the chicken open by cutting into and across the breast but not all the way through. Pound out the cutlets and season chicken with salt and pepper. Fill breasts with stuffing, roll and secure with toothpicks.
- Heat olive oil and butter in large skillet over med-high heat. Brown braciola all over 7 to 8 mins, remove, set aside. Deglaze pan with wine, scraping up drippings. Stir in tomatoes and tarragon, add chicken back, cover and simmer 15 mins. Slice and serve.

96. Chicken En Croute Recipe

Serving: 4 | Prep: | Cook: 45mins | Ready in:

Ingredients

- 1 package frozen puff pastry dough (see note below)
- 4 organic chicken breasts
- 1 large bag fresh baby spinach
- 1 large shallot, minced
- 2 tablespoons unsalted butter
- olive oil
- zest of one small lemon
- pinch of freshly grated nutmeg
- 1 package boursin cheese (I used garlic & Fine herbs)
- 1 container marsarpone cheese
- 2 sweet red bell peppers, roasted, peeled and seeded
- 1 1.5 oz. package "More than Gourmet" roasted chicken Demi-Glace
- egg wash: one egg and a little water, beaten
- kosher salt & freshly cracked black pepper
- white pepper

Direction

- For dough: Cut puff pastry into 4 pieces. On lightly floured surface, roll out each piece to slightly thin out (has to be big enough to wrap chicken). Chill until ready to use.
- For peppers: Set oven on broil and move rack to the top. Place peppers on top rack and broil until skin is blackened on that side. With tong, flip peppers over to blacken on other side. Remove from oven and place in brown paper bag and close. This steams the peppers and makes removal of skin easy. Once cooled, remove skin, discard of seeds and cut each pepper in half.
- For Chicken: In a large non-stick skillet, add 1 tablespoon of butter and a splash of olive oil. You may need to pound out the chicken breasts if they are too thick. Season chicken on both sides with kosher salt and pepper. Place breasts in pan and sear on each side, about 4

minutes per side, until you get a nice golden colour. Transfer chicken to plate, tent with foil, set aside.

- In same pan, add shallot and sauté until soft. Remove to a small bowl. To same pan again, add all the spinach (this will cook down to almost nothing!) Once spinach is wilted, transfer to bowl to cool. Squeeze all the liquid out the spinach with your hands over the sink. You must not skip this step; you'll wind up with soggy wet crust if you do! Add shallots with drippings and spinach to the pan. Season to taste with salt and white pepper, lemon zest and nutmeg. Return to bowl and let cool.
- For cheese: Mix boursin with mascarpone in bowl. Set aside.
- Assembly: Place all four squares of puff pastry back on lightly floured board. Place about 1/4 cup of cheese mixture on each pastry; divide the spinach among each as well. Top with red bell pepper halves and lastly the seared chicken breasts. Take each corner and fold in, completely cover the inside, trimming away any extra dough. Don't worry if it's not pretty, this is the bottom. Flip filled pastries over and onto a baking sheet lined with parchment. Cover with plastic wrap and freeze for at least 4 hours. This helps the crust really puff up and the crust doesn't get too soggy from the juices.
- Brush with egg wash. Bake at 400 degrees for 45 min or up to an hour. Once out of oven, let rest for 15 minutes.
- Serve with demi-glace: dissolve demi-glace in small saucepan with 1 1/2 cups water. Reduce to 1 cup.
- Note: The two most available brands of frozen puff pastry are definitely not alike. Dufour, sometimes available at Whole Foods markets, is made with all butter and is 100% natural; Pepperidge Farm, always in the freezer case of my local supermarket, contains no butter (how wrong!). Yes, Dufour tastes better, and rises higher when baked. It's also twice as expensive, and much harder to find, than Pepperidge Farm. Trader Joe's also carries "artisan" puff pastry in fall and winter seasons, which would be a good middle option. And

lastly, if you got the skills and time, just make it from scratch ;-)

97. Chicken Enchiladas Recipe

Serving: 6 | Prep: | Cook: 35mins | Ready in:

Ingredients

- 1 tablespoon butter
- 1/2 cup chopped green onions
- 1/2 teaspoon garlic powder
- 1 (4 ounce) can diced green chiles
- 1 (10.75 ounce) can condensed cream of mushroom soup
- 1/2 cup sour cream
- 1 1/2 cups cubed cooked chicken breast meat
- 1 cup shredded cheddar cheese, divided
- 6 (12 inch) flour tortillas
- 1/4 cup milk

Direction

- Preheat oven to 350 degrees F (175 degrees C). Lightly grease a large baking dish.
- In a medium saucepan over medium heat, melt the butter and sauté the green onion until tender (about 3 to 4 minutes). Add the garlic powder, then stir in the green chiles, cream of mushroom soup and sour cream. Mix well. Reserve 3/4 of this sauce and set aside. To the remaining 1/4 of the sauce in the saucepan, add the chicken and 1/2 cup of shredded Cheddar cheese. Stir together.
- Fill each flour tortilla with the chicken mixture and roll up. Place seam side down in the prepared baking dish.
- In a small bowl combine the reserved 3/4 of the sauce with the milk. Spoon this mixture over the rolled tortillas and top with the remaining 1/2 cup of shredded Cheddar cheese. Bake in the preheated oven for 30 to 35 minutes, or until cheese is bubbly.

98. Chicken Enchiladas Suizas Recipe

Serving: 4 | Prep: | Cook: 40mins | Ready in:

Ingredients

- 8 corn tortillas, stacked and wrapped in foil
- 1 1/4 cups green salsa (salsa verde)
- 1/2 cup reduced-fat sour cream
- 1/4 cup chopped cilantro
- 1 1/2 cups (8 oz) diced cooked chicken breast
- 6 oz (about 1.5 cups) swiss cheese,shredded
- 1 jar (7 oz) roasted red peppers, sliced
- Garnish: diced tomato and sliced scallion

Direction

- Place tortillas in oven. Heat to 425°F. Have a shallow 2- to 2 1/2-qt baking dish ready.
- Mix salsa, sour cream and cilantro in a medium bowl. Spread 1/2 cup over bottom of baking dish. In another bowl, combine chicken, 1 cup cheese and the roasted peppers. Remove tortillas from oven.
- Spoon scant 1/2 cup chicken mixture down center of each tortilla. Roll up; place seam side down in baking dish. Pour remaining salsa mixture over top.
- Cover with foil and bake 15 minutes until bubbly. Uncover; sprinkle with remaining cheese and bake 10 minutes, or until cheese has melted.

99. Chicken Enchiladas With Mole Sauce Recipe

Serving: 4 | Prep: | Cook: 25mins | Ready in:

Ingredients

- 3 tablespoons vegetable oil
- 1 1/2 pounds skinless boneless chicken breast
- salt and pepper
- 2 teaspoons cumin powder
- 2 teaspoons garlic powder
- 1 teaspoon Mexican spice Blend
- 1 red onion, chopped
- 2 cloves garlic, minced
- 1 cup frozen corn, thawed
- 5 canned whole green chiles, seeded and coarsely chopped
- 4 canned chipotle chiles, seeded and minced
- 1 (28-ounce) can stewed tomatoes
- 1/2 teaspoon all-purpose flour
- 16 corn tortillas
- 1 cup enchilada sauce, canned
- 1 cup shredded cheddar & jack cheese
- Garnish: Chopped cilantro leaves, scallions, sourcream, tomatoes.
- Mole Sauce:
- 2 teaspoons vegetable oil
- 1/4 cup finely chopped onion
- 1 tablespoon unsweetened cocoa powder
- 1 teaspoon ground cumin
- 1 teaspoon dried cilantro
- 1/8 tablespoon dried minced garlic
- 1 (10.75 ounce) can condensed tomato soup
- 1 (4 ounce) can diced green chile peppers

Direction

- Coat large sauté pan with oil. Season chicken with salt and pepper. Brown chicken over medium heat, allow 7 minutes each side or until no longer pink. Sprinkle chicken with cumin, garlic powder and Mexican spices before turning. Remove chicken to a platter, allow to cool.
- Sauté onion and garlic in chicken drippings until tender. Add corn and chilies. Stir well to combine. Add canned tomatoes, sauté 1 minute.
- Pull chicken breasts apart by hand into shredded strips. Add shredded chicken to sauté pan, combine with vegetables. Dust the mixture with flour to help set.
- Microwave tortillas on high for 30 seconds. This softens them and makes them more pliable. Coat the bottom of 2 (13 by 9-inch)

pans with a ladle of enchilada sauce. Spoon 1/4 cup chicken mixture in each tortilla. Fold over filling, place 8 enchiladas in each pan with seam side down. Top with mole sauce and cheese.

- Bake for 15 minutes in a preheated 350 degree F oven until cheese melts. Garnish with cilantro, scallion, sour cream and chopped tomatoes before serving. Serve with Spanish rice and beans.

- Mole Sauce: Heat the oil in a medium saucepan over medium heat, and cook the onion until tender. Mix in cocoa powder, cumin, cilantro, and garlic. Stir in the tomato soup and green chili peppers. Bring to a boil, reduce heat to low, cover, and simmer 10 minutes. Transfer to a gravy boat or pour directly over food to serve.

100.   Chicken Fettucine Alfredo Recipe

Serving: 4 | Prep: | Cook: 40mins | Ready in:

Ingredients

- 16 oz boneless skinless chicken breasts or tenderloin strips
- 1 cup cream
- 1/4 cup butter
- 1/2 cup grated or shredded parmesan cheese
- 1 tbsp onion flakes
- 1/2 tsp garlic powder
- 4 oz sliced mushrooms (small can or jar)
- 1 cup broccoli florets (fresh or thawed frozen)
- 4 slices bacon
- 6 oz fettucine

Direction

- Fry the bacon slices until crisp. Remove the bacon, drain on paper towel, cool and crumble. Pour off any excess drippings (preferably into a jar in the fridge for future flavoring).

- Cut the chicken breasts into approximately one inch pieces
- Chop the broccoli florets into small pieces about the size of a dime.
- Fill a pasta colander or large pot with water and bring to a boil.
- While the water is heating melt the butter and parmesan cheese together in the skillet over medium heat. Add garlic powder & onion flakes. Stir together.
- Add the mushrooms and broccoli florets. Mix together and simmer.
- Put fettucine in the pasta cooker and cook to just soft enough to cut through with the side of a fork. Remove the fettucine and drain.
- Meanwhile, back at the stove, add the cream to the mixture and stir together. Add the chicken pieces and simmer until everything is tender.
- Finally add the fettucine and toss together to coat the pasta. Serve hot and top each serving with a tablespoon or two of crumbled bacon.

101.   Chicken Florentine Recipe

Serving: 4 | Prep: | Cook: 25mins | Ready in:

Ingredients

- 2 whole chicken breasts, boned and halved
- 1/3 c flour
- 1/2 tsp salt, or to taste
- 1 egg ,beaten
- 1 to 2 Tbs. olive oil
- 10 oz pkg frozen chopped spinach
- 2 Tbs parmesan cheese
- 2 oz. Mozzarella or swiss cheese, sliced
- 1/3 c white wine
- juice of 1/2 lemon
- 1/2 c chicken broth

Direction

- Pound chicken breasts to uniform thickness. Dredge chicken in flour mixed with salt. Dip in beaten egg. Heat oil in frying pan and sauté chicken 6 to 7 mins on each side. While chicken is cooking, cook spinach according to package directions; drain and set aside.

- Remove chicken from pan and place in a greased ovenproof dish. Cover with spinach. Sprinkle Parmesan cheese over spinach. Cover with sliced Mozzarella or Swiss cheese
- Bake at 350 for 10 to 15 mins, or until chicken is tender and cheese melted. While chicken is baking, make sauce by adding wine and lemon juice to frying pan. Simmer and scrape up bits in the pan, until liquid is reduced to half. Add chicken broth, stir and simmer 2 mins. more.
- Pour over chicken or serve separately.

---

102. Chicken In Cream Sauce With Broccoli And Fettuccine Recipe

Serving: 4 | Prep: | Cook: 35mins | Ready in:

Ingredients

- 10 ounces uncooked fettuccine (1 package)
- 2 to 2-1/2 pounds boneless, skinless chicken breasts, cut into chunks
- 1 onion, diced / chopped
- 1 rib of celery, diced / chopped,
- 1 green or red bell pepper, chopped
- 3-4 garlic cloves, finely chopped / minced
- 3 Tbsps. butter
- 1 can (10-3/4 ounces) condensed cream of chicken soup, undiluted
- 1-1/2 cups chicken broth
- 2 cups frozen broccoli florets, thawed
- 1 can (4 ounces) mushroom stems and pieces, drained
- 1 can(small) water chestnuts, sliced
- 1 tsp. onion powder
- 1 tsp. pepper
- 3/4 cup shredded Parmesan / romano cheese

Direction

- Cook fettuccine according to package directions.
- In a very large frying pan, sauté onion, celery, bell pepper, garlic and mushrooms in butter until soft.
- Remove and set aside.
- Place chicken in the same frying pan and fry until no longer pink.
- Pour the can of soup into a bowl first and thoroughly mix it.
- Add the onion, celery, bell peppers, garlic, mushrooms with water chestnuts to the chicken.
- Stir in the soup, broth, broccoli, onion powder and pepper.
- Bring to a boil.
- Drain fettuccine and either add to the chicken mixture or place the mixture over top of the fettuccine before serving.
- Reduce heat. Cover and simmer for 5 minutes or until heated completely through.
- Sprinkle with Parmesan or Romano cheese.

---

103. Chicken Italiano Recipe

Serving: 14 | Prep: | Cook: 10mins | Ready in:

Ingredients

- 3 cups dried penne pasta, cooked according to package directions, and drained, omitting salt
- 1 pound chicken breast, skinless and boneless, cubed
- 2 cups broccoli florets
- 2 red bell peppers, sliced
- 2 yellow squash, sliced
- 1 14-oz. can no-salt-added diced tomatoes, drained
- 1/4 cup white cooking wine (or water)
- 1/2 teaspoon basil
- 1/2 teaspoon oregano
- 1/2 teaspoon black pepper
- 1/4 cup fat free Parmesan cheese, grated

Direction

- 1. Spray a non-stick skillet with cooking spray
- 2. Over medium high heat, cook chicken until done and set aside in a bowl.
- 3. Add broccoli, peppers and cooking wine to skillet.
- 4. Cover with a lid and simmer for 4 to 5 minutes.
- 5. Toss chicken, vegetable mixture and pasta in skillet.
- 6. Sprinkle with Parmesan cheese.

104. Chicken Kebabs With Creamy Pesto Recipe

Serving: 4 | Prep: | Cook: 30mins | Ready in:

Ingredients

- 2 tsp grated lemon rind
- 4 tsp fresh lemon juice
- 2 tsp bottled minced garlic
- 2 tsp olive oil
- 1/2 tsp salt
- 1/4 tsp black pepper
- 8(1") pieces yellow bell pepper
- 8 cherry tomatoes
- 1 lb. skinless,boneless chicken breasts,cut in 1" pieces
- 1 small red onion,cut in 8 wedges
- cooking spray
- 2 TB low-fat plain yogurt
- 2 TB reduced-fat sour cream
- 1 TB commercial pesto

Direction

- Preheat broiler or grill
- Combine rind, 1TB juice, garlic, oil, salt and pepper. Toss with bell peppers, tomatoes, chicken and onion. Thread vegetables and chicken onto 4 (12") skewers. Place on broiler pan coated with spray or an oiled grill rack.

Broil or grill 12 mins or till chicken is done, turning occasionally.
- Combine 1 tsp. juice, yogurt, sour cream and pesto. Serve sauce with kebabs.

105. Chicken Korma Recipe

Serving: 8 | Prep: | Cook: 45mins | Ready in:

Ingredients

- 2 c plain yogurt; non-fat
- 4 whole chicken breasts; skinless
- 4 tsp curry powder
- 2 tsp canola oil
- 2 tsp ground coriander
- 1 medium onion; peeled & cubed
- 2 tsp ginger; minced
- 2 large tomatoes; peeled & chopped
- 4 cloves garlic; peeled & minced
- 4 each bay leaves
- 1/2 tsp salt
- 1 teaspoon lemon juice
- 1 teaspoon cayenne pepper; ground

Direction

- Mix together yogurt, spices, garlic, and lemon juice in a medium bowl.
- Add chicken, turning to coat.
- Let stand at room temperature for 30 minutes.
- Heat oil in a skillet over medium heat. Add onion and cook, stirring about 3 minutes or until lightly browned.
- Stir in tomato and bay leaves; cook 5 minutes.
- Add chicken and marinade mixture to pan and mix thoroughly.
- Cover and simmer over medium-low heat, stirring frequently, for about 20-30 minutes, or until chicken is done.
- 150 calories, 29% calories from fat, 5 g fat, 1 g saturated fat, 38 mg cholesterol, 238 sodium, 2 meat, 1/2 milk, 1 fat

106. Chicken Marengo Recipe

Serving: 2 | Prep: | Cook: 40mins | Ready in:

Ingredients

- 2 deboned chicken breasts
- 1 onion
- 1 clove of garlic
- 1/2 cup flour
- 2 cans stewed tomatoes
- 8 large mushrooms
- cayenne pepper
- salt
- black pepper
- 1 tablespoon fresh tarragon
- 8 ozs. dry sherry
- olive oil or other cooking oil
- rice (I prefer boil-n-bag), vermicelli or similar pasta

Direction

- Step 1 - Brown the chicken
- Cut chicken breasts into bite size pieces.
- In a small paper bag, add flour, tarragon, salt, pepper, cayenne pepper and chicken pieces.
- Shake vigorously. In a large iron skillet, heat oil on medium high and add chicken pieces.
- Cook until golden brown and remove the chicken for later use.
- Step 2 - Making the sauce
- Using the drippings in the skillet, add minced onion, crushed garlic and sliced mushrooms.
- Simmer until onions are clear.
- Add flour then sherry, stirring frequently.
- Let simmer until sauce is of the desired consistency.
- Step 3 - The end game
- In a large casserole dish, put chicken pieces and pour sauce on top. Pour stewed tomatoes on top of the dish.
- Sprinkle parsley on the very top and bake for 30 minutes at 350 degrees. Serve on pasta or rice......

107. Chicken Nuggets Recipe

Serving: 3 | Prep: | Cook: 15mins | Ready in:

Ingredients

- 2 tbsp. vegetable oil
- 1 tbsp. Dijon prepared mustard
- 3 chicken breasts, boneless, skinless
- Crumb Coating:
- 1 cup whole brown rice flour
- 1 tsp. chili powder
- ½ tsp. paprika
- salt and pepper to taste
- ¼ tsp. oregano

Direction

- Coating:
- Place all coating ingredients in a shaker bag and mix well.
- Mix oil and mustard in a bowl. Cut the chicken into nugget sized pieces and add to mixture. Coat thoroughly. In a plastic bag with crumb coating, put a few pieces at a time, shaking well to coat them.
- On a baking sheet lined with tin foil, place the pieces so they don't touch, in a single layer. Bake at 400F for 15 mins. or until done.

108. Chicken Parisienne Recipe

Serving: 6 | Prep: | Cook: 480mins | Ready in:

Ingredients

- 6 skinless, boneless chicken breast halves
- salt and pepper to taste
- paprika to taste
- 1/2 cup dry white wine

- 1 (10.75 ounce) can condensed cream of mushroom soup
- 1 (4.5 ounce) can sliced mushrooms, drained
- 1 cup sour cream
- 1/4 cup all-purpose flour

Direction

- Sprinkle chicken breasts lightly with salt, pepper and paprika.
- Place in slow cooker.
- Combine wine, soup and mushrooms in a mixing bowl.
- In another bowl, mix together the sour cream and flour.
- Stir sour cream mixture into the mushrooms and wine.
- Pour over chicken in slow cooker.
- Sprinkle with additional paprika, if desired.
- Cover and cook on Low for 6 to 8 hours.

109. Chicken Parmesan Recipe

Serving: 6 | Prep: | Cook: 60mins | Ready in:

Ingredients

- 4 to 6 boneless, skinless chicken breasts
- 1/3 cup melted margarine
- 1 cup grated parmesan cheese

Direction

- Roll chicken in melted margarine first and then in parmesan cheese until well coated. Place chicken in a greased baking pan and drizzle a little extra margarine over each piece. Bake at 350F for 1 hour or until tender.

110. Chicken Parmigiana Recipe

Serving: 6 | Prep: | Cook: 40mins | Ready in:

Ingredients

- 2 large eggs
- 1 tsp. salt
- 1/8 tsp. black pepper
- 6 boneless, skinless chicken breast halves
- 1 cup crushed club crackers
- 1/2 cup vegetable oil
- 1 (15-oz.) can tomato sauce
- 1/4 tsp. dried basil
- 1/4 tsp. garlic powder
- 1 Tbsp. butter
- 1/2 cup grated parmesan cheese
- 6 slices mozzarella cheese

Direction

- Preheat the oven to 350 degrees.
- Spray a 13x9" baking dish cooking spray.
- Whisk eggs, salt and pepper until blended. Dip chicken pieces in egg mixture and coat with cracker crumbs.
- Heat oil in a large skillet over medium until hot. Add chicken=ken, cook chicken until browned on both sides, about 3 minutes per side, drain. Arrange in single layer in prepared baking dish.
- Wipe skillet with paper towels.
- Combine tomato sauce, basil and garlic powder in the skillet and mix well.
- Bring to a boil stirring occasionally reduce heat.
- Simmering stirring occasionally until mixture is thickened, about 6 minutes.
- Stir in butter. Pour over the chicken. Sprinkle with the Parmesan cheese.
- Baked covered for 30 minutes, remove the cover. Top each chicken breast with mozzarella cheese. Bake for 10 minutes longer

111. Chicken Pasta Bowl With Asparagus And Sugar Pod Peas. Recipe

Serving: 4 | Prep: | Cook: 10mins | Ready in:

Ingredients

- 1 lb pasta (450g)fettucini
- 2 large chicken breasts cut in half and pounded to 1/2 inch thick.
- salt and pepper to taste
- 1 lb fresh asparagus (450g)
- ½ lb sugar pod peas (225 g)
- 3 cloves garlic finely minced
- 2 tsp olive oil
- 2 cup Half and Half (236 ml)
- 1 cup parmesian cheese (100g) grated
- 4 tbsp butter

Direction

- Cook the pasta and grill the chicken breasts while the vegetables are roasting.
- Roast the Vegetables
- Preheat oven to 450°°F. Snap the tough ends off of the asparagus and cut the asparagus into 2 inch pieces.
- Spread the asparagus and sugar-pod peas on a roasting pan. Sprinkle with the minced garlic. Drizzle with the olive oil. Add Salt and Pepper to taste. Roast for 8 - 10 minutes or until fork-tender.
- Grill the Chicken Breast
- Season the Chicken Breast with salt and pepper and grill until the internal temp is 170°F, or the juices run clear when it is cut into.
- Cook the Pasta and Assemble
- Bring 4-6 quarts of salted water to a full rolling boil. Add the pasta and cook to desired doneness. 6-7 minutes for al-dente. If pasta is freshly made, 90 seconds to 2 minutes for al-dente.
- Once pasta is done drain, split between 4 serving bowls. Heat the half with the butter in a bowl until hot in the microwave. Stir in the

parmesan cheese to combine and pour 1/4 portions over each bowl of pasta. Divide the roasted vegetable equally between the pasta bowls. Slice the grilled chicken breast and place it on top. Garnish with some fresh-grated parmesan cheese and Italian parsley.

112. Chicken Pepper Pasta Recipe

Serving: 0 | Prep: | Cook: 30mins | Ready in:

Ingredients

- 6 Tbs butter
- 1 medium onion, sliced
- 1 red pepper, cut into strips
- 1 tsp minced garlic
- 1 rotisserie chicken, breast meat torn into pieces
- 1 Tbs dried tarragon
- 1/4 tsp pepper
- 3/4 tsp salt
- 1/2 cup parmesan cheese
- 1 cup penne

Direction

- Melt butter in skillet until sizzling.
- Stir in onion, peppers and garlic.
- Cook over medium high heat for 2-3 minutes until peppers are crisp/tender.
- Reduce heat to medium low.
- Add chicken, tarragon, salt and pepper.
- Stir to combine and heat through.
- Prepare pasta and drain.
- Toss with chicken mixture.
- Add parmesan cheese and toss.

113. Chicken Picata Recipe

Serving: 4 | Prep: | Cook: 20mins | Ready in:

Ingredients

- 2 full boneless chicken breasts or 8 boneless tenders.
- 1 cup flour
- 1/2 tsp lemon pepper
- 1/2 tsp paprika
- 1/4 tsp salt
- 1 egg
- 1/4 cup milk
- 6 tbsp butter
- 3 tbsp olive oil
- 1 cup wine
- juice of 2 fresh lemons
- 3 tbsp capers and juice

Direction

- 1. If fresh breasts, place each breast between wax paper to pound chicken flat. Then cut in half, then cut each length wise. If you are using the frozen chicken tenders, defrosted of course, just use from the bag. Thawed frozen taste just fine.
- 2. TO 1 CUP FLOUR ADD LEMON PEPPER, PAPRIKA, and SALT.
- 3. BEAT 1 EGG AND ¼ CUP MILK. DIP EACH BREAST IN MIX, THEN DIP EACH BREAST IN FLOUR MIX AND LAY IN A SINGLE LAYER ON WAX PAPER.
- 4. IN A LARGE NON-STICK FRYING PAN HEAT 3 TABLESPOONS BUTTER AND 3 TABLESPOONS OLIVE OIL (OIL HELPS PREVENT BUTTER BURNING). BROWN AND COOK ALL CHICKEN BREASTS. WHEN DONE PLACE BREASTS ON A PLATE.
- 5. COOK ON "HI" 1 CUP WHITE WINE. BRING TO A BOIL THEN ADD JUICE OF 2 LEMONS, 3 TABLESPOONS CAPERS AND JUICE, AND 3 TABLESPOONS BUTTER. BOIL A LITTLE, THEN RETURN CHICKEN TO PAN. REDUCE HEAT TO MEDIUM AND COOK FOR ABOUT 5 MINUTES.
- 6. SERVE TO PLATES, SPOONING ON CAPERS AND LEFT OVER SAUCE. THIS IS A KILLER DISH.

114. Chicken Pot Pie Lasagne Recipe

Serving: 10 | Prep: | Cook: 75mins | Ready in:

Ingredients

- 12 pieces Lasagne, uncooked
- 1 pound boneless, skinless chicken breasts, diced
- 3 cups sliced fresh mushrooms
- 1 cup thinly sliced carrots
- 1/2 cup sliced spring onions
- 1 cup frozen green peas, thawed and well drained
- 1 tsp. ground thyme
- 1/2 tsp. salt
- 1/2 cup all-purpose flour
- 3 1/2 cups skim milk
- 1/2 cup dry sherry
- 1/4 tsp. ground red pepper (cayenne)
- 1 15-oz. carton low-fat ricotta cheese
- 1 1/2 cups grated part-skim mozzarella cheese, divided
- 1/2 cup grated reduced-fat swiss cheese

Direction

- Prepare pasta according to package directions. Spray a Dutch oven or large skillet with cooking spray; place over medium-high heat until hot. Add chicken and sauté 4 minutes or until cooked through. Drain well and set aside. Recoat Dutch oven with cooking spray and place over medium-high heat until hot. Add mushrooms, carrots and onions; sauté 6 minutes. Set aside.
- Place flour in a medium saucepan. Gradually add milk, stirring with a wire whisk until blended; stir in sherry. Bring to a boil over medium heat and cook for 5 minutes or until thickened, stirring constantly. Stir in salt and red pepper. Reserve one cup of sauce and set aside.

- In a bowl, combine ricotta cheese, 1 cup mozzarella cheese and Swiss cheese.
- Preheat oven to 350° F. Spread 1 cup of the sauce over the bottom of a 13 x 9 x 2-inch pan. Arrange 4 pieces of the lasagne (3 lengthwise, 1 widthwise) over the sauce. Top with half of ricotta cheese mixture, half of chicken mixture and half of remaining sauce mixture. Repeat layers, ending with 4 pieces of lasagne. Spread reserved 1 cup of sauce over the last complete layer of lasagne, being sure to cover the lasagne completely.
- Cover lasagne with foil and bake 1 hour. Uncover lasagne, sprinkle remaining 1/2 cup mozzarella cheese on top and bake an additional 5 minutes uncovered. Re-cover and let stand 15 minutes before serving.

115.   Chicken Pot Pie Recipe

Serving: 6 | Prep: | Cook: 70mins | Ready in:

Ingredients

- Filling
- 1-lb boneless skinless chicken breasts
- 1 can cream of chicken soup
- 1 can cream of celery soup
- 1 can cream of potato soup
- 2 cans mixed vegetables (drained)
- salt
- pepper
- Crust
- 1 cup self-rising flour
- 1 cup milk
- 1 cup mayonnaise

Direction

- Preheat oven to 350 degrees. Cut up chicken and combine with all the filling ingredients. Pour into a buttered 9 x 13 pan. Mix the crust ingredients and pour over the filling. Bake on a sheet pan for 1 hour.
- ***NOTE***

- You can put the chicken in raw as recipe states or use rotisserie chicken. I sometimes cook my chicken it the crockpot and then add it to the casserole. Either way it is delicious!

116.   Chicken Ragu W Rigatoni Recipe

Serving: 6 | Prep: | Cook: 60mins | Ready in:

Ingredients

- •1 lb rigatoni (or other short cut pasta)
- •3 tbsp olive oil
- •1 1/2 lb. boneless chicken breasts (or thighs), chopped into small bite-sized pieces
- •1 medium onion, chopped
- •1 carrot, peeled and grated
- •4, 5 pieces Baby Bella mushrooms, sliced
- •1, 2 bay leaf
- •1 tsp dried oregano
- •2 garlic cloves, finely chopped
- •1/2 tsp black pepper
- •1/4 cup marsala
- •1/2 cup white wine
- •1 28 oz. jar spaghetti sauce of choice
- •1 26 oz. diced tomatoes
- •1/2 cup fresh parmesan cheese, grated (mandatory!)
- •A handful of fresh basil leaves, torn
- •1/4 pound pancetta or bacon, diced (optional)

Direction

- 1. In a large skillet or non-stick pan, heat 1 tbsp. olive oil over medium high heat and brown the chicken pieces on all sides. Cook until slightly browned and any pink spots are removed.
- 2. Meanwhile, cut the vegetables into desired pieces or use a grater for smaller sizes. Lower the heat and add the basil, onions, carrots, mushrooms, garlic and cook, stirring

frequently, until the veggies are softened, about 10 minutes.

- 3. Stir in the bay leaves, tomato sauce, tomato paste, Marsala, white wine, and herbs. Semi-cover with lid and cook on low with a slight bubble for about 30 minutes to infuse all ingredients. Sample the sauce and add salt and pepper according to taste. Discard bay leaves before combining with chicken pieces.
- 4. Cook the rigatoni according to package directions, but don't forget to add salt to the boiling water. In addition, do not rinse under cold water; drain in colander hot and set aside.
- 5. After rigatoni pasta and sauce are finished, combine the two and plate. Grate plenty of fresh parmesan cheese and garnish with extra basil leaves. Enjoy!

117. Chicken Ratatouille Recipe

Serving: 2 | Prep: | Cook: 60mins | Ready in:

Ingredients

- 2 whole chicken breasts, quartered, boned and skinned
- 1 -10 oz chicken broth or water
- 4 tbsp olive oil
- 1 clove garlic, minced
- 1 medium onion, chopped
- 1/2 green pepper, chopped
- 10 mushrooms, sliced
- 2 tomatoes, chopped
- 1 small zucchini, sliced
- 1/2 small eggplant, chopped
- 1 - 5 1/2 oz tomatoe paste
- 1 tsp salt
- 1/4 tsp dried chervil
- 1/4 tsp dried basil

Direction

- Place chicken in a large skillet and tight-fitting lid. Cover with chicken broth or water. Bring

to a boil. Reduce heat. Simmer, covered, for 10 minutes, or until done, turning chicken breasts once. Remove chicken to platter. Reserve broth.

- In a large saucepan, heat. Add oil, sauté garlic, onion and green pepper until transparent. Add remaining oil. Sauté mushrooms, zucchini, tomatoes and eggplant for 15 minutes. Add tomato paste and reserved broth. Mix well. Add salt and herbs. Simmer, covered, for 1 hour, adding a little more broth or water if it gets too dry. Taste and adjust for seasonings. Return chicken to the vegetable stew. The dish may be made ahead and refrigerated at this point.
- Just before serving gently simmer until heated through.

118. Chicken Riggies Recipe

Serving: 8 | Prep: | Cook: 1mins | Ready in:

Ingredients

- 8 tbs chopped garlic
- 16 oz sliced mushrooms
- 4 chicken breasts, cut into cubes
- 1 jar of sweet red peppers
- 3 tbs butter or margarine
- 1/4 cup cooking sherry, or sherry
- 3 cups parmesan cheese
- 2 tbs sweet basil
- 1 tbs black pepper
- 2-4 hot cherry peppers (for mild heat 2 or really hot use all 4)
- 3 cups parmesan cheese
- 1 cup of your favorite preparedI tomato sauce
- 1 quart half and half
- 1 lb cooked rigatoni

Direction

- Deseed the peppers and slice them. Put them aside.

- Mix the half and half and parmesan cheese together and Put aside. Put oil in preheated pan and cook garlic and onions on medium high heat.
- Add the mushrooms. When the mushrooms are cooked add the chicken.
- When chicken is done cooking, add sherry and butter. Add all of you peppers.
- Sprinkle with the basil and black pepper.
- Add the parmesan cheese and half and half mixture.
- Stir through chicken and cooked vegetables.
- Add the tomato sauce.
- Put sauce on low and bring it up to temperature, stirring regularly. (The parmesan cheese will stick to the bottom and burn if you don't stir regularly)
- Add the cooked noodles to the sauce and cook for 10 minutes to allow the sauce to thicken.

119.   Chicken Roll Ups Recipe

Serving: 8 | Prep: | Cook: 25mins | Ready in:

Ingredients

- 8 boneless skinless chicken breast halves
- 8 thin slices deli ham
- 4 slices provolone cheese, halved
- 2/3 cup seasoned bread crumbs
- 1/2 cup grated Romano or Parm
- 1/4 cup minced fresh parsley
- 1/2 cup milk
- cooking spray

Direction

- Flatten chicken to 1/4 inch thickness
- Place a slice of ham and half of a slice of provolone cheese on each piece of chicken
- Roll up from a short side and tuck in ends; secure with a toothpick
- In a shallow bowl, combine the crumbs, Romano and parsley
- Pour milk into another bowl

- Dip chicken rolls in milk, then roll in crumb mixture
- Wrap each of four chicken roll ups in plastic wrap; place in a large freezer bag
- Seal and freeze for up to 2 months
- Place remaining roll-ups, seam side down, on a greased baking sheet
- Spritz chicken with cooking spray
- Bake, uncovered, at 425 degrees for 25 minutes or until meat is no longer pink
- Remove toothpicks
- TO USE FROZEN CHICKEN
- Thaw in the refrigerator
- Unwrap roll-ups and place on a greased baking sheet
- Spritz with cooking spray
- Bake, uncovered, at 425 degrees for 30 minutes

120.   Chicken Salad Croissant Sandwiches Recipe

Serving: 4 | Prep: | Cook: 5mins | Ready in:

Ingredients

- 3 cooked, boneless, skinless chicken breasts, cut in very small bite size pieces
- 1 small granny smith apple, peeled, cored and diced
- 20 red, seedless grapes, quartered
- 2 stalks celery, diced
- 1 green onion, chopped
- 1/2 cup roasted pecans or walnuts, chopped
- 1/2 tsp. paprika
- 1/2 tsp. garlic powder
- 1 tsp. parsley
- salt and pepper to taste
- 1/4 cup plain yogurt
- 1/4 sour cream
- 1/3 cup mayonaise
- 4 croissants, split
- butter

Direction

- Combine first ten ingredients.
- Mix yogurt, sour cream and mayonnaise together, add to the chicken mixture. It depends on how creamy you like your salad and if you want it a bit dryer or wetter, start with half the amount of yogurt mixture and add more as needed. Also, you may play with the seasonings, some people even enjoy a bit of curry.
- Butter the inside of croissants and lightly toast in a frying pan.
- Fill the croissants with the salad. You can add some lettuce and sliced tomato on top of salad if so desired.

cool. (**try not to cut into the chicken you'll let all the juices run out)
- When the chicken is cool, dice the chicken and set aside.
- For the dressing, mix together the mayonnaise, sour cream, 1 teaspoon salt and 1/2 teaspoon of pepper. Fold in the tarragon leaves.
- Place the diced chicken in a bowl, add the celery and scallions. Pour the dressing over the chicken and toss well.
- Assemble:
- Toasted white bread
- Chicken salad, then the bacon slices
- Lettuce and Tomato
- Smear the mayo on the top slice, serve!

121. Chicken Salad My Way Recipe

Serving: 4 | Prep: | Cook: 8mins | Ready in:

Ingredients

- 4 chicken breasts
- olive oil
- salt and pepper
- 3/4 - 1 cup of diced celery
- 1/4 cup of chopped scallions
- 4 slices of bacon, cooked
- 1/2 cup of mayonnaise
- 1/2 cup of sour cream
- 1 teaspoon of tarragon or 1 Tablespoon fresh tarragon
- lettuce leaves
- tomato, sliced
- bread slices, of course

Direction

- Heat a large skillet with a couple TBS of olive oil. Meanwhile season chicken with salt and pepper. Fry the chicken about 4 minutes per side (**important tip: watch the clock for 4 minutes turn over for another 4 minutes, you will always end up with the chicken cooked through without drying it out!) Set aside to

122. Chicken Sandwich Recipe

Serving: 4 | Prep: | Cook: 68mins | Ready in:

Ingredients

- 1 Tbs olive oil
- 4 tsp. chili powder
- 1/2 tsp. garlic powder
- 1/2 tsp. cayenne pepper
- 4 boneless chicken breast ahlves{4 oz. each}
- 1 1/2 cups Mexican blend cheese {divided}1/3 cup mayoniase
- 8 slices sourdough bread
- 1/2 cup salsa

Direction

- In a small bowl combine oil and seasonings brush on chicken breast
- GRILL covered over medium heat 6-8 minutes on each side till juice runs clear
- THEN: combine 1 cup cheese and mayonnaise set aside: then grill bread slices on one side till brown spread with cheese mixture grill until cheese is melted. Place chicken on four slices of bread
- Top with Salsa and cheese and remaining bread cheese side down

123.   Chicken Scampi Recipe

Serving: 6 | Prep: | Cook: 10mins | Ready in:

Ingredients

- 1/2 cup butter, no substitutions
- 1/4/ cup olive oil
- 1/4 cup finely chopped scallions
- 1 Tbs. minced garlic
- juice of 1 lemon
- 2 pounds boneless, skinless chicken breasts, cut into 1/2" pieces
- 1 tsp. salt
- 1/2 tsp. freshly ground black pepper
- 1/4 cup minced fresh parsley
- 1 tomato, chopped

Direction

- In a skillet, heat together butter and olive oil. Sauté scallions and garlic. Add lemon juice, chicken, salt, pepper and parsley. Continue cooking, stirring constantly for 8-10 minutes or till chicken is done. Add tomato and heat through. Pour onto a platter and sprinkle with additional parsley and chopped scallion, if desired.

124.   Chicken Schnitzel Recipe

Serving: 4 | Prep: | Cook: 10mins | Ready in:

Ingredients

- 4 boneless, skinless chicken breast halves
- Note: You can follow this recipe for veal or pork.
- 2/3 cup all-purpose flour
- 1/2 tsp. garlic or onion powder
- 1/2 tsp. salt
- fresh ground pepper

- 1 tsp. paprika
- 2 large eggs, beaten
- 1 cup seasoned bread crumbs
- 1/4 cup vegetable oil
- 2 Tbsp. butter
- *Note: I always add butter to the cooking oil.
- 1 lemon, cut into wedges

Direction

- Place the chicken breasts between 2 pieces of cling wrap and pound to a desired texture and thickness.
- In a shallow pie plate or dish, mix together flour, garlic or onion powder, salt, pepper and paprika.
- In second shallow bowl, beat eggs.
- In third shallow dish or plate, place seasoned breadcrumbs.
- One at a time, dip each pounded chicken breast first into the seasoned flour mixture, coating thoroughly and shake to dust off excess.
- Next, dip chicken breast in well beaten eggs, covering completely.
- Then coat chicken with bread crumbs.
- Place each breaded chicken breast on a plate or a small cooking sheet pan.
- In a large non-stick skillet, place vegetable oil and butter.
- Heat over a medium element.
- Place chicken in the skillet, and brown for about 5 minutes per side.
- Make sure the chicken is cooked thoroughly before transferring it to a plate that has been lined with about 4 sheets of paper towel.
- Serve with boiled, baked or mashed potatoes and your favorite vegetables.
- Garnish with lemon wedges.
- Serves 4

125.   Chicken Spaghetti Recipe

Serving: 4 | Prep: | Cook: 20mins | Ready in:

Ingredients

- 2 boneless, skinless chicken breast halves
- 26 oz. jar spaghetti sauce
- 4 oz. can sliced mushrooms, drained
- 7 oz. pkg. spaghetti pasta
- 1/2 cup grated parmesan cheese

Direction

- Cut chicken breasts into 1" pieces. In large saucepan, place chicken, spaghetti sauce, and drained mushrooms. Bring to a boil, then reduce heat to low and simmer for 15-20 minutes until chicken is thoroughly cooked.
- While sauce is simmering, cook spaghetti according to package directions and drain.
- Serve sauce over cooked and drained spaghetti and sprinkle with Parmesan cheese.

126. Chicken Strips Recipe

Serving: 0 | Prep: | Cook: 10mins | Ready in:

Ingredients

- 1 cup mayonnaise
- 2 teaspoons dried minced onion
- 2 teaspoons dry mustard
- 2 cups Panko crumbs
- 1/2 cup sesame seeds
- 2 pounds of boneless, skinless chicken breasts cut into strips or you can use the all ready prepped chicken strips
- Sauce
- 1 cup mayonnaise
- 2 tablespoons honey

Direction

- 1. Preheat oven to 425 degrees F/ 220 degrees c
- 2. Combine in a shallow dish 1 cup mayonnaise, onion and mustard and mix together and set aside.

- 3. In a separate dish combine the panko crumbs and sesame seeds.
- 4. Dip the chicken in the mayonnaise mixture and then into the crumb mixture to coat.
- 5. Place the coated strips in a single layer on a lightly greased baking sheet.
- 6. Bake in the preheated oven for 15-18 minutes, or until juices run clear.
- 7. Mix 1 cup of mayonnaise and the honey together in a small bowl and serve with the chicken strips to dip.

127. Chicken Strips With Bleu Cheese Dressing Recipe

Serving: 4 | Prep: | Cook: 10mins | Ready in:

Ingredients

- Chicken:
- 1/2 cup low-fat buttermilk
- 1/2 teaspoon hot sauce
- 1/2 cup all-purpose flour
- 1/2 teaspoon paprika
- 1/2 teaspoon ground red pepper
- 1/2 teaspoon freshly ground black pepper
- 1/4 teaspoon salt
- 1 pound chicken breast tenders
- 1 tablespoon canola oil
- Dressing:
- 1/2 cup fat-free mayonnaise
- 1/4 cup (1 ounce) crumbled blue cheese
- 1 tablespoon red wine vinegar
- 1 teaspoon bottled minced garlic
- 1/4 teaspoon salt
- 1/4 teaspoon freshly ground black pepper

Direction

- To prepare chicken, combine buttermilk and hot sauce in a shallow dish. Lightly spoon flour into a dry measuring cup; level with a knife. Combine flour and next 4 ingredients (through salt) in a shallow dish. Dip chicken in buttermilk mixture, and dredge chicken in flour mixture.

- Heat oil in a large nonstick skillet over medium-high heat. Add chicken; cook 4 minutes on each side or until done. Remove from pan. Set aside, and keep warm.
- While chicken cooks, prepare the dressing. Combine fat-free mayonnaise and next 5 ingredients (through black pepper) in a small bowl. Serve with chicken strips.

128. Chicken Stroganoff Recipe

Serving: 8 | Prep: | Cook: 360mins | Ready in:

Ingredients

- 2 pounds skinless, boneless chicken breast halves and/or thighs
- 1 cup chopped onion
- 2 10 3/4-ounce cans condensed cream of mushroom soup with roasted garlic
- 1/3 cup water
- 12 ounces dried wide egg noodles
- 1 8-ounce carton dairy sour cream
- Freshly ground black pepper (optional)

Direction

- Cut chicken into 1-inch pieces. In a 3-1/2- or 4-quart slow cooker combine the chicken pieces and onion. In a medium bowl stir together the soup and water. Pour over chicken and onion.
- Cover and cook on low-heat setting for 6 to 7 hours or on high-heat setting for 3 to 3-1/2 hours.
- Cook noodles according to package directions. Drain. Just before serving, stir sour cream into mixture in cooker. To serve, spoon stroganoff mixture over hot cooked noodles. If desired, sprinkle with black pepper.

129. Chicken Stuffed Shells With A Spinach Cream Sauce Recipe

Serving: 6 | Prep: | Cook: 75mins | Ready in:

Ingredients

- 3 chicken breasts
- 25-30 jumbo pasta shells
- ½ onion diced
- 1¼ c. milk
- 1 c. chicken broth
- ½ c. white wine
- ½ bag of fresh spinach
- 2 tbsp butter
- Shredded parmesan cheese
- 1 tbsp garlic minced
- 1 tbsp cornstarch mixed with 1 tbsp water
- 1/8 tsp hickory smoke salt (optional)
- salt and pepper

Direction

- Preheat oven to 350°.
- Melt butter over medium heat in a frying pan.
- Add onion and sauté until almost translucent.
- Add garlic and sauté another 2 minutes.
- Add the broth and wine, and salt and pepper to your preference.
- Add the chicken breasts and cover and simmer until chicken is done 10-15 minutes.
- Meanwhile cook pasta until al dente.
- Drain noodles and place on waxed paper.
- Remove chicken from the pan when it is done and set aside to cool.
- Add the spinach and milk to the frying pan.
- Simmer until the spinach is almost wilted 3-5 minutes.
- Add the cornstarch and hickory salt.
- Simmer another 5 minutes to slightly thicken.
- Lightly coat a 9x13 pan with cooking spray.
- Shred the chicken and stuff the shells placing in the 9x13 as you go.
- Cover the noodles with the sauce then top each with a little parmesan.

- Cover the pan and cook in the oven for 20-25 minutes or until the cheese is melted.
- OPTIONAL: When the shells are done you can top them with fresh diced tomatoes and/or crumbled bacon.

130. Chicken Tikka Masala Recipe

Serving: 4 | Prep: | Cook: 20mins | Ready in:

Ingredients

- 1 1/2 chicken breast skinned and cut into 1 in cubes
- 6 tbs tikka paste
- 1/2 cup plain yogurt
- 1 TBS oil
- 1 onion chopped
- 1 garlic clove
- 3 serrano's chopped
- 1 in piece of ginger grated
- 1 tbs tomato paste
- 1 cup of chicken stock
- 1 tbs lemon juice
- Tikka paste ingredients recipe below
- 2 tbs corriander seeds
- 4 tbs cumin seeds
- 1 tbs garlic
- 2 tbs paprika
- 1 tbs garam masala
- 1 tbs ground ginger
- 2 tsp chili powder
- 1/2 tspturmeric
- 1 tbs dried mint
- 1/2 tsp salt
- 1 tsp lemon juice
- 2/3 cup wine vinegar
- 2/3 cup of oil

Direction

- Grind all the whole spices to a fine grind. Add the remaining spices and mix. Mix in the

lemon juice, vinegar and a little water to form a paste. Heat the oil in a large pan and add the paste and fry for ten minutes or until the moisture has been absorbed.
- Put 3 tbsp. tikka paste and 1/4 cup of yogurt in a bowl and add chicken pieces and leave marinate for 1/2 hour. Heat 1 tbsp. oil in a pan and fry the onions for 5 minutes. Add the ginger, chilies and garlic and continue frying for 5 minutes. Add the tomato paste, 3 tbsp. tikka paste and chicken stock and bring to a boil and simmer for 15 minutes. Put this mixture in a blender and puree till smooth. Grill the chicken until done (around 12 minutes) then put sauce back in the pan with the remaining yogurt and add the chicken and cook on medium heat for around 5-10 minutes. You can also broil the chicken if you don't grill it.

131. Chicken Valdostana For Two Recipe

Serving: 2 | Prep: | Cook: 20mins | Ready in:

Ingredients

- Two 8 oz. boneless, skinless chicken breasts.
- 1/2 cup flour
- 2 Tbl. butter
- 2 slices prosciutto
- 1/2 cup dry vermouth
- 2 slices Fontina cheese
- 1/2 cup tomato sauce
- 3 Tbl. heavy cream
- salt
- pepper

Direction

- Coat the chicken breasts in flour.
- Sauté the chicken in the butter for about 4 minutes on a side.
- Add the salt and pepper to taste.

- Cover chicken breast with a slice of prosciutto and fontina cheese.
- Pour the vermouth over the chicken and reduce until vermouth evaporates.
- Add the tomato sauce and bring to a boil.
- Add the heavy cream and blend together.
- Reduce the heat and cook for another 5 minutes or until the sauce is heated through again.
- Serve this over a little pasta or risotto if you like.

132. Chicken Vegetable Lo Mein Recipe

Serving: 4 | Prep: | Cook: 20mins | Ready in:

Ingredients

- 6 oz. udon noodles
- 2 (4oz.) chicken breasts cut into strips
- 1/2tsp crushed red pepper
- 2 cloves garlic minced
- 2tsp sesame oil
- 3c sliced bok choy
- 3/4c low-sodium Chicken broth
- 2Tbsp low-sodium soy sauce
- 1Tbsp oyster sauce
- 1/2c shredded carrots
- 1/3c sliced green onion
- 2tsp toasted sesame seeds

Direction

- Cook pasta
- Meanwhile, combine Chicken, Red Pepper, and Garlic, tossing well. In a Wok add 1tsp oil. Add Chicken mixture, stir-fry 2 min. Add Bok Choy, stir-fry 2min. Add Broth, Soy Sauce, and Oyster Sauce, stir-fry 1 min. Add Carrot and Green Onion, stir-fry 1 min.
- Add Pasta and remaining oil, toss until heated. Sprinkle with Sesame Seeds.

133. Chicken Veggie Stew With Mushroom Gravy Recipe

Serving: 4 | Prep: | Cook: 1hours | Ready in:

Ingredients

- About 2 Tbsps oil to fry, I used Safflower oil
- 2 large chicken breast fillets, trimmed of fat and chopped into cubes
- 1 large onion or 2 small, chopped
- 1 large carrot or 3 small, peeled and chopped
- 1 head of broccoli, chopped. Yes, the entire head, just do it.
- 1 small pkg of whole or chopped white button mushrooms. In fact, add as many mushrooms as you want. Go crazy putting in all different kinds, as many as you have available. Add the whole forest; see if I care.
- I used a fistful of snowpeas, but in retrospect, celery would've been better. I wasn't even trying to go running back to the store.
- 3 garlic cloves, minced
- 1/2 can (or about a cup) chicken stock
- 1 entire can of Campbell's Cream f Mushroom Soup (condensed)
- About 2 Tbsps of flour, in case gravy doesn't thicken
- My secret weapon: 1 Washington's Golden Seasoning and broth packet
- 1 Tbsp dried Parsley
- Salt and white pepper to taste

Direction

- Heat the oil over medium flame, putting the chicken cubes and onion slices first. Let the onions soften and caramel while the chicken browns.
- You must babysit it at this stage, making sure nothing burns and the chicken cubes cook on all sides. Throw in the garlic at this stage too. Add some water or chicken stock to kick up the nice caramel it leaves stuck to the bottom of your skillet.

- Add the carrots, broccoli, mushrooms and whatever other veggies you wanna throw in there. Mix well and let that simmer for a few minutes. When you feel like it, pour the chicken stock in, add the seasoning packet, the salt, white pepper and parsley.
- Mix well, cover it up, lower the flame, walk away and go finish your candy crush game, you shameless addicts. lol
- After that's had some time to simmer, (and you'll notice a volume difference to the dish too) about 15-18 minutes, it's time to add the soup.
- The rubber spatula is your friend!!!! No, really, guys. I love those things. Use 'em, they make your life so much easier. Just plop all that mushroom creamy goodness right in there with the chicken and veggies. Make the flame a bit higher if you want, but make sure it's all mixed in.
- If the gravy isn't thick enough for you, that's why the gods made flour. Take a separate bowl and a fork. Mix about 1/4 cup of cool water with about twice as much flour. (Use cold water, people. Hot water + flour = glue) Beat the daylights out of this mixture with the fork to get all the lumps out. Then move all the chicken and veggies to the sides and drizzle the flour mixture into the liquid part of your dish, little bits at a time, beating constantly. You still may get lumps, it happens. Beat up the gravy, not yourself because it'll still be delicious.
- Let the stew cook for a bit longer, maybe 3-5 minutes until all is blended. You may taste it with a separate spoon if you want to see what it needs. Just don't put the spoon back in if you're making this for another folks cos that's nasty.
- Cut the heat, serve hot over rice, pasta or mashed potatoes for optimum yumminess.
- It makes amazeballs leftovers to take to work the next day, or to have when you get home. Happy nomming!

134. Chicken Veronique Recipe

Serving: 4 | Prep: | Cook: 15mins | Ready in:

Ingredients

- 2 tablespoons vegetable oil
- 1 cup sliced mushrooms
- 3 tablespoons sliced green onions
- 1 pound boneless, skinless chicken breast cubed
- 1 tablespoon flour
- 1 cup chicken broth
- 1/4 cup dry white wine
- 1 cup seedless green grapes halved
- 1 tablespoon drained capers
- 1/2 teaspoon salt
- 1/2 teaspoon freshly ground black pepper
- 2 cups cooked rice warm

Direction

- Sauté mushrooms and green onions in oil in large skillet until tender.
- Add chicken and sauté 5 minutes then sprinkle with flour.
- Cook stirring constantly for 3 minutes then stir in broth and white wine.
- Heat to boiling then reduce heat and simmer covered 8 minutes.
- Stir in grapes and capers then season with salt and pepper and serve over rice.

135. Chicken With Apricot Picante Recipe

Serving: 4 | Prep: | Cook: 15mins | Ready in:

Ingredients

- 4 medium skinless,boneless chicken breast halves
- salt

- 3/4 cup salsa or picante sauce (Or in my case 1 1/2 cups)
- 1/4 cup apricot preserves (or in my case 1/2 cup)

Direction

- Rinse chicken breast and pat dry and lightly salt. Place chicken on the unheated rack of a broiler pan. Broil 4 to 5 inches from heat for 10-15 minutes, turning once after half the broiling time.
- In a small saucepan combine salsa and preserves and cook just until heated through and preserves are melted.
- Spoon Salsa/Preserve mixture over chicken breast and serve.

---

136.   Chicken With Creamy Herb Sauce Recipe

Serving: 6 | Prep: | Cook: 25mins | Ready in:

Ingredients

- 6 skinned, boned chicken breasts
- 1/3 cup balsamic vinegar
- 1 teaspoon dried oregano
- 1/2 teaspoon salt
- 1/2 teaspoon pepper
- 3 garlic cloves, unpeeled
- 1/4 cup buttermilk
- 2 tablespoons minced fresh parsley
- 3 tablespoon mayonnaise
- 1 tablespoon water
- 1 1/2 teaspoons minced fresh or 1/2 teaspoon dried thyme
- 1/8 teaspoon salt
- 1/8 teaspoon pepper

Direction

- Preheat oven to 375 degrees.
- Arrange chicken in a single layer baking dish.

- Pour vinegar over chicken and sprinkle with oregano, 1/2 teaspoon salt and 1/2 teaspoon pepper.
- Place garlic cloves in dish.
- Bake at 375 degrees for 25 minutes, basting occasionally with pan drippings.
- Remove garlic from dish and peel.
- Place garlic in a bowl, and mash into a paste.
- Add buttermilk and next 6 ingredients; stir with a wire whisk until well blended.
- Cut each breast diagonally across the grain into thin slices.
- Then pour herb sauce over chicken slices.

---

137.   Chicken With Nuts In Hoisin Sauce Recipe

Serving: 2 | Prep: | Cook: 5mins | Ready in:

Ingredients

- 1 whole chicken breast,bones,skinned and cut in 1" cubes
- 6 water chestnuts
- 2 med size dried Chinese mushrooms
- 1/2c bamboo shoots
- 1/2c nuts(cahews or almonds)
- 1Tbs. dry sherry
- 1tsp cornstarch
- 2Tbs hoisin sauce
- 2Tbs peanut oil

Direction

- Marinate chicken breast in sherry and cornstarch for 10 mins.
- Soak mushrooms in warm water for 20 mins. Cut same size as water chestnuts. Cut bamboo shoots into 1" pieces
- Heat oil in fry pan over high flame. Add chicken, stir fry 2 mins till chicken turns white. Add mushrooms, water chestnuts and bamboo shoots and stir another minute. Add 2 Tbsp. hoisin sauce and mix well. Just before serving add nut mixture and stir.

- Note: If you can't find Chinese mushrooms, use regular mushrooms.

138. Chicken With Sherry And Cream Sauce Recipe

Serving: 6 | Prep: | Cook: 20mins | Ready in:

Ingredients

- 4 boneless skinless chicken breasts cut into 2 inch pieces
- 3 shallots peeled and sliced
- 1lb chestnut mushrooms
- 1 clove garlic smashed
- 1 bay leaf
- 2 cloves
- ½ cup sherry or white wine
- 1-cup heavy cream
- canola oil for frying and a little butter for taste

Direction

- Heat a couple of tablespoons of oil and butter into large skillet.
- Add garlic and onions. Cook until the edges begin to brown. Remove and set aside.
- Add mushrooms to skillet and cook until beginning to caramelize. Remove and add to onions.
- Add chicken to skillet and a little more butter if needed to keep the chicken pieces from sticking, cook until opaque and beginning to brown slightly.
- Remove and add to onion and mushroom mixture.
- Deglaze pan with wine or sherry, reduce by half.
- Return chicken, onions mushrooms to skillet. Add bay leaf and cloves.
- Stir to combine, then add heavy cream and continue cooking, stirring often until chicken is cooked through.

139. Chicken Wrap Recipe

Serving: 4 | Prep: | Cook: | Ready in:

Ingredients

- 1/3 cup mayoniase
- 4 whole wheat tortillas
- 2 cups cooked chicken breast
- 1/4 cup roasted sweet red peppers
- 1/4 cup crumbled feta chesse
- 1/4 cup sliced basil leaves

Direction

- Spread mayonnaise on tortillas top with chicken peppers cheese and Basil Roll up.
- Enjoy

140. Chicken And Bacon Kabobs Recipe

Serving: 0 | Prep: | Cook: 20mins | Ready in:

Ingredients

- 1/4 cup soy sauce
- 1/4 cup cider vinegar
- 2 tbsp honey
- 2 tbsp canola oil
- 2 green onions, minced
- 10 large mushrooms, cut in half
- 3 skinless, boneless Chicken Breast halves, cut into chunks
- 1/2 pound thick slice bacon, cut in half
- 1 can pineapple Chunks, drained
- skewers

Direction

- The first step towards making chicken and bacon kabobs is to mix soy sauce, cider vinegar, honey, canola oil and green onions in a large bowl.

- Add mushroom and chicken pieces to the bowl. Stir it well, so that the pieces get coated with the mixture.
- Cover the bowl and keep in the refrigerator for about an hour.
- Now, preheat the grill on high temperature.
- Cover the chicken chunks with bacon and thread them onto skewers, alternating with mushroom halves and pineapple chunks.
- After oiling the grill grate, arrange the skewers on it.
- Cook it for 15 to 20 minutes and brush it with soy sauce mixture, until bacon is crisp and chicken juices run clear.

141.   Chicken And Melon Kabobs Recipe

Serving: 4 | Prep: | Cook: 20mins | Ready in:

Ingredients

- 1 tablespoon olive oil
- 2 garlic cloves, minced
- 1/2 teaspoon dried rosemary
- 1/4 teaspoon ground cumin
- 1/8 teaspoon salt
- 1/8 teaspoon ground coriander
- 1/8 teaspoon black pepper
- ground red pepper, to taste
- 2 tablespoons balsamic vinegar or red wine
- 4 boneless skinless chicken breast halves
- 1/2 cantaloupe, 1 1/2-inch dice
- 16 green onions (1/2-inch pieces)
- 2 tablespoons peach preserves or apricot preserves

Direction

- Heat oil in a small saucepan, add spices and cook 1 minute.
- Remove from heat, cool and add vinegar.
- Cut each breast 1/2 into 1" pieces.
- On four skewers alternate chicken cantaloupe and green onion.

- Brush all surfaces with vinegar mixture.
- Place skewers over medium coals and grill 4-5 inches from heat for 5 minutes turning as needed.
- Stir preserves into remaining vinegar mixture.
- Brush on kabobs, turn kabobs and brush again. Broil 3-5 minutes longer or until chicken is tender and no longer pink.

142.   Chicken And Mushroom Kabobs Recipe

Serving: 46 | Prep: | Cook: 15mins | Ready in:

Ingredients

- 1 1/4 tsp. freshly ground pepper
- 1 tsp. dried sage
- 1/2 tsp. dried thyme
- 1/2 tsp. cayenne pepper
- 1 clover garlic, minced
- 4 chicken breast halves, skinned and boned
- 1 tblsp. vegetable oil
- 12 large fresh, cultivated (button) mushrooms, stemmed
- 12-16 fresh sage leaves, optional
- 2 tblsp. olive oil
- 1/4 tsp. salt

Direction

- In a small bowl stir together 1 tsp. salt, pepper, sage, thyme, cayenne pepper and garlic. Set aside.
- Cut the chicken breasts into strips about 3 inches long and 1 inch wide. Pat them dry with absorbent paper towels and place in a large bowl. Add the vegetable oil and toss to coat the chicken strips evenly. Add the herb mixture and toss again to coat completely. Let stand for about 1 hour.
- Prepare a fire in a grill. Position the oiled grill rack sticks 4 - 6 inches above the fire. Toss the mushroom caps with the sage leaves and olive oil and the remaining 1/4 tsp. salt. Thread

chicken strips onto skewers alternately with the mushroom caps and sage leaves. Arrange the skewers on the rack. Grill, turning frequently until the chicken and mushrooms are lightly browned and the chicken is cooked through. 8 - 15 minutes, depending on size of chicken breasts.

143. Chicken And Spinach Pasta With Creamy Red Sauce Recipe

Serving: 4 | Prep: | Cook: 20mins | Ready in:

Ingredients

- 4 boneless skinless chicken breasts cut into bite size pieces
- olive oil
- 2 handfuls fresh baby spinach
- 2 cans stewed tomatoes
- 8 ounce package cream cheese cut up
- 2 cloves minced garlic
- 1 teaspoon basil
- 1/4 teaspoon freshly ground black pepper
- 16 ounces bow tie pasta

Direction

- In large deep frying pan brown chicken over medium heat in small amount of olive oil.
- Add garlic and let cook just until garlic begins to brown.
- Add tomatoes, cream cheese, basil and pepper.
- Reduce heat to medium low and let simmer stirring occasionally.
- Start boiling noodles and when almost done add spinach to water.
- Continue cooking until pasta is done.
- When cream cheese has melted and sauce is creamy add pasta and spinach to pan.
- Stir well then serve immediately.

144. Chicken And Stuffing Casserole Recipe

Serving: 12 | Prep: | Cook: 60mins | Ready in:

Ingredients

- 1 lb. boneless, skinless chicken breast halves
- 12 slices of swiss cheese
- 1 cup of unsweetened apple juice
- 1 can (10¾ oz) cream of chicken soup
- 1½ cups plain stuffing
- 1 stick of butter (melted)

Direction

- Preheat oven to 325 degrees.
- Spray a casserole dish with non-stick cooking spray.
- In a bowl mix together soup and apple juice and pour over chicken in the casserole dish.
- In a separate bowl mix together stuffing and butter. Spread over the top of chicken in the casserole dish.
- Layer Swiss cheese on top and bake covered for around 50 minutes and uncovered for 10 minutes.

145. Chicken Balti Recipe

Serving: 4 | Prep: | Cook: 20mins | Ready in:

Ingredients

- 2tbsp oil
- 3 garlic cloves peeled and chopped
- 1/2tsp cumin seeds
- 1 onion peeled and chopped
- 4tbsp balti masala paste
- 1lb boneless chicken breasts skinned and cut into strips
- 1 x14oz can chopped tomatoes
- 1 mango peeled and cubed
- 3tbsp fresh chopped mint
- 7floz chicken stock

Direction

- Heat the oil in a large pan, add the chopped garlic and cumin seeds and cook for 30 seconds
- Reduce the heat and add the onion cook for 2-3 minutes, add masala paste and chicken, mix well and cook for further 5 minutes stirring frequently
- Drain the tomatoes and reserve the juice.
- Add the tomatoes to the pan with the mango and 2tbsp of the mint and the stock, bring to the boil then reduce the heat and simmer for 20 minutes stirring frequently.
- If the mixture becomes too dry add the reserved tomato juice

---

146. Chicken In Parcement Recipe

Serving: 4 | Prep: | Cook: 25mins | Ready in:

Ingredients

- 2 ea boneless, skinless chicken breasts
- 1 ea waxy potato, sliced into 1/8" thick rounds
- 4 oz shredded savoy cabbage
- 1/2 small spanish onion, sliced into 1/4" rings
- 1 ea large garlic clove, sliced thin
- 2 ea rosemary sprigs
- 2 tbsp olive oil (I recommend a highly-flavored oil such as Goya.)
- 1/2 ea lemon, juiced
- 1 tbsp lemon zest
- 4 tbsp white wine
- salt & pepper

Direction

- Heat oven to 400F.
- Bring 3 cups water to a boil over high heat.
- Add cabbage and cook for two minutes then drain thoroughly. (This will minimize the sulfur compounds in the cabbage produced by heating from affecting the main dish.)
- Heat olive oil, garlic, lemon zest, and rosemary in a small skillet over medium low heat until aromatics infuse oil.
- Set aside.
- Prepare two sheets of parchment paper for pouches.
- Place 1/2 of cabbage on each parchment sheet and layer with onion slices.
- Toss potatoes in flavored oil and layer on onions.
- Season potatoes with salt and pepper.
- Toss chicken in flavored oil and lay on top of potatoes.
- Season chicken with salt and pepper.
- Pour remaining oil over each breast, taking care to distribute garlic and rosemary evenly.
- Add 2 tbsp. white wine to each pouch.
- Seal pouches and bake for 25 minutes

---

147. Chicken With Angel Hair Pasta Recipe

Serving: 6 | Prep: | Cook: 60mins | Ready in:

Ingredients

- 6 boneless skinless chicken breast halves
- 1/4 cup butter
- 1 package dry Italian salad dressing mix
- 1/2 cup white wine
- 1 can golden mushroom soup
- 4 ounces cream cheese with chives
- 1 pound angel hair pasta

Direction

- 1. Preheat oven to 325 degrees F (165 degrees C).
- 2. In a large saucepan, melt butter over low heat. Stir in the package of dressing mix. Blend in wine and golden mushroom soup. Mix in cream cheese, and stir until smooth. Heat through, but do not boil. Arrange chicken breasts in a single layer in a 9x13 inch baking dish. Pour sauce over.

3. Bake for 60 minutes in the preheated oven. Twenty minutes before the chicken is done, bring a large pot of lightly salted water to a rolling boil. Cook pasta until al dente, about 5 minutes. Drain. Serve chicken and sauce over pasta.

148. Chicken With Creamy Apple Sauce Recipe

Serving: 6 | Prep: | Cook: 30mins | Ready in:

Ingredients

- 6 boneless chicken breasts
- 1 teaspoon salt
- 1 teaspoon freshly ground black pepper
- 1 teaspoon dried thyme
- 2 tablespoons olive oil
- 3/4 cup apple cider
- 2 cups thinly sliced apples
- 1 cup half and half

Direction

- Sprinkle each chicken breast with salt, pepper and thyme.
- Heat oil in a skillet then cook chicken breasts on each side until juices run clear.
- Remove chicken from skillet and cover to keep warm.
- Add apple cider to pan and cook over medium heat for several minutes.
- Add apples and half and half then cook on low heat until tender.
- Place chicken on a serving platter and pour sauce over top then serve over hot rice or pasta.

149. Chicken With Garlic Zucchini Cream Recipe

Serving: 3 | Prep: | Cook: 40mins | Ready in:

Ingredients

- 1/4 cup butter
- •3 whole chicken breasts, halved
- •3 cups zucchini, sliced 1/8-inch thick
- •1/2 cup diced green onions
- •.
- •garlic Cream:
- •2 tablespoons butter
- •1 large clove garlic, minced
- •3 tablespoons flour
- •1 (3 oz) package of cream cheese
- •1 can chicken broth
- •1/2 tsp. pepper

Direction

- Chicken:
- In skillet, melt 1/4 cup butter; add chicken breasts.
- Cook, turning once, until chicken is browned and fork tender.
- Add zucchini and onions. Continue cooking, stirring until zucchini is crisp-tender.
- Garlic Cream Sauce:
- In 2 quart saucepan, melt 2 tablespoons butter; add garlic.
- Cook for 1 minute, then stir in flour and cook until smooth and bubbly.
- Add remaining ingredients and continue cooking, stirring occasionally, until sauce is smooth and thickened.
- This is pretty served on a bed of rice - layer the zucchini and then the chicken breasts on top then pour sauce over each chicken breast

150. Chicken With Green Chili Sauce Recipe

Serving: 2 | Prep: | Cook: 30mins | Ready in:

Ingredients

- 2 boneless,skinless chicken breast halves(5 oz ea)
- 1/2 tsp cajun seasoning
- 2/3 c reduced-sodium,reduced-fat cream of chicken soup
- 1/4 c water
- 1/4 c canned chopped green chilies
- 1/2 tsp lemon juice
- 2 Tbs reduced fat sour cream
- 1 c hot cooked rice

Direction

- Sprinkle chicken with Cajun seasoning.
- In large, nonstick skillet coated with spray, brown chicken on both sides.
- In small bowl, combine soup, water, chilies and lemon juice. Stir into skillet.
- Bring to a boil. Reduce heat; cover and simmer for 8-10 mins or till chicken juices run clear. Remove from heat; stir in sour cream. Serve with rice.

151. Chicken With Jalapeno Cheese Sauce Recipe

Serving: 4 | Prep: | Cook: 45mins | Ready in:

Ingredients

- • 1/4 cup chopped green bell pepper
- • 2 jalapeno peppers, finely chopped
- • 1 large clove garlic, minced
- • 1 tablespoon canola oil
- • 4 boneless chicken breast halves
- • 2 tablespoons butter or margarine
- • 2 tablespoons flour
- • 1 1/2 cups milk
- • 1 cups shredded sharp cheddar cheese, divided
- • few drops hot pepper sauce, or to taste, or a dash of ground cayenne pepper
- • 1/4 teaspoon salt
- • ground black pepper
- • jalapeno pepper rings
- nacho chips, optional

Direction

- Combine bell pepper, jalapeno pepper, garlic, and olive oil. Place chicken breasts in a shallow baking pan sprayed lightly with nonstick cooking spray; add pepper and oil mixture. Bake chicken at 350°, uncovered, 20 minutes.
- While chicken bakes, melt butter or margarine in saucepan. Add flour and stir for 1 minute. Whisk in milk, stirring until sauce starts to thicken. Remove from heat; stir in Cheddar cheese, hot pepper sauce, salt, and pepper.
- Pour sauce over chicken. Continue baking, uncovered, for 15 to 20 minutes longer, or until chicken is done and juices run clear. Remove chicken from oven; turn oven to broil. Return chicken to oven; broil just until lightly browned. Arrange on a serving platter with cheese sauce spooned over chicken breast halves. Garnish with jalapeno pepper rings and nacho chips, if desired.
- Jalapeno chicken and cheese recipe makes 4 servings.

152. Chicken With Lemon Cream Pasta Recipe

Serving: 4 | Prep: | Cook: 10mins | Ready in:

Ingredients

- 3 skinless, boneless chicken breast halves
- 1 lemon, quartered
- 2 teaspoons garlic powder, divided
- 1 teaspoon ground black pepper, divided

- 1 (14.5 ounce) cans chicken stock
- 1/4 cup fresh lemon juice
- 8 ounces rotelle pasta OR pasta shape of your choice
- 1 cup heavy cream
- 1 teaspoon grated lemon zest

Direction

- Preheat oven to 350 degrees F.
- Place chicken in lightly greased baking dish.
- Squeeze lemon juice over breasts and season with 1 1/2 teaspoons garlic powder and 3/4 teaspoon pepper.
- Bake for 40 minutes OR until juices run clear.
- In a saucepan large enough to cook the pasta, place broth with 1/2 teaspoon garlic powder and 1/4 teaspoon pepper.
- Bring to a boil.
- Add lemon juice and pasta.
- Cook over medium heat, stirring occasionally, until liquid is absorbed, about 25 minutes.
- Cut cooked chicken into bite-sized pieces.
- Stir into cooked pasta, along with cream and lemon zest.
- Cook, stirring, over low heat for 5 minutes OR until chicken is heated through.
- Remove from heat.
- Let stand 5 minutes.
- Stir before serving.

153. Chicken With Poblano Cream Sauce Recipe

Serving: 4 | Prep: | Cook: 10mins | Ready in:

Ingredients

- 1 poblano chili
- 2 Tbs canola oil
- 1/2 smallonion,chopped
- 1 garlic clove,minced
- 1/3 cup heavy cream coarse salt and pepper

- 4 boneless,skinless chicken breast halves. (6oz. ea.)

Direction

- Roast the chili over gas burner or under broiler, until charred all over. Wrap in paper towel; steam 5 mins. Rub off skin; remove the seeds and ribs. Chop coarsely.
- Heat 1 Tbsp. of canola oil in a small saucepan over med. heat; add the onion and garlic; cook till soft, 5 to 7 mins. Add chili and cream.
- Puree in blender; add water if too thick. Season with salt and pepper.
- Season chicken with salt and pepper. Heat remaining Tbs. canola oil in large skillet over med-high heat. Cook the chicken until it is golden and juices run clear, 4 to 5 mins per side. Serve with sauce.

154. Chicken With Prosciutto Rosemary And White Wine Recipe

Serving: 4 | Prep: | Cook: 35mins | Ready in:

Ingredients

- chicken with prosciutto, rosemary, and white wine
- Pollo con prosciutto, Rosmarino, Vino Bianco
- Ingredients:
- 2 tablespoons extra-virgin olive oil
- 3 large chicken breast halves with ribs and skin, cut crosswise in half
- 3 chicken drumsticks with skin
- 3 chicken thighs with skin
- 1 cup 1/4-inch cubes prosciutto (about 5 ounces)
- 6 garlic cloves, thinly sliced
- 2 tablespoons chopped fresh rosemary
- 1 and 1/4 cups dry white wine
- 1 cup low-salt chicken broth

- 1 cup canned crushed tomatoes with added puree
- Fresh rosemary sprigs

Direction

- Directions:
- Preheat oven to 325°F.
- Heat extra-virgin olive oil in heavy large ovenproof pot over medium-high heat.
- Sprinkle chicken with salt and pepper.
- Working in 2 batches, sauté chicken until golden, about 4 minutes per side.
- Transfer chicken to platter.
- Add prosciutto, sliced garlic, and chopped rosemary to same pot.
- Stir 1 minute.
- Add dry white wine, chicken broth, and crushed tomatoes with puree.
- Bring to boil, scraping up browned bits.
- Boil 5 minutes.
- Return chicken to pot, arranging in single layer.
- Return to boil.
- Cover pot and place in oven.
- Bake until chicken breasts are cooked through, about 20 minutes.
- Remove chicken breasts.
- Continue baking until drumsticks and thighs are cooked through, about 10 minutes longer.
- Remove pot from oven.
- Return chicken breasts to pot. (Can be prepared 1 day ahead. Cool slightly. Refrigerate uncovered until cold, then cover and keep refrigerated.)
- Bring chicken mixture to simmer.
- Transfer chicken to platter; tent with foil.
- Boil until sauce is reduced to 2 cups and coats back of spoon, about 5 minutes.
- Season sauce to taste with salt and pepper.
- Pour sauce over chicken.
- Garnish with rosemary sprigs and serve. Makes 6 servings.
- That's it!

155.   Chicken Stuffing Rolls Recipe

Serving: 4 | Prep: | Cook: 67mins | Ready in:

Ingredients

- 4 large boneless, skinless chicken breasts
- 1 large pint French-Onion flavored tub of sour cream
- 2 large packets pre-made stuffing mix
- salt
- black pepper
- 1 T garlic powder
- chopped chives
- butter
- fresh chopped parsley

Direction

- Pre-heat oven to 325 degrees.
- Rinse chicken in cold water to drain off any blood, trim away all the excess fat.
- On a cutting board, slice the breasts horizontally from the thick side, like you would to filet a fish. This will create 8 thin slices.
- Add the chives and seasonings to the sour cream mixture.
- With a rubber spatula, thoroughly spread the sour cream mixture onto both sides of the chicken breasts.
- Pat both sides down into the stuffing mix, then carefully roll, placing the open side down.
- Layer pats of butter on top and bake for approx. 60-75 minutes.
- Do not turn over while baking. Bake until golden.
- Before removing from the oven, sprinkle with fresh parsley and more butter pats.
- Serve with your favorite side dishes.
- Yield: 2 per person.

156. Chili Chicken With Avocado Mango Relish Recipe

Serving: 4 | Prep: | Cook: 20mins | Ready in:

Ingredients

- 1/4 cup olive oil
- 2 tablespoon red chili powder
- 1/2 teaspoon ground cumin
- 1 teaspoon fresh garlic minced
- 1/2 teaspoon fresh oregano
- 4 boneless skinless chicken breasts
- 1/4 cup olive oil
- 1 leek white part only chopped
- 1 clove garlic minced
- 1 pound fresh spinach
- Relish:
- 1 large mango diced
- 1/2 medium red onion diced
- 1/2 bunch cilantro chopped
- 1 avocado diced
- 1 small red bell pepper seeded and diced
- juice of 1 lime
- 1/2 teaspoon salt

Direction

- Combine first 5 ingredients in a mixing bowl then put chicken in bowl and toss.
- Marinate chicken refrigerate for 3 hours.
- Combine all relish ingredients and set aside.
- When ready to prepare meal get two sauté pans.
- In one pan heat oil and add leeks and cook until tender then add garlic and cook until brown.
- Add spinach and sauté until almost wilted.
- In the other pan pull chicken from marinade and discard marinade.
- Sauté chicken 4 minutes per side then drain and put on a bed of spinach on each plate.
- Top with relish and serve immediately.

157. Chinese Almond Chicken Recipe

Serving: 2 | Prep: | Cook: 20mins | Ready in:

Ingredients

- 1 large chicken breast half boned and skinned
- 3 tablespoons vegetable oil
- 1/2 cup whole blanched almonds
- 2 tablespoons sherry
- 2 tablespoons soy sauce
- 2 teaspoons cornstarch
- 1 teaspoon granulated sugar
- 1/2 teaspoon ground ginger
- 6 ounce package frozen snow peas thawed
- 2 tablespoons sliced green onions

Direction

- Cut chicken into 3/4 inch cubes.
- Set aside.
- Heat oil in wok over medium high heat.
- Add almonds and toss until browned about 5 minutes.
- Remove with slotted spoon and set aside.
- Add chicken to wok and toss 3 minutes.
- In small bowl mix sherry soy sauce, cornstarch, sugar and ginger.
- Stir into chicken then cook and stir until thickened.
- Stir in snow peas, onion and reserved almonds.
- Heat through then serve with hot steamed rice.

158. Citrus Buttery Herbed Chicken And Rice Recipe

Serving: 6 | Prep: | Cook: 45mins | Ready in:

Ingredients

- 1 and 1/4 cup of extra virgin olive oil

- 8 - 10 large garlic cloves, crushed, peeled, and chopped
- juice from 6 lemons
- 1/4 to 1/3 can of orange juice concentrate (depending on how sweet you want this)
- 1 and 1/2 large vidalia sweet onions
- 3/4 stick of butter
- 1 and 1/2 cups of clear beef broth
- meat from 6 large chicken breasts, skins removed,and cut into strips.
- 3/4 cup chopped fresh basil leaves
- 1/2 cup chopped fresh cilantro leaves
- 3/4 cup fresh parsley
- 4 - 5 teaspoons of louisiana hot sauce (or more - depending on how spicy you want this)
- 1/3 cup red wine

Direction

- Caramelize onions and garlic in olive oil, butter, 1/2 cup beef broth.
- Add herbs and stir.
- Boil - 3 minutes.
- Add orange juice concentrate, lemon juice and 1 cup of beef broth. Stir again.
- Bring to boil - 3 minutes.
- Add hot sauce and wine and let boil two more minutes.
- Remove pan from stove and let cool, covered, for 10 minutes.
- Put in blender (hand blender works well) and let blend until you are left with a creamy looking sauce.
- Put sauce back in pot and add raw chicken strips.
- Bring to a boil, stirring constantly - about one to two minutes on high.
- Turn off stove and let chicken strips remain in the sauce for 30 minutes. Cover on pot.
- Stir contents of pot and boil again for one minute only.
- Stir and serve.
- NOTE: If you are not going to serve this right away, remove the chicken from the sauce and cover in a separate bowl or chicken will continue to cook.

159. Coco Ichibanya Cocos Style Chicken Cutlet Curry Recipe

Serving: 4 | Prep: | Cook: 20mins | Ready in:

Ingredients

- 4 servings short grain white rice, cooked and kept warm
- 4 boneless, skinless chicken breasts
- 2 cups fine breadcrumbs(panko, if possible)
- 2 eggs, beaten
- 1 block S&B Golden® curry sauce mix(med/hot)*
- 12oz sliced fresh mushrooms(variety, if possible)
- 2 cups shredded Monterey or pepperJack cheese
- 2 1/2 cups water
- 2 pieces of bacon, chopped or 1T bacon grease
- 2T peanut oil
- salt, pepper and cayenne
- *there are 3 heat variations of S&B...if you're looking for a "level 1 or 2", please try the MILD version of the curry block.

Direction

- In large stir fry pan or wok, cook bacon (or just add the bacon grease) until just crispy.
- Add mushrooms and sauté about 5 minutes.
- Add water and entire brick of curry sauce mix to mushrooms.
- Let simmer on high to thicken, stirring occasionally while preparing chicken.
- Pound chicken breasts out to about 1/2 inch thickness. Season with salt and pepper.
- In pie plate, combine breadcrumbs with salt, pepper and other desired seasonings (i.e. garlic or onion powder, cayenne, parsley, etc.)
- Dredge chicken in egg then in breadcrumbs until evenly coated.
- Cook chicken in large skillet with peanut or vegetable oil.

- Cook about 5 minute each side, until chicken is cooked through.
- To arrange dish, place serving of rice on plate, top with sliced chicken breast, then about 1/2 cup shredded cheese, then top with sauce.
- **CoCo's curry is a messy dish of yummy goodness according to those who've tasted the real thing. You can adjust the heat of this recipe by the use of cayenne or the pepper jack cheese, but I don't suggest using any commercial curry powders...they will change the flavor, noticeably. **

---

160. Collard Green Wraps Recipe

Serving: 4 | Prep: | Cook: 15mins | Ready in:

Ingredients

- 4 large collard greens (or 8 small ones)
- ¾ cup shredded carrots
- ¾ cup shredded purple cabbage (the thinner the better)
- 1 large avocado (or 2 small ones)
- 8 tablespoons of kale & basil pesto
- 2 15-Minute Pesto chicken breast
- water

Direction

- In a large skillet or frying pan, simmer about 1" of water.
- Remove the thick stems from the bottom of the collard leaf and quickly immerse it into the water for about 10 seconds (5 seconds on each side). Set aside on a plate until all leaves have been immersed. They should turn bright green and slightly waxy.
- Lay 1 large leaf (or 2 small overlapped leaves) on a plate and spread 2 tablespoons of Kale & Basil Pesto. Add a small handful of purple cabbage, carrots, chicken, and avocado. (I also like to add a bit more pesto on the top). Be mindful of how much you put in, leaving

enough space around the edges of the leaf to roll them up.

- Position the open-faced wrap so the spine of the leaf is horizontal to your body. With the top of the leaf in your left hand and the bottom of the leaf in your right hand, fold it towards the center and slip your thumbs under the flap closest to you. Simultaneously using your ring finger and pinkies to hold down the opposing flap and ingredients, begin to roll the wrap away from your body. It takes patience and practice.
- Secure collard wrap in a piece of parchment paper, saran wrap, or tin foil.
- Repeat for 3 other wraps. If storing for a "next-day" lunch or snack, be sure to put the wrap in a ziplock or glass lock container. The juices will begin to leak.

---

161. Copycat TGIFridays Sizzling Chicken And Cheese Recipe

Serving: 2 | Prep: | Cook: 15mins | Ready in:

Ingredients

- 2   (4 oz.) boneless, skinless chicken breasts
- 2   Tbsp. olive oil
- 1   tsp. chopped garlic
- 1/2 cup shredded Chihuahua white cheese
- 2   slices American chees3
- prepared mashed potatoes
- -------------------------
- ---Marinade:
- 2   Tbsp. chopped garlic
- 2   Tbsp. chopped parsley
- 2   ozs. olive oil
- 1   tsp. crushed red pepper
- 1/8 tsp. pepper
- 1/4 tsp. salt
- -------------------------
- ---pepper and onion Medley:
- 1   green pepper, julienned

- 1 red pepper, julienned
- 1 small yellow onion, julienned

Direction

- Pound chicken breasts to even thickness, between 2 sheets of wax paper.
- In a small dish, combine all marinade ingredients.
- Place chicken breasts in marinade and refrigerate for 2-4 hours.
- Sauté peppers and onion in olive oil for 2 minutes.
- Then add 1 tsp. garlic, and continue to sauté 2 more minutes.
- Season with salt and pepper.
- Sauté chicken in olive oil over medium heat; cook evenly on both sides to a golden brown color.
- Heat cast iron skillet on burner over medium heat until very hot then remove from heat.
- Place the mashed potatoes in half of the skillet.
- Place cheeses on the other half of skillet and cover with pepper and onion medley,
- Add chicken to top of pepper and onion medley, resting on the potatoes.
- Top with parsley.
- Serve directly from skillet for authenticity or transfer to plates.

---

162. Corn And Bell Pepper Chicken Bake Recipe

Serving: 6 | Prep: | Cook: 30mins | Ready in:

Ingredients

- 1 2/3 cups hot water
- 1 pkg (6 ounces) Stove Top cornbread stuffing mix
- 1 1/2 pounds boneless skinless chicken breast, cut into 6 serving-size pieces
- 16 ounce package fromen stir-fry pepper and onion blend, thawed
- 10.75 ounce can cream of chicken soup
- 10 ounce package frozen corn

Direction

- Preheat oven to 425.
- Mix stuffing mix with hot water and set aside.
- In a 13x9 baking dish, place chicken pieces, then cover with the stir-fry vegetables.
- Mix corn and soup together and spoon over the chicken and vegetables in dish.
- Top with moistened stuffing.
- Bake until chicken is cooked all the way through, about 30 minutes.

---

163. Cream Of Mushroom Chicken Recipe

Serving: 4 | Prep: | Cook: 30mins | Ready in:

Ingredients

- 4 chicken breast pieces
- 1 can of Campbell's Cream of Mushroom Soup
- 1 tbsp. fresh ground black pepper (or powder)
- 1 tbsp. all purpose seasoning
- 1 tbsp. cold butter
- 1 tbsp. soy sauce

Direction

- Butter a glass or foil baking dish with the cold butter well
- In a bowl sprinkle chicken with pepper, seasoning and soy sauce
- Pour some soup into bottom of baking dish and spread evenly
- Place chicken side by side in dish and pour rest of soup over chicken
- Cover loosely with foil and bake at 360 degrees for 30 minutes or until chicken is tender when cut into and sauce is bubbly.

164. Creamy Chicken Enchiladas Recipe

Serving: 6 | Prep: | Cook: 25mins | Ready in:

Ingredients

- 1/2 pound skinless, boneless chicken breasts
- 4 cups torn fresh spinach or 1/2 of one 10-ounce package frozen chopped spinach, thawed and well-drained
- 1 8-ounce carton light dairy sour cream
- 1/4 cup plain fat-free yogurt
- 2 tablespoons all-purpose flour
- 1/4 teaspoon ground cumin
- 1/4 teaspoon salt
- 1/2 cup fat-free milk
- 1 4-ounce can diced green chili peppers, drained
- 6 7-inch flour tortillas
- 1/3 cup shredded reduced-fat cheddar or monterey jack cheese (1-1/2 ounces)
- Chopped tomato or salsa (optional)
- Thinly sliced green onions (optional)
- 1/4 cup thinly sliced green onions

Direction

- In a 3-quart saucepan place chicken in enough water to cover. Bring to boiling; reduce heat. Cover and simmer about 15 minutes or until chicken is no longer pink. Remove chicken from saucepan. When cool enough to handle, use a fork to shred chicken into bite-size pieces. (You should have about 1-1/2 cups.) Set aside.
- If using fresh spinach, place spinach in a steamer basket over boiling water. Reduce heat. Steam, covered, for 3 to 5 minutes or until tender. (Or, cook in a small amount of boiling water, covered, for 3 to 5 minutes.) Drain well.
- In a large bowl combine chicken, spinach, and green onions; set aside. In a bowl combine sour cream, yogurt, flour, cumin, and salt. Stir in milk and chili peppers. Divide sauce in half. Set one portion aside.
- For filling, combine one portion of the sauce and the chicken-spinach mixture. Divide the filling among the tortillas. Roll up tortillas. Place, seam side down, in an ungreased 2-quart rectangular baking dish.
- Spoon reserved portion of sauce over tortillas. Bake, uncovered, in a 350 degree F oven about 25 minutes or until heated through. Sprinkle with cheese; let stand for 5 minutes. Transfer to a serving platter.
- To serve, if desired, garnish with chopped tomato or salsa and additional green onion.

165. Creamy Farfalle & Pepper Chicken Recipe

Serving: 10 | Prep: | Cook: 1hours | Ready in:

Ingredients

- 1 box whole wheat farfalle (bowtie) pasta
- 3 boneless, skinless chicken breasts (thawed)
- 2 cups grape tomatoes
- 2 large zucchini, chopped.
- 2 small white onions
- 2 garlic cloves
- 1/2 cup shredded mozzarella
- 1 cup freshly shaved parmesan
- 1/2 cup whole milk
- white wine of your choice
- olive oil
- 1 lemon
- several leaves fresh basil, thinly sliced
- oregano, salt, freshly ground black pepper

Direction

- Heat a Dutch oven on high, and coat bottom with olive oil until smoking. Rub chicken breasts liberally with oregano, salt, and lots of freshly ground black pepper. Carefully place chicken in Dutch oven (tongs are handy).
- Chop up one onion & one garlic clove, add to Dutch oven. Brown chicken on both sides, then turn burner to medium, add a splash of

white wine and cover. Chicken is done when juices run clear; about 25-30 minutes.

- In a large, heavy-bottomed pan, heat more olive oil, and add tomatoes, second onion & garlic clove, and basil. Season with salt & pepper. Cook until tomatoes begin to burst.
- Boil water for the pasta. When draining al dente pasta, reserve 1/4 cup of starchy water.
- When chicken is done, remove from Dutch oven and let rest on a cutting board (at least 10 minutes), then slice very thin. Transfer pasta to Dutch oven, and pour in reserved water. Add the tomato-basil mixture to pasta. Add mozzarella, parmesan, & milk; mix well. Keep warm on low.
- In the same large pan, heat more olive oil and add zucchini. Season with salt and pepper. Zest the lemon and add to zucchini. Halve the lemon and squeeze one half of the juice over zucchini.
- Serve farfalle, chicken, and zucchini together on a plate, and garnish with fresh basil & parmesan.

166.   Creamy Italian Chicken In The Crock Pot Recipe

Serving: 4 | Prep: | Cook: 240mins | Ready in:

Ingredients

- 4 boneless skinless chicken breast halves
- 1 envelope Italian salad dressing mix
- 1/4 cup water
- 8 ounce package cream cheese softened
- 1 can cream of chicken soup undiluted
- 4 ounce can mushroom stems and pieces drained
- Hot cooked noodles

Direction

- Place chicken in a slow cooker.
- Combine salad dressing mix and water then pour over chicken.

- Cover and cook on low for 3 hours.
- In a small mixing bowl beat cream cheese and soup until blended then stir in mushrooms.
- Pour over chicken then cook 1 hour longer then serve over noodles.

167.   Creole Chicken Fried Chicken With Creole Ranch Dressing Recipe

Serving: 6 | Prep: | Cook: 20mins | Ready in:

Ingredients

- 1/2 cup paprika
- 1/2 cup granulated garlic
- 1/4 cup granulated onion
- 3 tablespoons ground black pepper
- 2 teaspoons ground white pepper
- 2 teaspoons cayenne pepper
- 1/4 cup dried oregano
- 1/4 cup dried thyme
- 2 tablespoons ground cumin
- 2 tablespoons sugar
- 2-1/4 pounds small boneless skinless chicken breasts
- 1-1/2 cups buttermilk
- 2 cups flour
- 2 tablespoons kosher salt
- vegetable oil for frying
- Dressing:
- 1-1/4 cups mayonnaise
- 1 cup buttermilk
- 1 tablespoon red wine vinegar
- 2 teaspoons minced garlic
- 1/4 cup finely chopped chives
- 1 tablespoon lemon pepper
- 1/4 cup freshly grated parmesan
- 1 teaspoon kosher salt
- 1/2 teaspoon freshly ground black pepper
- 1 teaspoon spice mix used to coat chicken

Direction

- Combine all spice ingredients.
- Pull off chicken tenders from the breasts then sprinkle both sides of tenders with spice mix.
- Line them up in a non-reactive baking pan and pour on the buttermilk.
- Cover and let marinate in the refrigerator for at least 4 hours.
- Mix flour, 1/4 cup spice mix and salt then spread out in a flat pan.
- Remove chicken pieces out of buttermilk and press into the flour mixture coating them well.
- Pour 1/4" of oil in bottom of a heavy skillet then heat over medium high until almost smoking.
- Add chicken pieces without crowding the pan.
- Turn down heat to medium and fry 5 minutes on each side.
- Serve hot until crisp and golden with some ranch dressing ladled on top.
- To make dressing whisk all dressing ingredients together in a bowl.
- Transfer to a container with a lid and store in refrigerator until needed.

168. Creole Chicken And Vegetables Recipe

Serving: 4 | Prep: | Cook: 15mins | Ready in:

Ingredients

- cooking spray
- 1 pound chicken breast tenders
- 2 cups frozen pepper stir-fry (such as Bird's Eye brand), thawed
- 1 cup frozen cut okra, thawed
- 3/4 cup thinly sliced celery
- 3/4 teaspoon sugar
- 1/2 teaspoon salt
- 1/2 teaspoon dried thyme
- 1/4 teaspoon ground red pepper
- 1 (14.5-ounce) can diced tomatoes, undrained
- 1/4 cup chopped fresh parsley
- 1 tablespoon butter

Direction

- Heat a large nonstick skillet over medium-high heat. Coat pan with cooking spray. Add chicken; cook 3 minutes on each side or until browned. Add pepper stir-fry and next 6 ingredients (through red pepper), stirring to combine. Pour tomatoes over chicken mixture; bring to a boil. Cover, reduce heat, and simmer 5 minutes. Uncover; cook 3 minutes. Add parsley and butter, stirring until butter melts

169. Crisp Coconut Chicken With Mango Salsa Recipe

Serving: 2 | Prep: | Cook: 30mins | Ready in:

Ingredients

- CHICKEN:
- 1 clove garlic, crushed
- 1 TBS Dijon mustard
- Pinch ground ginger
- 2 skinless, boneless chicken breasts
- all-purpose flour
- 1/4 tsp salt
- 1/4 tsp pepper
- 1 egg
- 3/4 cup sweetened flakes coconut
- 1 TBS vegetable oil
- 2 TBS fresh lime juice
- MANGO SALSA:
- 1 ripe mango, diced
- 1/4 cup diced red onion
- 1 TBS fresh lime juice or white wine vinegar
- 1 TBS chopped fresh coriander or parsley
- salt & pepper
- Pinch hot pepper flakes

Direction

- Preheat oven to 375°F. Combine garlic, mustard and ginger in a small bowl. Spread mixture lightly on both sides of each chicken breast. Place chicken on waxed paper and sprinkle both sides lightly with flour, salt and pepper. Stir egg with 1 tsp cold water in shallow bowl.

- Place coconut on waxed paper. Dip chicken breasts in egg wash then in coconut, pressing to make it adhere. Heat oil over medium-high heat in oven proof skillet.
- Add chicken and cook two minutes a side. Add lime juice to skillet and place in preheated oven for 12 to 15 minutes or until chicken in no longer pink inside.
- To make Salsa: Combine mango, red onions, lime juice and coriander in bowl. Season to taste with salt and pepper. Stir in hot pepper flakes, Divide salsa between two dinner plates and place cooked chicken on top.

---

170. Crispy Chicken Breasts With Sage And Proscuitto Recipe

Serving: 4 | Prep: | Cook: 15mins | Ready in:

Ingredients

- 4 boneless chicken breasts, with skin (about 5 ounces each)
- 16 whole sage leaves
- 4 slices prosciutto
- 2 tablespoons extra virgin olive oil, or as needed
- salt and freshly ground pepper, to taste

Direction

- Heat oven to 400 degrees F.
- Carefully peel back the chicken skin leaving one side attached. Season with salt and freshly ground pepper, then place the sage leaves on top. Top with the slices of prosciutto; fold the chicken skin back over and pat down.
- Heat an oven-proof sauté pan over medium-high heat. Add the oil; when hot add the

chicken breasts skin side down. Cook until nicely browned, then turn and place the pan in the oven to finish cooking, about 10 minutes more . (I find finishing the chicken in the oven helps it to remain moist and tender.) Let sit for a couple of minutes, then slice and serve.

- Per Serving: 269 Calories; 18g Fat (4g Sat, 10g Mono, 3g Poly); 26g Protein; trace Carbohydrate; 0mg Dietary Fiber; 78mg Cholesterol; 529mg Sodium.

---

171. Crock Pot Pizza Chicken Recipe

Serving: 5 | Prep: | Cook: 23mins | Ready in:

Ingredients

- 4 skinless, boneless chicken breast halves - cut into bite size pieces
- 1 onion, chopped
- 1 green bell pepper, chopped
- 1 (10.75 ounce) can condensed tomato soup
- 1 (10.75 ounce) can condensed cream of mushroom soup
- 2 tablespoons tomato paste
- 1/2 cup water
- 1 tablespoon dried parsley
- 1 tablespoon dried oregano
- 1 tablespoon dried basil
- 1 bay leaf
- salt and pepper to taste

Direction

- Place chicken, onion, bell pepper in a slow cooker.
- In a medium bowl, combine the tomato soup, cream of mushroom soup, tomato paste, water, parsley, oregano, basil, salt and pepper.
- Mix well and pour mixture over chicken and vegetables in slow cooker.
- Stir to coat and add bay leaf.
- Cook on Low setting for 8 hours, until chicken and vegetables are tender.

172. Crockpot Amaretto Chicken Recipe

Serving: 6 | Prep: | Cook: 360mins | Ready in:

Ingredients

- 4-6 chicken breasts, boneless and skinless
- 1/2 cup flour
- 1 teasopon curry powder
- 1 teaspoon garlic powder
- 1/4 teaspoon salt
- 1/4 teaspoon pepper
- 1 Tablespoon vegetable oil
- 1 can cream of mushroom soup
- 1 can of mushrooms (4 oz. or more - or use fresh sliced)
- 1/4 cup Amaretto
- 1 teaspoon Kitchen Bouquet or Gravymaster
- 2 Tablespoons lemon juice

Direction

- Mix flour, curry powder, garlic powder, salt and pepper in zip lock bag. Add rinsed and patted chicken breasts and toss to coat.
- Heat vegetable oil in skillet.
- Brown coated chicken breasts in hot oil over medium heat.
- Transfer to crockpot.
- Mix remaining ingredients and spoon over chicken.
- Cover and cook on low for 6-8 hours.
- Serve with rice.

173. Crockpot Chicken Delicious Recipe

Serving: 6 | Prep: | Cook: 28mins | Ready in:

Ingredients

- 4-6 whole boneless skinless chicken breasts, cut into thirds
- 2-3 tablespoons lemon juice
- black pepper
- celery salt (may use just iodized salt)
- paprika
- 1 (10 3/4 ounce) can condensed cream of mushroom soup
- 1 (10 3/4 ounce) can condensed cream of celery soup
- 1/3 cup dry sherry or white wine
- grated parmesan cheese
- rice or egg noodles

Direction

- Rinse chicken and pat dry.
- In a large bowl or meat platter, season chicken with lemon juice, pepper, celery salt and paprika.
- Place in crock-pot.
- In medium bowl or pan, mix the soups with the sherry.
- Pour over chicken breasts.
- Sprinkle generously w/parmesan cheese.
- Cover and cook on low 7 to 10 hours or on high 4 to 5 hours.
- Serve over noodles or rice

174. Crockpot Chicken Parmesan Recipe

Serving: 4 | Prep: | Cook: 420mins | Ready in:

Ingredients

- 2 tsp olive oil
- 4 skinless, boneless chicken breasts (about 3 oz each)
- 1and 1/4 crushed tomatoes
- 2 lg cloves garlic, crushed
- 1 tsp sugar
- Pinch of celery seed
- 2 tbl dry red wine

- 1/2 cup shredded mozzarella
- 2 Tbl grated parmesan cheese

Direction

- Heat oil in nonstick skillet over medium high heat. Add chicken and sauté, stirring occasionally, until lightly browned, about 10 minutes.
- Combine chicken, tomatoes, and garlic, sugar, celery seeds and wine in crockpot. Cover and cook on low until chicken is 6-8 hours.
- Combine cheeses in a small bowl and sprinkle them over chicken. Do not stir. Cook until cheeses are melted, about 15 minutes.

175. Crunchy Chicken Bake Recipe

Serving: 8 | Prep: | Cook: 30mins | Ready in:

Ingredients

- 8 boneless, skinless chicken breast halves
- 4 slices muenster cheese, halved
- 1 can cream of broccoli soup
- 1 large ripe tomato, cut into 8 slices
- 1/2 cup seasoned breadcrumbs (I use panko)
- 2 tablespoons butter, melted

Direction

- Arrange chicken breasts in a greased 13x9 inch baking dish.
- Top each chicken breast with half a cheese slice.
- Spread soup over all.
- Arrange one tomato slice on top of each chicken breast.
- Combine breadcrumbs and butter. Sprinkle over.
- Bake at 400 degrees for 25 to 30 minutes or until chicken juices run clear.

176. Curried Chicken And Vegetable Pasta Recipe

Serving: 2 | Prep: | Cook: | Ready in:

Ingredients

- 1 skinless chicken breast fillet, chopped into bite-sized pieces (not too small). Feel free to substitute with other parts of the chicken, I just prefer breast.
- 1/2 medium zucchini, diced
- 1 bacon rasher, (rind removed) diced into tiny pieces
- 4-5cm stalk of celery, tiny dice (optional)
- 3-4 button mushrooms, tiny dice
- 1/2 medium brown onion, tiny dice
- approx 4-5 florets of broccoli, chopped into halves or quarters
- approx 2 cups of uncooked pasta, enough for two people when cooked (I prefer penne for this recipe, but used spirals this time around)
- milk (only a splash needed)
- marinade:
- 1 heaped teaspoon Keens dry curry powder
- 3/4 teaspoon of mixed dried herbs
- 1/2 teaspoon dried parsley
- 1 teaspoon minced garlic
- A good splash of tamari, or soy (if it isn't to be GF friendly)
- olive oil

Direction

- The chicken doesn't need to marinade long, so I usually mix it up first, add the chicken pieces, turn them through, and leave to sit while I prep the other ingredients. By the time I'm ready, it's been long enough. The amount of tamari and olive oil aren't precise (and the powder ingredients are flexible if you want to add more or less of any), I often need to add a little more oil once the chicken is added, to make sure it acts as a nice even coating paste in consistency.

- Once everything is prepared, I add broccoli, zucchini and celery to a steamer and leave until par cooked. While they are steaming, I put chicken (and any excess marinade) into a hot frying pan and stir to seal. Add more oil if needed.
- Add bacon to the frying pan next, allowing it and the chicken to brown a little before adding the onion. Give it all a regular stir, to keep it evenly colored. Once the onion has softened, turn the heat down before adding the mushroom and continue to stir until it's cooked.
- Next, add a splash of milk to the pan. Just a small one, to deglaze the bottom of the pan a little and help to merge the flavors a bit. After a moment or two, I usually add another splash. This a visual thing, just enough so there's a bit of something to work through the pasta. I'd say no more than a 1/4 of a cup at the most).
- Note: Milk is all I had at hand, cooking cream would be lovely, I'm sure, or even a dollop of sour cream.
- Lastly, I add a small teaspoon of parmesan cheese to the mix and stir through, before adding the steamed veggies. Leave for around 3 minutes, stirring every so often, until the vegetables have joined the dish nicely.
- Serve with cooked pasta, either just on top, or you can mix it through the pan before dishing up.

177. Dawnas Stuffed Chicken Breasts Recipe

Serving: 4 | Prep: | Cook: 60mins | Ready in:

Ingredients

- 4 4-oz chicken breasts
- 1 block of cream cheese

- The following to taste: seasoned salt, pepper, garlic powder, italian seasoning, soul seasoning, oregano.
- bread crumbs

Direction

- Defrost chicken (I make this dish from frozen so that the chicken is still wet from defrosting - this way you don't need egg and milk to do breading. The water from defrosting is enough moisture to hold the breading on)
- Soften cream cheese and add the seasonings. Mix together well.
- Slice a pocket into each breast.
- Stuff a spoonful of the cheese mixture into the pocket (not so much that it is oozing out and you can't lay the top part of the pocket down, but as much as you can)
- Season bread crumbs (sometimes I throw parmesan cheese into the bread crumbs - adds a little something).
- Roll breasts in bread crumb mixture and pat on to make sure you have a nice covering on both sides.
- Place on sprayed cookie sheet.
- Bake at 350* for 1 hour.
- I usually serve with augratin or baked potatoes and veggies. MMM!

178. Delete Recipe

Serving: 4 | Prep: | Cook: 45mins | Ready in:

Ingredients

- 4 cups dry bread cubes
- 1 cup chopped onion
- 1 cup chopped celery
- 2 apples, cored, peeled and chopped very fine
- 1 cup chicken broth
- 1 tsp. allspice
- 1 T. sugar
- Four boneless, skinless chicken breasts, pounded flat

- 1/3 cup apple juice

Direction

- Preheat oven to 350 degrees. Combine first seven ingredients in large bowl and mix well
- Place about two tablespoons of stuffing on top of each chicken breast and roll up so that the stuffing is completely enclosed inside the chicken
- Secure with toothpicks or tie with kitchen twine and place, seam side down, in greased baking pan
- Pour apple juice over chicken and cover with tin foil. Bake for 20 minutes and then remove foil. Bake, uncovered for another 25 minutes.

179. Derek's Comfort Jambalaya Recipe

Serving: 4 | Prep: | Cook: 30mins | Ready in:

Ingredients

- 2 cups calrose rice - if you don't like sticky rice, any medium grain white rice will do
- 1 cup chicken broth
- 1 cup sherry
- 2/3 cup water
- 2 sticks unsalted butter
- 3 tbsp olive oil
- 1 cup cubed ham
- 1 chicken breast 1 in. slices
- 1 cup medium or large cooked shrimp
- OPTIONAL: If you don't mind a slight fishy odor, about a 1/2 cup of crawfish tailmeat can be added with the shrimp
- 1 14oz package (2 links) smoked sausage - 1/2 in. slices
- 1 green bell pepper diced
- 1 large yellow onion diced
- 5 green chiles finely sliced (not de-seeded)
- 1 bottle Guinness Draught
- 4 tsp minced or freshly pressed garlic
- paprika
- fresh ground black pepper
- cayenne pepper
- salt
- thyme
- 4 whole bay leaves
- your favorite creole or cajun seasoning

Direction

- Soak rice in chicken broth, sherry, and water,
- Place sliced sausage on a cookie sheet, sprinkle with Cajun seasoning, and place in oven set to broil. You want to achieve a nice crispy char to the edge of the slices. Just keep tabs on it while you're doing the next several steps, because this won't take long. You don't want to burn it! When it's done just remove and set aside.
- Over med. heat, begin to sauté half of the garlic.
- After garlic is heated, add sausage, ham, and chicken.
- Begin to sauté onion and green bell pepper in a whole stick of butter over med. heat on a separate burner. Just continue to watch your veggies and turn off the burner when they've reached that nice golden colour and are slightly tender.
- Add sliced chilies to meat mixture ---you may start to cough a little.
- Bring soaked rice to a boil on a separate burner. When liquid begins to boil, add bay leaves, the remaining garlic, and the last stick of butter, then reduce heat to simmer and cover.
- After meat mixture is thoroughly browned, add the sausage that you had set aside from the oven, spice to taste with seasonings, and add entire bottle of Guinness...well, minus a good sampling for yourself, of course.
- Bring beer to boil, then reduce heat to simmer and cover for five minutes.
- Uncover meat mixture, add shrimp, and raise heat so that the beer can boil off a bit. At this point you may want to sample a bit of the mixture and decide if you need to season a bit more. I usually end up adding a bit more salt and Cajun seasoning.

- Taste test the texture of the rice to make sure that it is cooked through.
- When the rice is tender enough, the meat mixture should be thickened. At this point you can add the meat mixture and peppers and onions to the rice, and stir thoroughly. Try to find and remove the bay leaves. No big deal though if one turns up in a serving. Just tell that friend they're a winner.
- Bring it to the table in your favourite serving dish with a bit of attitude, serve and enjoy!

180. Devas Funky Chicken Recipe

Serving: 8 | Prep: | Cook: 90mins | Ready in:

Ingredients

- 8 chicken breasts halves
- pack of bacon
- 1 (4 oz.) pkg. dried beef
- 2 can cream of chicken soup
- pt. sour cream
- Garden rotini pasta

Direction

- Soak dried beef in warm water for 30 seconds.
- Season chicken with salt and pepper to taste.
- Wrap each breast half in a 2-3 slices of dried beef, then 2 slices of bacon.
- Arrange the chicken breast wraps in the bottom of the 9 x 13 pan.
- Mix the cream of chicken soup and sour cream together (I prefer a bit of extra sour cream.
- Pour the sour cream/soup mix over the chicken breasts and dried beef.
- Cover
- Bake at 350 degrees for 1.5 hours or at 400 degrees for a little over one hour.
- Serve over garden rotini pasta. This makes a great sauce. Use rolls to sop it up!

181. Dijon Chicken Recipe

Serving: 2 | Prep: | Cook: 10mins | Ready in:

Ingredients

- 1 lb organic chicken breasts
- 1 tbs (or so!) of tarragon
- 2 tbs. (or so!) of chunky Dijon mustard
- 2 cloves of garlic
- olive oil
- lemon
- salt and pepper to taste

Direction

- Dice garlic and mix in a bowl with a bit of tarragon, the Dijon, a good glug of olive oil and the lemon juice.
- Pat dry the chicken breasts and salt and pepper both sides.
- Score the chicken and rub in the mixture.
- Broil for ten minutes and serve.

182. Dotties Chicken Piccata Recipe

Serving: 6 | Prep: | Cook: 15mins | Ready in:

Ingredients

- 6 to 8 chicken breast halves, boneless, no skin
- 1/2 cup flour
- 1 1/2 teaspoons salt
- 1/4 teaspoon freshly ground pepper
- 1/2 teaspoon paprika, or to taste
- 3 tablespoons butter
- 2 tablespoons olive oil
- 1/4 cup chicken broth or water
- 3 tablespoons fresh lemon juice
- 1 tablespoon of sugar (optional)
- 6 to 8 thin slices of lemon
- 3 tablespoons capers (optional)

Direction

- Put chicken breasts between 2 sheets of waxed paper or plastic wrap; pound to flatten to about 1/4-inch.
- In a shallow bowl, combine flour, salt, pepper and paprika; dredge chicken breasts to coat well.
- Heat butter and olive oil in a large skillet. Sauté chicken breasts in batches, about 3 minutes on each side.
- Drain off all but 2 tablespoons of fat.
- Stir in chicken broth, scraping to loosen browned bits.
- Add lemon juice and sugar to dissolve sugar and heat through.
- Return chicken to the skillet with the lemon slices; heat until sauce thickens.
- Add capers, if using.
- Serve with your favorite pasta and a green vegetable.
- Chicken Piccata recipe serves 6 to 8.

183. Dressed For Dinner Chicken Recipe

Serving: 4 | Prep: | Cook: 1hours | Ready in:

Ingredients

- 4 chicken breast
- 1 pakage reduced fat cream cheesee or reg cream cheese
- 2 lemons
- 2 cloves garlic
- 1 zucchini (or 2 small)
- salt & pepper
- olive oil
- 1 cup white wine
- 1 table spoon butter

Direction

- Butterfly the chicken breast
- Salt and pepper inside and out (lightly)

- Mix room temp cream cheese the zest of the lemon, crushed garlic and grated zucchini. (Grate and put in a strainer with a little salt let drain well and squeeze out all juice)
- Divide the cream cheese mixture between the chicken, fold and tie or pin with tooth pick.
- Heat olive oil and place the chicken in and brown 3 mi. aside on med low heat. While chicken is on stove top slice the lemon and the zested lemon. Place the lemons in the pan and bake for 20 to 25 mi. At 350.
- Remove and cover chicken put pan on stove and add 1 cup white wine cook for 5 min pull from heat add 1 tab. Soon butter and drizzle over the chicken. (Lemon can be served and eat or removed depending on your taste) wonderful over pasta.

184. Dried Beef Company Chicken Recipe

Serving: 6 | Prep: | Cook: 180mins | Ready in:

Ingredients

- 1/2 jar dried beef, cut up
- 6 boneless, skinless chicken breasts
- 3 slices of bacon
- 1 can cream of mushroom soup
- 1 cup sour cream

Direction

- Put the dried beef on the bottom of a baking dish
- Roll up the boneless chicken breast with 1/2 slice of bacon around it.
- Secure the roll with a toothpick.
- Lay the 6 rolls on top of the beef.
- Pour over a mixture of the soup and the sour cream.
- Bake uncovered 275 degrees for 3 hrs.

185. EASY CHICKEN AND POTATOES Recipe

Serving: 4 | Prep: | Cook: 60mins | Ready in:

Ingredients

- 4 boneless, skinless chicken breasts to equal 1 pound
- 3 medium scrubbed, unpeeled potatoes, cut into 1-inch or so pieces (about 3 cups)
- 1-1/2 cups baby carrots
- one 12 ounce jar homestyle chicken gravy
- garlic-pepper blend, to taste

Direction

- Heat oven to 400 degrees.
- Spray a 13X9 glass baking dish with no-stick cooking spray. Arrange the chicken breasts in the middle of the dish. Arrange potatoes and carrots around the edges (DO NOT cover up chicken!) In a small bowl, stir together chicken gravy and garlic-pepper blend. Pour over chicken and vegetables. Cover tightly and bake 50-60 minutes or until the vegetables are tender and the juice of the chicken is no longer pink when the centers of the thickest parts are cut.
- Note: Recipe is easily halved. You can find garlic-pepper blend in the spice aisle of your grocery store with the seasoned salt, lemon-pepper blend, etc.

186. Easy BBQ Chicken Recipe

Serving: 4 | Prep: | Cook: 7mins | Ready in:

Ingredients

- *4-6 boneless, skinless chicken breasts (quanity depends on size of crock pot)

- *Bottle of your favorite BBQ sauce (or you can try my homemade bbq recipe if you don't a bottle)
- Pack of frozen corn on the cob (baby ears)

Direction

- Clean your chicken. Set your crock pot on the Low setting. Pot your chicken in the pot and cover with the bbq sauce. Next, wrap the corn on the cobs in aluminum foil. Set atop the chicken and bbq sauce. Cook for 7 hrs. or until chicken is no longer pink! Wah-lah...dinner is served.

187. Easy Chicken Enchiladas Recipe

Serving: 10 | Prep: | Cook: 25mins | Ready in:

Ingredients

- 2 pounds chicken breasts
- 2 cans cream of chicken
- 1 cup salsa
- 10-12 flour tortillas
- 1 can cheddar cheese soup

Direction

- Preheat oven to 350
- Cook the chicken breasts in a skillet, drain and cube.
- Add chicken soup and 1/2 cup salsa.
- Bring to a boil and simmer 10 minutes
- Fill each tortilla with 1/3 cup of the mixture
- Roll up and place in a 9X13 sprayed pan
- Melt cheese soup with remaining salsa and pour over tortillas.
- Bake 25 minutes.

188. Easy Crock Pot Chicken Tacos Recipe

Serving: 46 | Prep: | Cook: 480mins | Ready in:

Ingredients

- 3 cans tomatoes (garlic, oregano and basil flavored)
- 2 cans diced green chiles
- 1 medium onion chopped
- 1/4 tsp pepper
- 1/4 tsp garlic salt
- 1 cup chicken broth
- 3 large frozen boneless-skinless chicken breasts

Direction

- Put all ingredients into a crockpot
- Set on low
- Cook for 8 hours and shred chicken with a fork
- Serve on tortilla shells with all of the fixings

189. Easy Egg Foo Yung Recipe

Serving: 6 | Prep: | Cook: | Ready in:

Ingredients

- 1/3 cup cooked and crumbled ground beef
- 1/3 cup chopped cooked chicken breast
- 1/3 cup chopped cooked pork
- 8 beaten eggs
- 1 cup sliced celery
- 1/2 cup diced mushrooms
- 1 cup bean sprouts
- 1 cup finely chopped onion
- 1 tsp salt
- 2 cubes chicken bouillon
- 1/4 tsp ground black pepper
- 1 1/2 tbspns cornstarch
- Foo Yung sauce

- 1 1/2 cups hot water
- 1 1/2 tsps white sugar
- 6 tbspns cold water
- 2 tbspns soy sauce

Direction

- Beat the eggs in a good sized bowl. Add the onion, celery, sprouts, chicken, mushrooms, pork, beef, salt and pepper. Mix all together.
- Heat a little oil in a medium-sized frying-pan (preferably wok) and then brown the egg mix 1/2 cup at a time. When all of the mix is brown, set it aside for later.
- Now to create the finishing sauce. Dissolve the bouillon cubes in hot water in a small saucepan. Then add sugar and some soy sauce and blend it all over medium heat. Add (cold) water and the cornstarch and stir it until it gets thick and smooth. Serve this with your delicious Egg Foo Yung!

190. Easy LemonLime Grilled Chicken Recipe

Serving: 8 | Prep: | Cook: 20mins | Ready in:

Ingredients

- chicken breasts (I buy the bulk from Costco and use the whole package)
- 1 cup lemon juice
- 1 cup lime juice
- 4-6 cloves finely chopped garlic
- 3 tbsp kosher salt
- 2 tsp fresh cracked black pepper
- red pepper flakes (however much you like ro can be omitted)

Direction

- I like to poke each chicken breast 4-5 times with a small paring knife to give the marinade a chance to penetrate the chicken

- In a gallon size plastic ziplock I add all the ingredients and squeeze out all the air
- Place bag in the fridge for at least 4-6 hours
- Grill and chop for tacos, burritos, salads or this stands on its own for a delicious meal

191. Easy Low Fat Chicken With Mushrooms Recipe

Serving: 6 | Prep: | Cook: 20mins | Ready in:

Ingredients

- 2lbs B/S fresh chicken breasts, cut to desired size (I diced mine)
- 8oz fresh mushrooms
- 8oz cooking sherry
- 2tbsp garlic pwdr or minced garlic (I loooove garlic, so less is fine)
- 1tbsp EVOO

Direction

- Add oil and chicken to med heat and cook until almost all the pink is gone
- Add sherry, garlic, and mushrooms and cook until mushrooms are tender and chicken is completely cooked through
- I set the sherry on fire to assure all the alcohol was removed (I'm not sure if this is necessary, but I didn't want to take any chances)
- Serve with pasta or potatoes, it is phenomenal :)

192. Easy One Dish Chicken Dinner Recipe

Serving: 4 | Prep: | Cook: 35mins | Ready in:

Ingredients

- 4 medium chicken breasts
- 3 large carrots
- 1 medium onion
- 3 sticks of celery
- 3 medium yellow potatoes
- 2 cloves garlic
- 1 tsp sage
- 1/2 tsp parsley
- 1 tbs olive oil
- 1/2 tsp salt
- 1/2 course black pepper
- 1 can chicken stock
- 1 can cambells French onion soup

Direction

- Preheat the oven to 400 degrees.
- Coat chicken in olive oil and herbs and place in a casserole dish.
- Chop veggies and add to dish.
- Mince garlic and sprinkle it over the mix along with salt and pepper.
- Add stock and French onion soup.
- Bake in the oven for 35 minutes.
- Eat.

193. Easy Raspberry Chicken Recipe

Serving: 6 | Prep: | Cook: 45mins | Ready in:

Ingredients

- 6 boneless, skinless chicken breasts
- 1 bottle Russian dressing
- 1 envelope onion soup
- 1 jar raspberry jam

Direction

- Mix the dressing, soup mix and jam together.
- Pour the mixture over the chicken and bake for 45 to 50 minutes at 350 degrees.

194. En Nogadar Roasted Poblano Pepper Stuffed With Chicken And Fruit Recipe

Serving: 2 | Prep: | Cook: 50mins | Ready in:

Ingredients

- 4 poblano peppers, roasted and peeled
- 2 skinless chicken breasts, diced into small pieces
- 1 tablespoon canola oil
- 2 teaspoon tomato paste
- 1 teaspoon dried apricots
- 1 teaspoon diced apple
- 1 teaspoon diced pears
- 1 teaspoon raisins
- 2 teaspoons diced onion
- 1clove garlic, minced
- 1cup sugar
- salt and pepper, to taste
- For Sauce:
- 2 cups heavy cream
- 1 cup white wine
- 1 clove garlic, minced
- 1 shallot, minced
- 1/4 cup almonds, ground
- salt and pepper to taste
- cilantro and pomegranate seeds for garnish

Direction

- Heat a large skillet on high. Add oil, and when hot add diced chicken breast. Sauté until chicken starts to turn white. Add diced onions and continue to sauté until onions are translucent. Add chopped garlic, apricots and all of the fresh and dried fruit, continue to sauté for 1 minute. Add chicken paste and continue to sauté until paste has covered all of the ingredients. Add white wine and continue to cook until chicken is tender. Season to taste.
- Stuff peppers with chicken-fruit mix. In a sauté pan add oil, shallots and sauté until shallots are translucent. At this point, add garlic and continue to sauté until garlic has turned to a light caramel colour. Add wine

and reduce until almost gone. Add heavy cream and simmer until reduced in half. Adjust seasoning and finish with almonds. Garnish with cilantro and pomegranates.

195. FUNKY CHICKEN Recipe

Serving: 4 | Prep: | Cook: 30mins | Ready in:

Ingredients

- 4 chicken breasts BONELESS
- 3 tangerines
- 1 sweet onion
- 6 cloves garlic
- 1 TSP. red pepper flakes
- 3 TSP. CAVENDER'S GREEK seasoning
- 2 TBSP. olive oil
- 1/2 CUP GREEK red wine
- 2 TBSP. butter
- 1/4 CUP duck SAUCE

Direction

- Wash chicken pat dry with paper towel
- Zest and juice the tangerines
- Smash garlic
- Chop onion into half moons
- Season chicken with Greek seasoning and a little of the tangerine juice
- Put olive oil into a sauté pan add in onions and cook until soft then add garlic cook well and remove
- Add chicken to the pan and cook thoroughly
- Deglaze pan with tangerine juice and wine reduce by half
- Add butter duck sauce and zest simmer until the oils from the zest are released
- Add chicken and onion and garlic into pan with sauce

196.   Fancy Chicken Cheese Rolls Recipe

Serving: 6 | Prep: | Cook: 40mins | Ready in:

Ingredients

- 3 large chicken breasts, boned and split
- 8 oz. whipped cream cheese with chives, divided
- 1 T butter or margarine, divided
- 6 slices bacon

Direction

- Place split breasts between waxed paper; pound to 1/2" thickness. Spread each with about 3 T cheese; dot with 1/2 tsp. butter. Fold ends over filling (some will ooze out during baking) Wrap 2 slice bacon around each roll. Place seam side down in shallow baking pan. Bake on top rack in 400 oven 40 minutes or until chicken is tender and juices run clear when meat is pierced. Broil about 5 minutes or until bacon is crisp and golden.

197.   Fannie Farmer's Chicken Pot Pie Recipe

Serving: 0 | Prep: | Cook: 1hours | Ready in:

Ingredients

- For the sauce:
- 6 Tbsp flour
- 6 Tbsp butter
- 2 c. chicken broth (if I don't have any I dissolve 4 bouillon cubes in 2 cups water)
- 1 c. heavy whipping cream
- 1/2 tsp fresh cracked pepper
- For the rest:
- 1 package pre-made refrigerated pie crusts (2 crusts)
- 2 chicken breasts (about 4 c. chicken), cooked

- 1/2 large onion, chopped and cooked; or 1/2 c. pearl onions, cooked
- 1/2 c. peas, cooked
- 1/2 c. carrots, sliced and cooked
- 1/2 c. celery, sliced and cooked
- 1 potato, peeled, cubed and cooked
- 9-inch deep dish pie pan
- 1-quart saucepan
- 2-cup microwave safe measuring cup or dish

Direction

- For the vegetables & chicken: (Fannie Farmer does not tell you how to cook them, so I'll give you my method.)
- **I recommend doing the prep work (but not the sauce) the day before you intend on making the pie. Put everything in the fridge and then just preheat the oven, make the sauce, assemble the pie, and bake.**
- Chop the onion up very chunky. Slice the carrots and celery about 1/2" thick. Combine these three and steam for 7 minutes. Run under cool water to stop the cooking process.
- Use frozen peas and soak them in warm water to defrost.
- Peel and cut the potato and boil for 3 minutes. Drain and run under cold water to stop the cooking process.
- Butterfly the chicken breasts, and dry rub with Lawry's season salt.
- Heat 2 Tbsp. olive oil in a large fry pan or skillet and cook the chicken until golden brown and cooked through. Cut into 1 inch cubes.
- Note: You can use frozen veggie mixes and canned potatoes and chicken to make your life REALLY easy.
- For the sauce:
- Put the broth in the microwave safe dish and heat on "high" for 2 minutes.
- Melt the butter in the saucepan and add the flour to make a roux. Cook, whisking, for 3 minutes.
- Slowly add the broth and whisk until incorporated into the roux.

- Add the cream and pepper and blend thoroughly. Cook until sauce it is very thick and smooth. Remove from heat.
- Assembling the pie:
- Preheat the oven to 425 degrees.
- Unroll the pie crusts on a lightly floured surface and repair any tears in them. Line the bottom of the pie pan with one crust and use a fork to perforate it in a few places.
- Put a layer of vegetables, potatoes, and chicken, and pour half of the sauce over them. Do this again until all of the vegetables, chicken and sauce have been added to the pan. (This is easier than trying to mix all of the ingredients together and it keeps you from accidentally putting holes in the crust while mixing.)
- Cover with the second crust and pinch the seams together. Flute the edges with a fork or crimp with your hands. With a sharp knife, cut 6 to 8 slits on the top crust to vent steam.
- Bake for 25 to 30 minutes, or until crust is golden brown.

198. Fantastic Grilled Chicken With A Mediterranean Twist Recipe

Serving: 6 | Prep: | Cook: 6mins | Ready in:

Ingredients

- 1 cup plain yogurt
- 1/4 cup extra-virgin olive oil
- 2 garlic cloves, chopped
- 1 teaspoon dried basil
- 1 teaspoon dried oregano
- 1 lemon, zested
- 2 teaspoons salt
- 1 teaspoon hot sauce
- 6 (6-ounce) boneless, skinless chicken breasts
- lemon slices, for garnish

Direction

- Mix the yogurt, olive oil, garlic, basil, oregano, lemon zest, salt and hot sauce together in a large bowl.
- Add the chicken and toss well to coat. Refrigerate for 1 hour.
- Preheat a cast iron grill pan over high heat for 4 to 5 minutes or preheat an outdoor grill.
- Place the chicken on the grill and cook for 4 minutes per side, until the chicken is firm to the touch.
- Platter and garnish with lemon slices. Serve warm or at room temperature with salsa on the side.

199. Fast,fun,easy Chicken Ranch Flakes Recipe

Serving: 0 | Prep: | Cook: 45mins | Ready in:

Ingredients

- 1- 6 pieces Boneless skinless chicken Breast
- 1 packet ranch dressing Powder
- 1-2 cups sugar free Kellogs Flakes cereal
- 1-2 eggs
- A quick small pour of milk

Direction

- Pre-Heat oven to 400 degrees
- Cover baking pan with foil
- Stir milk and eggs together in small bowl
- Put Kellogg's non frosted flakes in large Ziploc bag and crunch up as small as you want
- Pour packet of ranch dressing in bag with flakes
- Dip defrosted chicken in egg mix
- Place chicken in ranch flake mix and shake to coat
- (If you want a thicker coat dip in egg mix again and then shake again in ranch flake mix)
- Place chicken on foil covered pan and bake for 30- 40 minutes or until fully cooked
- Let cool then eat up

200. Fiesta Chicken Nachos Recipe

Serving: 4 | Prep: | Cook: 8mins | Ready in:

Ingredients

- 1 tablespoon olive oil
- 1 pound boneless, skinless chicken breasts
- 1 jar (1 pound) RAGÚ® cheese Creations!® Double Cheddar Sauce
- 1 bag (9 ounces) tortilla chips
- 2 green and/or red bell peppers, diced
- 1 small onion, chopped
- 1 large tomato, diced

Direction

- In 12-inch skillet, heat oil over medium-high heat and cook chicken, stirring occasionally, 8 minutes or until thoroughly cooked. Remove from skillet; cut into strips.
- In same skillet, combine chicken and Ragú® Cheese Creations! Sauce; heat through.
- On serving platter, arrange layer of tortilla chips, then 1/2 of the sauce mixture, bell peppers, onion and tomato; repeat, ending with tomato. Garnish, if desired, with chopped fresh cilantro and shredded lettuce.
- Recipe Tip: For a spicier dish, add chopped jalapeño peppers or hot pepper sauce to suit your taste.

201. Fire Roasted Mexicano Chicken Recipe

Serving: 2 | Prep: | Cook: 60mins | Ready in:

Ingredients

- 1/4 cup (50 mL) Kahlúa
- 1/4 cup (50 mL) fresh lime juice
- 1/4 cup (50 mL) extra virgin olive oil
- 1/4 cup (50 mL) hot sauce
- 2 cloves garlic
- 1 onion, quartered
- 1/4 cup (50 mL) cilantro
- 2 Tbsp (25 mL) fancy molasses
- 2 Tbsp (25 mL) ketchup
- 2 tsp (10 mL) Dijon mustard
- 2 Tbsp (25 mL) pickled jalapeños
- 1 tsp (5 mL) ground cumin
- 1 tsp (5 mL) chili powder
- 1 tsp (5 mL) salt
- 1/2 tsp (2 mL) cinnamon
- 1/2 tsp (2 mL) nutmeg
- 1/4 tsp (1 mL) freshly ground black pepper
- Pinch red pepper flakes
- 4 bone-in chicken breasts, skin on

Direction

- Combine Kahlua, lime juice, olive oil, hot sauce, garlic, onion, cilantro, molasses, ketchup, mustard, jalapeños, cumin, chili powder, salt, cinnamon, nutmeg, black pepper and red pepper flakes in food processor or blender and blend until smooth. Place chicken breasts in shallow baking dish and pour over marinade. Cover and refrigerate overnight.
- Preheat grill to medium-high and sear chicken, breast-side down, for 10 minutes, rotating to produce crisscross grill marks after 5 minutes. Reduce heat to medium, turn chicken, close lid and continue cooking until juices run clear, about 10 minutes.
- Bone of Contention
- Using chicken breasts with the bone-in increases flavor. A whole cut-up chicken, chicken wings or thighs can also be used. Leftover chicken is perfect for soup, sandwiches or a spicy chicken salad.

202. Foil Pack Chicken Fajita Dinner Recipe

Serving: 4 | Prep: | Cook: 35mins | Ready in:

Ingredients

- 1-1/2 cups instant white rice, uncooked
- 1-1/2 cups hot water
- 1 Tbsp. TACO BELL® HOME ORIGINALS® taco seasoning Mix
- 4 small boneless skinless chicken breast halves (1 lb.)
- 1 each green and red pepper, cut into strips
- 1 jalepeno pepper, seeded and sliced thinnly
- 1/2 cup TACO BELL® HOME ORIGINALS® Thick 'N chunky salsa 1/2 cup KRAFT Mexican Style Finely Shredded taco cheese
- sour cream, garnish

Direction

- Heat oven to 400°F.
- Fold up all sides of each of 4 large sheets of heavy-duty foil to form 1-inch rim; spray with cooking spray. Combine rice, water and taco seasoning; spoon onto foil. Top with remaining ingredients.
- Bring up foil sides. Double fold top and ends to seal each packet, leaving room for heat circulation inside. Place in 15x10x1-inch pan.
- Bake 30 to 35 min. or until chicken is done (165°F). Let stand 5 min. Cut slits in foil to release steam before opening packets.
- Garnish with sour cream, if desired.
- Nutrition Information
- Calories 350
- Total fat 8g
- Saturated fat
- 3.5 g Cholesterol
- 80 mg Sodium
- 510 mg Carbohydrate
- 37 g Dietary fibre
- 2 g Sugars
- 3 g Protein
- 31 g Vitamin A
- 25 %DV Vitamin C
- 70 %DV Calcium
- 15 %DV Iron

203.   Foolproof Easy White Chili Recipe

Serving: 8 | Prep: | Cook: 360mins | Ready in:

Ingredients

- 1-2 pounds boneless skinless chicken (breast or thighs your choice) we like a lot of meat so we use 2 pounds.
- 1 16 ounce jar medium, (or hot if you like spicy) picante sauce
- 2 large bell peppers (Green, yellow, red, orange, purple, your choice)
- 2 medium onions
- jalapenos
- 48 ounce jar of white beans
- 8-10 ounces of hot pepper jack cheese
- 3-4 cloves of garlic chopped fine
- 1 tablespoon black pepper
- 1 tablespoon ground cumin

Direction

- Cut chicken into small bite sized cubes, or small strips (think along the lines of Chinese food for the size of the pieces)
- Chop your bell peppers and onions to your liking
- Chop fine your jalapeno's (cook the recipe without as you can always add them for heat if not spicy enough for you)
- Cube, or shred your cheese
- Picante sauce
- Add all your ingredients to a large crock pot in this order: chicken, onions, bell peppers, jalapenos, garlic, beans with the juice they're in, black pepper, Cumin, pepper jack cheese, and finally picante sauce
- Cover and let cook on high for 4 hours and finish the last 2 hours on low stirring every hour "GENTLY" so as to not break up the beans, and chicken too much as they cook. Beans should get creamy and very soft.
- Alternate cooking method: put it together in the morning before you go to work, cook on

low heat for the 9-10 hours you will be gone. A hot dinner will await you.

- Garnish however you want.....maybe a little sour cream, or with a few sliced jalapenos set in the center of your bowl. Eat this like "normal" chili, or use it like a hot dip by scooping it up with Tortilla chips as this is how my family loves it.
- If you feel the need to salt it, keep in mind there is a lot of salt in the cheese.
- Even better the second day.
- Great for parties, card games, or watching the game on TV as people can serve themselves....and it goes great with beer!
- Makes a large batch but it freezes well in an airtight container.

204.   Forgotten Chicken Recipe

Serving: 6 | Prep: | Cook: 120mins | Ready in:

Ingredients

- 3-4 Boneless skinless chicken Breasts
- 1 Can mushroom soup
- 1 Can cream of celery soup
- 1 Can French onion soup
- 1 Soup can of milk
- 2 Cups uncooked rice
- 2 Tbsp. butter
- 1 Cup Shredded Motzerella cheese
- 1 Cup Shredded mild cheddar cheese

Direction

- In large bowl mix all soups, milk, and cheeses well; set aside
- Melt butter in 9x13 pan.
- Sprinkle 2 Cups of uncooked rice to cover the bottom of the pan.
- Place the chicken breasts onto the rice
- Pour soup mixture over chicken and rice
- Bake at 350 degrees. The first hour covered with aluminum foil; the 2nd hour uncovered.

Sprinkle a little more cheese on top the last 15 minutes.

205.   From Scratch Chicken Stroganoff Recipe

Serving: 5 | Prep: | Cook: 40mins | Ready in:

Ingredients

- 4 small chicken breasts, about 1lb.
- 1 teaspoon white pepper
- 1 teaspoon seasoned salt
- 8 oz egg noodles
- 2 tablespoons butter
- 2 shallots, minced
- 5 garlic cloves, minced
- 1/2 teaspoon italian seasoning
- 1/4 teaspoon thyme
- 1/4 teaspoon sage
- 3/4 cups chicken stock
- 4 heaping tablespoons sour cream
- 1/4 cup heavy cream
- 2-1/2 tablespoons white cooking wine
- chives for garnish
- *I also added a couple tablespoons canned portabella mushrooms for myself, becuase no one in my family like them. But fresh would be best, they could be sauted with the shallots and galic.

Direction

- Dice chicken into bite size pieces, and sprinkle salt and pepper onto it. Heat butter in large skillet, once hot add chicken and cook until light brown on all sides. Heat oven to warm and remove chicken from skillet and place onto baking dish and set in oven to keep warm. Reserve butter.
- Bring pot of water to boil and cook egg noodles as directed and set aside.
- In skillet add the shallots and garlic, sauté until tender and onion is beginning to become translucent. *If using mushrooms add them at

this time. Add Italian seasoning, thyme and sage, mix well. Slowly pour in chicken stock and white cooking wine. Slowly whisk in sour cream and heavy cream. Remove from heat and set aside covered.

- Remove chicken from oven and add back into skillet with sauce.
- Assemble plates with egg noodles and chicken stroganoff, garnish with chives.

206. GRILLED CHICKEN BREASTS WITH TOMATO OLIVE AND FETA RELISH Recipe

Serving: 4 | Prep: | Cook: 7mins | Ready in:

Ingredients

- 1 1/2 cups coarsely chopped cherry tomatoes (about 10 ounces)
- 1/2 cup pitted kalamata olives, chopped
- 3 tablespoons extra-virgin olive oil, divided
- 2 tablespoons chopped fresh mint
- 1 tablespoon red wine vinegar
- 3/4 cup crumbled feta cheese (about 3 1/2 ounces)
- 4 large skinless boneless chicken breast halves (about 6 to 7 ounces each)

Direction

- Mix cherry tomatoes, olives, 2 tablespoons extra-virgin olive oil, mint, and vinegar in medium bowl. Gently stir in feta cheese. Season relish to taste with salt and pepper.
- Prepare barbecue (medium-high heat). Brush chicken on both sides with remaining 1 tablespoon extra-virgin olive oil; sprinkle with salt and pepper. Grill chicken just until cooked through, about 7 minutes per side. Transfer chicken to plates and slice, if desired. Top with relish and serve.

207. Garlic Chicken Wcapers Recipe

Serving: 2 | Prep: | Cook: 15mins | Ready in:

Ingredients

- 2 pieces of bonless chicken breast
- 1/2 stick of butter (more or less)
- 1/4 cup fresh parsley coursely chopped
- 1 T capers
- 2-3 cloves of garlic - minced
- salt and pepper to taste

Direction

- Brown chicken.
- Remove from pan and melt butter.
- Add garlic until softened.
- Add parsley and capers.
- Pour mixture over chicken and put in 350 deg. oven for about 10 minutes to finish cooking the chicken.
- Serve with fettuccine noodles and good parmesan cheese.

208. Grande Chicken Quesadillas Recipe

Serving: 1 | Prep: | Cook: 20mins | Ready in:

Ingredients

- (Makes enough for (1) so multiply the ingredients according to how many you are feeding)
- ***NOTE*** I had a rotisserie chicken to use, which is perfect for this.
- Ingredients:
- 2 (12-inch) flour tortillas
- 1 T. vegetable oil
- 2 T. chipotle sauce
- 4 ounces grilled chicken breast, sliced

- QUESA FILLING (Use as desired)
- Shredded Jack and cheddar cheeses
- Diced jalapeno pepper
- Diced tomato
- Diced onion
- Minced cilantro
- Crumbled bacon (Throw a few slices of thick cut bacon in the oven at 350 degrees for 6 min. per side; set on paper towels to absorb grease and thin slice or crumble.)
- TOPPING:
- Shredded lettuce
- sour cream
- Chopped green onion
- salsa
- Crumbled bacon
- A little more chopped cilantro

Direction

- Brush one side of each tortilla with oil.
- Place one tortilla, oiled side down, on a work surface. Spread the chipotle sauce over the tortilla.
- Spread the chicken evenly on top of the sauce on the tortilla.
- Evenly spread the queso filling over the chicken. Cover with the other tortilla, oiled side up.
- Brown evenly on both sides in a non-stick pan until the filling is heat thoroughly.
- Serve with lettuce, sour cream, green onion, and salsa as accompaniments. Sprinkle crumbled bacon on top.
- Optional: Serve with guacamole.

209. Grill Chicken Fajitas Recipe

Serving: 4 | Prep: | Cook: 30mins | Ready in:

Ingredients

- 1 lbs boneless, skinless chicken breast, cut into strips

- 1 pkt fajitas seasoning
- 1 green pepper, remove seeds, cut into strips
- 1 red pepper, remove seeds, cut into strips
- 1 med onion, cut into strips
- 1 Large tomato, cut into slices
- Shredded cheese
- 6 tortillas
- Sourcream
- salsa
- guacamole
- 6 bamboo skewers

Direction

- In large bowl, pour 3 cups of water, pour fajitas seasoning in the water, and mix well. Dump the chicken strips in the seasoning marinate. Let it sit and marinate in fridge for about 5 hours.
- Half hour to 45 mins before marinate is done, go ahead and jump start your bbq grill.
- On each bamboo skewers, start to put on chicken, peppers, onion, tomato. (I would put on at least 3 chicken strips, 3 peppers strips, 3 onion strips, & 3 tomato slices per person/skewers).
- When grill is ready, lay the prepare skewers on the grill, let cook for about 15 mins, turn over, cook another 15 mins or till chicken is done.
- When done, take a tortilla, and slide the ingredients off the skewer onto the tortillas.
- Top with Sour cream, cheese, guacamole, and salsa.
- Enjoy!

210. Grilled Basil Marinated Chicken Recipe

Serving: 4 | Prep: | Cook: 20mins | Ready in:

Ingredients

- 1 Tbsp olive oil
- 1 Tbsp red wine vinegar

- 1 Tbsp chopped fresh basil leaves
- 1 Tbsp finely chopped red onion
- 2 tsps kosher salt (not table salt!)
- 1 tsp freshly ground pepper
- 1 garlic clove, finely chopped
- 4 boneless, skinless chicken breasts

Direction

- Whisk together the oil, vinegar, basil, onion, salt, pepper, and garlic in a bowl. Transfer the marinade to a gallon-sized sealable plastic bag with the chicken and shake to combine. Refrigerate for 12 hours. Then grill inside or outside.

211. Grilled Chicken Breasts With Mandarin Orange Salsa Recipe

Serving: 4 | Prep: | Cook: 12mins | Ready in:

Ingredients

- 1 (11-oz.) can mandarin orange segments, drained
- 1 (8-oz.) can crushed pineapple in unsweetened juice, drained
- 2 tablespoons fresh lemon juice
- 1 tablespoon chopped, seeded jalapeño chile
- 1/4 teaspoon salt
- Chicken:
- 1 tablespoon olive oil (I used peanut oil)
- 4 boneless skinless chicken breast halves
- 1/4 teaspoon salt
- 1/4 teaspoon pepper
- 1/4 teaspoon ground red pepper (cayenne)

Direction

- Heat gas or charcoal grill. In medium bowl, combine all salsa ingredients; mix well. Set aside.

- Brush oil over all sides of chicken breast halves. Sprinkle with 1/4 teaspoon salt, the pepper and ground red pepper.
- When grill is heated, place chicken on gas grill over medium heat or on charcoal grill 4 to 6 inches from medium coals. Cook 10 to 12 minutes or until chicken is fork-tender and juices run clear, turning once. Serve salsa with chicken.

212. Grilled Honey Mustard Chicken Recipe

Serving: 4 | Prep: | Cook: 20mins | Ready in:

Ingredients

- 4 skinless, boneless chicken breast halves
- 1 cup salad dressing or mayonnaise
- 1/4 cup dijon-style mustard
- 1/4 cup honey
- 1/2 teaspoon salt
- 1/2 teaspoon pepper

Direction

- In a bowl mix salad dressing, mustard, honey, salt and pepper.
- In a ziplock bag place chicken and pour honey mustard over chicken, reserving 1/2 cup.
- Let marinate at least 2 hours, overnight is even better.
- Remove chicken and discard the marinade.
- Grill chicken about 10 minutes each side.
- The last few minutes brush with reserved honey mustard.

213. Healthy Jambalaya 5 Points Plus! Recipe

Serving: 5 | Prep: | Cook: 25mins | Ready in:

Ingredients

- 1) 2 chicken andouille sausages cut into 1/8 inch slices
- 2) 1/2 TBS evoo
- 3) 2 ribs celery cut into a small dice
- 4) 1/2 cup of diced onion
- 5) 1 red bell pepper cut into a medium dice
- 6) 1 chicken breast cut into 1/4 inch pieces
- 7) 1-2 TBS Cajun spice
- 8) 1 cup of tomato sauce
- 9) 1 cup of uncooked bulgur wheat
- 10) 1-1/4 cups of chicken stock
- 11) 8 medium sized shrimp shelled and deveined

Direction

- Place 3 quart saucepan on a stove with medium to high heat and add the first 2 ingredients (1-2). Sauté about 3-5 minutes (to brown) then stir sausage with a wooden spoon briefly.
- Add the next 3 ingredients (3-5) to the sausage and stir frequently for about 2 minutes. Transfer to a bowl and set aside.
- Add the next ingredients (6-7) to the 3 quart saucepan and sauté for about 3 minutes stirring when necessary to brown chicken pieces.
- Add the next ingredient (8) and stir 30 seconds. Add the bowl of reserved sausage and vegetables to the chicken and stir for 30 seconds.
- Add the next 3 ingredients (9-11) and turn burner to high and bring to a boil, reduce heat to low cover pan and cook for 15 minutes.
- Makes 4-6 servings
- If you are a stick in the mud thinking the shrimp are over-cooked simply add them the last 3 minutes of cooking time and give it a quick stir. Then allow the pan to rest 5 minutes prior to serving.

214. Healthy Twice Baked Potato Skins Recipe

Serving: 1 | Prep: | Cook: 120mins |Ready in:

Ingredients

- Baking size potatoes, washed, skin on.
- 1 cooked, diced chicken breast (seasoned as you prefer)
- turkey bacon (4 slices per spud, 2 slices on each half)
- Finely shredded cheese, your favorite (I use cheddar)
- Your favorite condiments, i.e veggies, salsa, sour cream, herbs, spices, etc.

Direction

- Bake the spuds until they are done.
- Allow to cool enough to handle, so you can cut the spuds in half and scoop out the potato flesh. Meanwhile, put the turkey bacon in the over to cook (suggested temp of 350, monitored).
- Once hollowed, line the skins with 2 slices of the cooked turkey bacon.
- Fill with some of the chicken.
- Sprinkle with the shredded cheese (add any spices, herbs, or veggies you want cooked).
- Bake at 350 for about 20 - 30 minutes.
- Serve as is or topped with your favourite condiments.

215. Herbed Balsamic Chicken With Blue Cheese Recipe

Serving: 6 | Prep: | Cook: 20mins |Ready in:

Ingredients

- 6 skinless boneless chicken breast; halves (5 to 6 oz. each)
- 1/2 cup balsamic vinegar

- 3 tablespoons olive oil
- 2 teaspoons coarse kosher salt; divided
- 1 1/2 teaspoons freshly ground black pepper; divided
- 2 teaspoons herbes de provence
- 1 3-4 oz wedge blue cheese; cut into 6 slices

Direction

- Place chicken in large resealable plastic bag.
- Whisk vinegar, 3 tablespoons oil, 1 1/2 teaspoons coarse salt, and 1 teaspoon pepper in small bowl.
- Add to chicken; seal bag.
- Chill 2 hours, turning bag occasionally.
- Prepare barbecue (medium-high heat).
- Brush grill rack generously with oil.
- Arrange chicken on grill. Sprinkle with herbes de Provence, 1/2 teaspoon coarse salt, and 1/2 teaspoon pepper.
- Grill chicken until cooked through, about 6 minutes per side.
- Transfer to plates; top each with slice of cheese.
- Contributor: Bon Appétit - June 2009

216. Herby Stuffed Chicken Breasts Recipe

Serving: 2 | Prep: | Cook: 15mins | Ready in:

Ingredients

- 2 boneless skinless chicken breast halves
- 4 paper-thin slices speck or prosciutto
- 2-3 tsp. chopped fresh sage
- 2 tbs. hard cheese such as aged goat's cheese, grated, or even cheddar if you like
- salt and pepper
- flour, for dredging
- olive oil, a fairly good amount
- one lemon

Direction

- Pound each breast half out to an even thickness. Season with salt and pepper and set on a plate.
- Place the speck or prosciutto on the chicken, then sprinkle over the cheese and sage evenly on each half. Fold the chicken in half, so the stuffing stays in.
- Dredge the chicken in the flour.
- Heat the olive oil in a pan large enough to hold the chicken. You want it to come up the side about 1/4 inch.
- When hot, add the stuffed chicken and brown it nicely on both sides until it's cooked through. This may take a while and if it's getting too dry on the outside and isn't cooking through, you may want to finish them in the oven. It took me a couple of times to get it nice and browned on the outside without drying out.
- To serve, squeeze a bit of lemon juice over the chicken and maybe sprinkle with a bit more sage.

217. Honey Chipotle Chicken Recipe

Serving: 6 | Prep: | Cook: 15mins | Ready in:

Ingredients

- 2 chipotles, chopped (in adobo sauce)
- 1 clove garlic, chopped
- 1 tbls. cilantro, chopped
- 4-5 tbls. honey
- 2 tbls. ground mustard
- 1 tsp. cumin
- juice for 1 1/2 limes
- 2 tbls. canola oil
- 6 boneless chicken breasts

Direction

- In blender, combine first 7 ingredients and blend
- Add oil while blender is still on

- Heat grill to medium
- Brush both sides of chicken with sauce
- Cook 5-7 minutes on each side
- Brush with additional sauce before serving

218. Hot Browns Recipe

Serving: 4 | Prep: | Cook: 30mins | Ready in:

Ingredients

- 4 boneless chicken breasts
- 1 lb. bacon
- 6 to 8 pieces white bread
- 2 large tomatoes
- 2/3 cup bacon drippings
- 3 Tbsp. flour
- 6 oz. canned cream
- 3 cup water
- 2 to 3 heaping Tbsp. Cheez Whiz

Direction

- Cook chicken breasts until well done. Allow to cool.
- Tear chicken into tiny pieces and place to the side in a bowl.
- Cut bacon strips in halves.
- Fry bacon pieces until crisp, set aside to cool
- Save the bacon drippings.
- Brown flour in the drippings.
- Add cream and water; stir until mixture begins to thicken.
- Add cheese whiz and stir until desired thickness.
- Toast bread
- Place layer of chicken breast, layer of bacon, and slice of tomato
- Smother with cheese sauce.

219. House Fried Rice Recipe

Serving: 8 | Prep: | Cook: 15mins | Ready in:

Ingredients

- 1-1/2 cups uncooked white rice
- 1 small onion, chopped
- 1 cup small shrimp, peeled
- 2 stalks of celery, chopped
- 1 freen bell pepper, chopped
- 1 cup cooked chicken breast, chopped
- 1/4 cup (or more) soy sauce
- 3 tbs. sesame oil
- 1 clove garlic, chopped
- 1/2 cup diced ham
- 1/2 cup green peas
- 1 egg, beaten

Direction

- Cook rice according to package directions and then cool to room temperature.
- (The rest of the prep can be done while rice is cooling)
- Heat wok or skillet over medium heat
- Add sesame oil and then stir in onion
- Fry until golden, then add garlic
- When garlic is lightly browned, mix in shrimp, ham and chicken
- Continue to cook until shrimp are pink
- Lower heat to medium and stir in vegetables, frying until tender crisp
- Stir in beaten egg and cook until egg is scrambled and firm
- Mix rice with all ingredients and stir in soy sauce and adjust seasonings to your preference.

220. Irie Jerk Chicken Recipe

Serving: 2 | Prep: | Cook: 70mins | Ready in:

Ingredients

- 1 lb chicken, breasts, legs or thighs - I prefer skin on, but that's left to your discretion
- 1 Tbsp Walkerswood jerk seasoning, Hot & Spicy
- 2 Tbsp Italian dressing
- Jamaican Jerk Sauce

Direction

- Combine jerk seasoning and Italian dressing in a bowl.
- Pour over chicken in a ziplock style bag and seal with most of the air purged out.
- Turn and roll bag a few times to evenly coat.
- Marinade for 24 hours, turning the bag once in a while.
- Bake at 350 degrees, for 1 hour or until juices run clear, turning chicken once.
- Turn skin side up and broil until lightly browned.
- Serve with a Jamaican jerk sauce for dipping.

221. Irish Soda Breasts Recipe

Serving: 4 | Prep: | Cook: 27mins | Ready in:

Ingredients

- 2 SKINLESS, BONELESS chicken breasts, CUT IN HALF
- 6 TABLESPOONS honey
- 2 TEASPOONS sea salt
- 4 TABLESPOONS caraway seeds
- 4 TABLESPOONS butter

Direction

- I cook this in a toaster oven.
- Preheat it to 375
- Wash the chicken & cut the full breasts in half & dry
- On a dinner sized plate, spread the chicken out
- Prepare each side completely before doing the other side of the breast.

- Pour nearly a tablespoon of honey on each side of each breast.
- Over each breast sprinkle one half tablespoon caraway seeds per side.
- Sprinkle the sea salt to your taste.
- ***remember, sea salt has nearly half the sodium of regular salt. Until you're aware of the differences, remember, you can always add more, but you cannot ever undo your salting.
- Put your Irish soda breasts on the toaster oven tray.
- Just before you put them into the toaster oven, cut 1 tablespoon worth of butter
- Cut this in half again and put 3 or 4 dollops of your 1/2 tablespoon of butter all over 1 breast, saving the other half for when you turn it over.
- Do the same for the 3 other breasts.
- Put them into the toaster oven and bake for 12 to 15 minutes.
- Pull them out & turn them over.
- (If you are so inclined you can add a little more honey & a couple more seeds to the uncooked side,
- It's not necessary, but if you want to pump up the flavor, do so with a soft touch.)
- Add the remaining butter in the same fashion you did to the first side & put them back in to finish cooking.
- ****toaster ovens vary, so check them after they've cooked for 5 to 7 minutes.
- Over cooked chicken stinks, even if it's divine and under cooked chicken's just dangerous.
- ***I recommend that the first time you make this, sacrifice 1 breast by cutting it in half to test for doneness.
- Center white chicken is cooked & translucent chicken isn't. Cut at thickest part.
- Remember that smaller pieces will cook more quickly and larger pieces will take longer.
- When cooked, plate, serve & enjoy.
- I happen to like them cold as well so I make them ahead of time for picnics.

222. Island Chicken And Rice Recipe

Serving: 6 | Prep: | Cook: 1hours | Ready in:

Ingredients

- 4 chicken breasts
- pinch, salt and peppers
- 1/2 tsp ground allspice
- 1/4 tsp ground ginger
- 5 cloves garlic, minced
- 1 jalapeno pepper, minced
- 1 red bell pepper, chopped
- 1 400mL can unsweetened coconut milk
- 1 cup chicken stock
- 1/2 cup chopped fresh coriander or Italian parsely
- 1 green onion, chopped
- 1 cup long grain rice

Direction

- Remove all skin and fat from chicken if necessary. Sprinkle with salt, pepper, allspice, and ginger.
- In a large shallow Dutch oven, heat oil over medium heat and brown chicken. Place chicken on plate - don't worry if it isn't fully cooked at this point.
- Add garlic and jalapeno to pan and sauté until garlic is golden.
- Add red pepper and rice.
- Stir in coconut milk and chicken stock, stirring to include the brown bits from the chicken on the bottom of the pan. Bring to a boil.
- Return chicken to pan, reduce heat and simmer. Cover the pan and simmer about 25 minutes, turning the chicken once halfway through.
- Sprinkle with coriander and green onion and serve.

223. Italian Chicken Mozzarella Melt Recipe

Serving: 4 | Prep: | Cook: 30mins | Ready in:

Ingredients

- 4 boneless skinless chicken breast halves
- 2 tablespoons olive oil
- 1/4 teaspoon salt
- 1/2 teaspoon dried oregano divided
- 1 cup pizza sauce
- 1/2 teaspoon dried basil
- 4 French rolls halved and toasted
- 1 small zucchini shredded
- 1/4 cup shredded mozzarella cheese
- 1/4 cup grated parmesan cheese

Direction

- Brush each piece of chicken with olive oil then sprinkle with salt and 1/4 teaspoon oregano.
- Cook chicken in lightly greased nonstick skillet over medium high heat 4 minutes on each side.
- Set chicken aside then combine pizza sauce, basil, and remaining oregano in skillet,
- Cook over medium high heat until thoroughly heated then remove from heat and add chicken.
- Spread rolls on a baking sheet and spread sauce evenly on bottom half of each roll.
- Top evenly with chicken, zucchini and cheeses then broil 3" from heat for 3 minutes.
- Cover with tops of rolls and serve.

224. Italian Pizza Bake Recipe

Serving: 2 | Prep: | Cook: | Ready in:

Ingredients

- 1/3 cup Bisquick Heart Smart mix
- 2 T. fat-free egg product, or 2 T. egg white
- 1 T. water

- 1/8 t. or more garlic powder
- 1/4 cup diced green or yellow bell peppers
- 1/4 cup chopped onion
- 1/2 cup cooked cut up chicken breast
- 1/4 t. italian seasoning (Frontier makes "pizza seasoning")
- 1/2 cup canned diced tomatoes w/ Italian herbs, drained
- 1/4 cup reduced fat mozzarella cheese, shredded

Direction

- Heat oven to 400. Spray a loaf pan 8 X 4 inches. Stir Bisquick mix, egg product water and garlic powder; spread in pan.
- Cook pepper and onion in nonstick skillet over med-high heat. Stir frequently until onion tender. Stir in chicken, tomatoes and seasonings. Spoon over batter in pan. Sprinkle with cheese.
- Bake 20 to 23 minutes until golden brown. Loosen from sides of pan. 2 servings.

225.   Italian Slow Chicken Recipe

Serving: 6 | Prep: | Cook: 8mins | Ready in:

Ingredients

- 3 pounds boneless, skinless chicken breast, cut into fingers
- 16 ounce bottle Italian salad dressing
- 1/2 cup parmesan cheese, freshly grated
- 2 or 3 crushed chopped garlic pods

Direction

- Place chicken fingers in bottom of slow cooker. Pour Italian salad dressing and garlic over chicken and sprinkle with Parmesan cheese. Cover and cook on low for 8 hours.

226.   JK's Herb Stuffed Chicken Breasts With Sage Cream Recipe

Serving: 4 | Prep: | Cook: 60mins | Ready in:

Ingredients

- 4 boneless, skinless chicken breasts
- 10 sage leaves
- 1 large sprigs of rosemary
- 2 cloves garlic, finely minced
- 1/4c olive oil, divided
- salt & pepper to tasts
- For Sauce
- 1/4c chicken broth
- 5-10 sage leaves
- 1 clove garlic finely minced
- 1 sprig of rosemary, chopped
- 1/4c half and half
- 2 tsb finely minced Italian parsley
- 2 tsb parmesan cheese
- salt & pepper to taste

Direction

- Preheat oven to 375
- Pound out chicken breasts to about 1/4" thickness
- Season liberally with salt and pepper on both sides
- On the pounded side, sprinkle breasts evenly with 2 cloves minced garlic, rosemary leaves, lemon zest, and sage leaves.
- Roll seasonings inside breast and secure with a toothpick.
- Heat half of the olive oil in a heavy bottom skillet and sere rolled chicken breasts, turning as needed to sear all sides.
- Place pan in oven and roast for 15-20 minutes until breasts are cooked thoroughly and juices run clear.
- Remove chicken from pan and place back on stovetop. Add remaining olive oil and remaining clove of garlic.

- Deglaze pan with 1/4c chicken stock.
- Add remaining sage, rosemary, and parsley and let reduce.
- Finish sauce with half and half and parmesan cheese.
- Salt and pepper to taste.
- Enjoy!

227. Jambalaya Ala Everything Recipe

Serving: 8 | Prep: | Cook: 40mins | Ready in:

Ingredients

- 2 Tbls. olive oil
- 1 lb. boneless, skinless chicken breast, cut into chunks
- 1/4 thick sliced, smoked ham, cubed
- 1 lb. smoked sausage, preferably cajun style, sliced
- 1/2 lb. to 1 lb. of fresh shrimp, peeled and deveined
- 2 c. chopped onion
- 1 c. chopped celery
- 1 c. chopped red bell pepper
- 2 cloves minced garlic
- 2 cups of long grain rice
- 1 tsp. each salt, fresh ground black pepper, paprika
- 1/4 tsp. hot red pepper flakes or more if you like it spicy
- 1 1/2 tsp. dried thyme or 3/4 tsp. fresh thyme
- 2 crushed bay leaves
- 1/4 tsp. allspice
- 4 - 5 c. hot chicken broth
- 1 14 oz. can diced tomatoes, drained
- rind of 1 lemon

Direction

- Heat olive oil in LARGE heavy skillet.
- Fry chicken and ham in olive oil until well browned, remove from pan and set aside.

- Fry sausage in same pan until browned, remove and set aside.
- Sauté onion, celery, red pepper and garlic in same pan until wilted about 5 minutes.
- Stir in the rice and all of the seasonings and sauté 3 to 4 minutes to coat rice grains with oil.
- Add hot chicken broth to pan followed by the meats and stir to mix.
- Cover and simmer over low heat just until the rice is barely tender, about 15 minutes.
- Add the tomatoes, shrimp and lemon rind and remove from heat.
- Let stand, covered, until shrimp is cooked and turns pink about 10 minutes.
- Enjoy!

228. Jazzy Dressed Up Chicken Recipe

Serving: 6 | Prep: | Cook: 30mins | Ready in:

Ingredients

- 4-6 chicken breast halves, skinned
- 8 oz shredded mozzarella
- 1 cup grated or shredded parmesan
- 2 tablespoons parsley flakes
- 3/4 cup seasoned bread crumbs
- 2 eggs
- olive oil
- salt, pepper, garlic powder
- SAUCE:
- 1 pt. sour cream
- 1 cup grated or shredded parmesan
- 1 can cream celery soup (or your fave cream soup)
- 1/2 cup milk
- 2 tablespoons parsley flakes
- 4 pieces sun-dried tomatoes, chopped finely
- salt, pepper, garlic powder

Direction

- Using a mallet, plastic tumbler, can of beans or whatever, flatten breasts just a bit. You're not going for 1/2 inch here, just flatten them a bit. Maybe about 3/4 inch all over or whatever.
- Season the breadcrumbs with a bit of salt and garlic powder, stir in the parmesan. Place breadcrumbs on a plate suitable for breading.
- Pepper the breasts, and dip them into the beaten eggs, then the crumbs.
- Fry them until lightly browned in the hot olive oil.
- Place into baking dish sprayed with Pam, or buttered.
- Sprinkle with mozzarella.
- SAUCE:
- Mix all sauce ingredients and season to taste with salt, pepper and garlic. Pour over chicken in baking pan.
- Bake at 350 for 25-30 minutes, until bubbly, slightly browned. ENJOY!

229. Jennie's Heavenly Slow Cooker Chicken Recipe

Serving: 4 | Prep: | Cook: 4hours | Ready in:

Ingredients

- 2 tablespoons butter
- 1 (.7 ounce) package dry Italian-style salad dressing mix
- 1 (10.75 ounce) can condensed mushroom soup
- 8 oz. cream cheese
- 1/2 cup dry white wine
- 4 skinless, boneless chicken breast halves cut into pieces
- 8 oz. fresh mushrooms, sliced
- dried onions
- onion powder
- cayenne
- dried dill

Direction

- Melt the butter in slow cooker, add mushrooms, and stir in the salad dressing mix, mushroom soup, cream cheese, and wine until the sauce mixture is hot, smooth and well combined.
- Place the chicken breasts into the slow cooker, and stir the sauce mixture over the chicken. Cover and cook on Low setting until chicken is tender, about 3 hours.

230. Jenny Craigs Italian Chicken Rolls Recipe

Serving: 6 | Prep: | Cook: 35mins | Ready in:

Ingredients

- 6 (4 oz) skinned, boneless chicken breast halves
- 1/4 tsp salt
- 1/4 tsp pepper
- 1/2 cup chopped roasted red pepper or from a jar (rinsed and drained)
- 1/4 cup pesto (homemade or in a jar)
- 1/3 cup light cream cheese, softened
- 3/4 cup crushed corn flakes
- 3 tbsps chopped fresh parsley (or 2 tsp dried)
- 1/2 tsp paprika
- vegetable cooking spray
- fresh thyme sprigs (optional)

Direction

- Place chicken between 2 sheets of heavy-duty plastic wrap; flatten to 1/4 inch thickness using a meat mallet. Sprinkle salt and pepper, set aside.
- Combine red pepper, cream cheese and pesto in a small bowl, stirring until smooth. Spread cheese mixture evenly over the chicken breasts. Roll up, jellyroll fashion, secure with wooden picks.
- Dredge chicken pieces in combined corn flakes, parsley and paprika. Place in an 11 by 7 inch baking dish coated with cooking spray.

- Bake, uncovered, at 350 degrees F for 35 minutes. Let stand 10 minutes and remove tooth picks. Slice each roll into 6 rounds or slices for each person. Garnish with thyme sprigs if desired.
- Serve with rice and/or a salad.

231. Judys Stuffed Chicken Breasts Recipe

Serving: 6 | Prep: | Cook: 60mins |Ready in:

Ingredients

- 3 lbs chicken boneless skinless chicken breasts, flattened. (Please refer to the picture that I provided for an example)
- 2 lg shallots
- 4 garlic cloves
- 6 slices of prosciutto, chopped
- 1 cup Italian bread crumbs
- 1/3 cup fresh sage leaves, chopped
- 1 tsp. fresh thyme, chopped (use less if using dried thyme)
- 1 tsp fresh oregano, chopped (use less if using dried oregano)
- 3 tblsps chopped parsley
- 3 tblsps chopped basil
- 1/4 tsp red pepper flakes
- 1 cup Fontina cheese
- 2 small vine sweet mini peppers, chopped
- 1 box chopped frozen spinach (squeeze out all liquid through a paper towel or cheese cloth). You can use fresh as well if you like.
- 2 1/2 cups chicken broth
- salt and pepper to taste
- garlic powder
- extra virgin olive oil
- 2 tblsps unsalted butter
- 1 8 oz. box of white buttom mushrooms sliced

Direction

- In a deep frying pan that has been heated coat the bottom with the olive oil and 1 tbsp. butter. Add the prosciutto and sauté for about 3 minutes, stirring occasionally.
- Next add the shallots and sauté for about 4 minutes and then the chopped garlic and sauté for about 1 minute
- Next add the following: chopped sage, thyme and oregano, salt and pepper and sauté for about 1 minute then add 1/2 cup of the chicken broth to deglaze the pan and continue to cook on medium low heat for about 15 minutes. Next stir in the chopped parsley and basil and immediately remove from the heat.
- Add the vegetable mixture to the bread crumbs. Then add the grated fontina cheese, chopped peppers, the chili flakes and mix thoroughly. Add 1 cup of the chicken broth to the stuffing mixture, enough to make sure that your stuffing is moist. (Please refer to my picture for an example). Set your stuffing aside and let completely cool. I put my stuffing in the refrigerator while I prepared the chicken breasts.
- This is when I actually flattened the chicken breasts myself (you refer to the photo that I provided; however prior to flattening them, remove the tenders, this is the bonus part to the chicken breasts that you can use for another recipe, (smile). I used the flat side of the mallet even though the picture shows the spiked side). (Smile) Now season the inside of the flatten chicken breasts with salt, pepper and garlic powder.
- Now you can get your chilled stuffing mixture and get ready to roll. If you used fresh spinach leaves then layer several leaves on first. If you used the frozen chopped spinach (after squeezing out all of the liquid), add about 1 tbsp. of the spinach to the chicken breast first and then 1 tbsp. of the stuffing, then roll up carefully and secure with a couple of toothpicks. After all of the breasts have been filled and rolled, season the outside of the roll with salt, pepper and garlic powder. You will have dressing left over and you will be using some of it later. :o)

- Reheat the pan you sautéed your vegetables in for the stuffing and coat with the olive oil and another tbsp. of unsalted butter.
- Brown the rolled chicken breasts on all sides to seal in the juices. Once browned on all sides, remove from the pan and set aside.
- Add the remaining chicken broth to deglaze the pan, add the sliced mushrooms and cook for about 5 minutes. Add about an ice cream scoop of the left over dressing to the pan, stir to thoroughly mix and it will make a nice gravy. Next add the chicken breasts back to the pan and simmer on low to medium heat for about 30 minutes. At this point if you need to prepare other side dishes you can remove the pan from the stove top, cover it and put in a 300 degree preheated oven to keep warm. Or, you can do what I did and transfer everything into a large lasagna type baking dish, cover with foil and put in the oven until you are ready to serve. The chicken will be so moist and full of flavor because the herbs and spices continue to intensify.

232. Kennedys Pub Chicken Vienne Recipe

Serving: 2 | Prep: | Cook: 15mins | Ready in:

Ingredients

- 1c all pupose flour
- 2(6oz.each)boneless chicken breasts,pounded to 1/4" thickness
- 3Tbs. olive oil
- 1/2c. white wine
- 1c chicken broth
- 1/4c julienned sun-dried tomatoes
- 11/2tsp chopped fresh garlic
- salt and pepper to taste
- 3/4c chopped fresh spinach

Direction

- Dredge the chicken in the flour until coated on all sides. Heat the oil in a sauté pan. Sauté the chicken until brown on both sides. Leaving the chicken in the pan, add the white wine and let simmer until the liquid is reduced by half.
- Add the chicken broth, sun-dried tomatoes, garlic, salt and pepper. Simmer on medium heat till sauce thickens. Add the spinach and cook for 2 mins. Serve over linguine or rice.

233. King Ranch Chicken Casserole Recipe

Serving: 6 | Prep: | Cook: 55mins | Ready in:

Ingredients

- 6 chicken breast halves, cooked and diced
- 12 corn tortillas, cut into strips
- 1 medium onion, chopped
- 1 green bell pepper, chopped
- 1 can (10 3/4 ounces) condensed cream of mushroom soup
- 1 can (10 3/4 ounces) condensed cream of chicken soup
- 8 ounces shredded cheddar cheese
- 1 can diced tomatoes with green chile's
- 1/2 teaspoon garlic powder
- salt
- dash cayenne pepper
- 2/3 cup chicken broth

Direction

- Pour about 1/3 cup of broth over bottom of a 13x9-inch baking pan.
- Layer half of the tortillas on the bottom, then half of the chicken, onion, bell pepper, and dollops of about 1/2 of both soups.
- Sprinkle with a little garlic powder, salt, and cayenne pepper.
- Repeat layers.
- Spread tomatoes over the top and drizzle with remaining chicken broth.

- Cover with foil and bake at 350° for 45 to 55 minutes, until bubbly.

234. Kissgetti Recipe

Serving: 10 | Prep: | Cook: 40mins |Ready in:

Ingredients

- 4 chicken breasts
- 2 jars Cheese Whiz
- 2 jars chicken gravy
- 1 can Rotel tomatoes
- 3 celery stalks
- 1 box family size spaghetti noodles

Direction

- Cut chicken into bite size pieces and cook on stove for 10 minutes. Cut celery into small pieces. While cooking chicken start spaghetti to cook per directions on box. When chicken is done add all other ingredients and cook an additional 10 minutes. Drain spaghetti.
- In a casserole dish put a layer of spaghetti on the bottom of the dish and add enough of the mixture to cover the spaghetti continue this step one more time (similar to lasagna). Put into oven at 375 for 40 minutes.

235. Kumquat Chicken Recipe

Serving: 4 | Prep: | Cook: 90mins |Ready in:

Ingredients

- 4 chicken breasts
- 1/4 cup of brown sugar
- 1/2 cup of catsup
- 1/4 cup of cider vinegar
- 2 tbsp of cornstarch
- 1 small green pepper, chopped
- 1 can (8 ounces) pineapple chunks with juice

- 8 or 9 sliced kumquats, seeds removed

Direction

- Kumquats are very unusual. The flesh is tart/sour and the rind is sweet. They are small and have two seeds that are quite bitter.
- Place chicken in a casserole dish.
- Mix all ingredients and pour over the chicken.
- Cover with foil.
- Bake at 375 degrees for 1 1/2 hours.
- Serve over rice or noodles.
- I think this could be adapted to slow cooker and use the instructions above and use your crockpot and let it cook on low for 8--9 hours.
- Kumquats cost about $3.00 a pint. They should be vibrant orange and firm. Green indicates they are under ripe and if they are faint orange, they may be past their prime. In season from November to March.
- They can be dried in a dehydrator and they will keep in your freezer.
- They can be used in place of raisins or dried cranberries.

236. Lemon Chicken Recipe

Serving: 4 | Prep: | Cook: 20mins |Ready in:

Ingredients

- 1 tsp. cornstarch
- 1 Tbsp. low sodium soy sauce
- 12 0z. chicken breast tenders, cut in thirds
- 1/4 cup fresh lemon juice
- 1/4 cup low sodium soy sauce
- 1/4 cup fat free chicken broth
- 1 tsp. fresh ginger, minced
- 2 cloves garlic, minced
- 1 Tbsp. Splenda sweetener, granulated
- 1 tsp. corn starch
- 1 Tbsp. vegetable oil
- 1/4 cup red bell pepper, sliced into 2-in. strips
- 1/4 cup green bell pepper, sliced into 2-in. strips

Direction

- Mix 1 tsp. cornstarch and 1 Tbsp. soy sauce in a small mixing bowl. Add sliced chicken tenders. Place in refrigerator and marinate for 10 minutes.
- Stir the lemon juice, 1/4 cup soy sauce, chicken broth, ginger, garlic, Splenda and 1 tsp. cornstarch together in a medium sized mixing bowl.
- Heat oil in a medium frying pan. Add chicken and cook over medium- high heat for 3 -4 minutes or until just done. Add sauce and sliced peppers.
- Cook 1-2 minutes more or until sauce thickens and peppers are slightly tender.

---

237. Lemon And Olive Chicken Recipe

Serving: 8 | Prep: | Cook: 25mins |Ready in:

Ingredients

- 8 bone-in chicken breast halves
- salt and pepper
- 3 tablespoons olive oil
- 2 lemons
- 2 mediums onions, chopped
- 4 cloves garlic, minced
- 1 cup green olives, pitted and halved
- 2 cups chicken broth
- 1 teaspoon dried thyme
- 1/2 teaspoon crushed red pepper

Direction

- Sprinkle chicken with 1 teaspoon each salt and pepper.
- In large skillet heat 2 tablespoons olive oil over medium heat.
- Sear chicken (in two batches), skin-side first until golden brown or about 3 minutes per side.
- Transfer chicken to a plate.

- Cut lemons in half lengthwise and then into thin slices crosswise.
- If skillet is dry add remaining 1 tablespoon oil.
- Add onions and garlic; cook over medium heat until soft, about 3 minutes.
- Stir in lemon slices, olives, stock and 2 cups water.
- Bring to a boil, reduce heat and simmer for 10 minutes.
- Put chicken on top of mixture and pour in accumulated juices from plate.
- Sprinkle with thyme and crushed red pepper.
- Cover and simmer until chicken is cooked through, about 15 minutes.

---

238. Lemongrass And Garlic Chicken Marinade Recipe

Serving: 2 | Prep: | Cook: 10mins |Ready in:

Ingredients

- 2 chicken breasts.
- 1 lemongrass Stalk.
- 2 Table spoons of plain yogurt.
- 1 lemon, juiced.
- 2 cloves of garlic, sliced.
- 1/2 onion, chopped roughly.
- 1/4 tea spoon of ginger.

Direction

- 1. Cut breasts in 3 parts, length ways. (Repeat with both breasts.)
- 2. Cut lemongrass into 2 cm circles then half and break apart.
- 3. Slice up garlic and onion.
- 4. Get a big silver bowl or plastic marinade container and put the chicken bits in along with the lemongrass, onion, garlic and ginger.
- 5. Put the yogurt and lemon juice in, mix well.
- 6. Cover and leave in fridge for about 30 minutes to an hour.
- 7. Heat pan to a medium/low heat. Add a fair amount of olive oil.

- 8. Cook half the strips at a time until golden brown.
- 9. They make take a while to cook but make sure they are cooked the whole way through.
- Note: The bottom on the pan will burn very quickly and easily. Don't worry about it because it forms a barrier for the chicken so it won't burn as easily, the flavor is a lot better and it gives it a really nice color.

239. Lemony Chicken In A Flash Recipe

Serving: 10 | Prep: | Cook: 30mins | Ready in:

Ingredients

- 10 boneless,skinless chicken breasts
- 1/2 tsp salt
- 1/4 tsp pepper
- 1 medium red onion,sliced
- 3 Tbs extra virgin olive oil
- 2 jars (8oz ea.) quartered artichokes,drained
- 1 lemon,cut in 10 slices
- 1 tsp each oregano and thyme

Direction

- Heat oven to 350 degrees. Season chicken with salt and pepper. In skillet over medium - high heat, cook onions in 1 Tbsp. oil 5 mins, stirring occasionally; remove from skillet.
- In same skillet over med-high heat, cook chicken (in batches, if necessary) in remaining oil 5 mins.
- Divide onions, chicken and artichokes between 2 baking dishes coated with spray. Top with lemon slices and sprinkle with oregano and thyme. Cover with foil and bake 10 to 15 mins.

240. Light And Zesty Chicken And Rice Recipe

Serving: 4 | Prep: | Cook: 55mins | Ready in:

Ingredients

- 4 chicken breasts
- 1/3 cup Italian dressing
- 1 3/4 cups chicken broth
- 16 oz. (1 bag) frozen vegetables [carrots, water chesnuts, broccoli, red pepper]
- 2 cans fried onion rings
- 1/2 tsp. Italian dressing
- cooked rice (still figuring out how much)

Direction

- Place chicken in baking pan.
- Pour Italian dressing over chicken.
- Bake at 400 degrees for 20 minutes.
- Put rice, vegetables and 1 can of fried onion rings around and under the chicken.
- Combine broth and Italian seasoning and pour over the top of the chicken.
- Bake at 400 degrees for another 25 minutes.
- Put the rest of the fried onion rings and bake for another 2-3 minutes.
- Let rest for 5 minutes.

241. Lime And Honey Mustard Chicken Recipe

Serving: 4 | Prep: | Cook: 10mins | Ready in:

Ingredients

- * 1/2 cup honey mustard
- * zest from 1 lime
- * juice from 1 lime (about 2 tablespoons)
- * 2 garlic cloves, minced
- * 1 tablespoon soy sauce
- * 4 boneless, skinless chicken breasts (each about 4 ounces)

Direction

- Stir together first five ingredients in a bowl and spread on top chicken breasts, covering evenly.
- Broil chicken until cooked through, 3 – 4 minutes for each side.
- Serve with Screaming Potatoes (My Recipe), mixed vegetables and have a grand meal. *wink*

---

242.   Lip Smackin Finger Lickin Good Chicken Recipe

Serving: 4 | Prep: | Cook: 35mins | Ready in:

Ingredients

- 4 boneless chicken breasts
- 1 1/2 cups chili sauce
- 3/4 cup red wine vinegar
- 1 1/2 tablespoons prepared horseradish
- 2 teaspoons roasted minced garlic, from jar
- 1 teaspoon salt

Direction

- Mix chili sauce, vinegar, horseradish, garlic and salt in a bowl. Transfer 1/2 of marinade to a gallon size zip top bag.
- Place 1/2 remaining marinade into a small sauce pan.
- What remains in bowl will be used as a baste for chicken while it is cooking.
- Add chicken to marinade in ziptop bag and seal.
- Turn and shake bag to coat chicken.
- Lace marinating bag in refrigerator for at least 20-30 minutes, however overnight works even better.
- Preheat grill.
- Remove chicken from marinade and place chicken on grill.
- Discard remaining used marinade in bag.

- Grill chicken, turning and basting frequently with half the reserved marinade, until juices run clear when meat is pierced with a knife. This should take about 30 minutes. (165 with instant ready meat thermometer)
- Heat reserved marinade in sauce pan, stirring occasionally.
- Serve this sauce hot alongside chicken.

---

243.   MEDITERRANEAN CHICKEN BREAST SANDWICH Recipe

Serving: 1 | Prep: | Cook: 5mins | Ready in:

Ingredients

- two slices of country bread toasted
- softened goat cheese.
- cooked chicken breast half (grilled, poached or pan-fried)
- balsamic vinegar.
- bottled sun-dried tomatoes in olive oil.
- baby spinach leaves.

Direction

- Toast two slices of country bread.
- Spread each slice with softened goat cheese.
- Slice a cooked chicken breast half (grilled, poached or pan-fried) into strips (or buy cooked chicken strips from the supermarket).
- Drizzle chicken lightly with balsamic vinegar.
- Arrange chicken strips on bottom half of sandwich.
- Cover chicken with bottled sun-dried tomatoes in olive oil.
- Top with baby spinach leaves.
- Cover with remaining slice of country bread.

244.   MY Butter Chicken Recipe

Serving: 4 | Prep: | Cook: 45mins | Ready in:

Ingredients

- 1 lb chicken thighs, chopped into bite size pieces (half may be substituted with chicken breast, however, it will be dryer and less flavourful)
- 8 oz tomato paste
- 1 white onion, diced
- 1/2 cup plain yogurt (or 1/2 cup heavy cream; i like to use both)
- 1/4 cup heavy cream, half and half (or homo milk),
- 4 tbsp butter, divided
- 1 1/2 tbsp garam masala (or more, if you like it a little more spicy)
- 1/2 tsp turmeric (optional)
- 1/4 tsp ground coriander (optional)
- up to 1/2 tbsp chili powder (depending on heat)
- 1/2 tbsp cumin (i like the extra cumin, just cause)
- 3 cups rice of choice - jasmine is the usual rice, however, i like brown or black (forbidden) rice.

Direction

- In a large frying pan (at least twice as much room than the chicken will need), place about 1 1/2 tbsp. butter, and chicken, and cook on medium heat until sealed (white on the outside, still pink inside)
- Start making your rice now so it's done at about the same time
- Add diced onion, garam masala, turmeric, coriander, chili powder and cumin, stir and cook until onions are transparent but not limp (about 3 minutes)
- Add tomato paste and the rest of the butter, stir and cook about 2 minutes.

- Mound chicken in the middle of the frying pan, and while stirring, pour in heavy cream and plain yogurt.
- Cover and cook about 15 minutes on medium-low heat, sauce will thicken and possibly separate a little - it may look like red oil top
- Serve hot over or beside rice.
- This recipe can also be made in a slow cooker for potlucks and office parties - just double the recipe, keeping the fully cooked chicken separate from the sauce, and combine in crockpot on high heat for 4 hours before the start of the party/function.

245.   Mandarin Chicken Stir Fry Recipe

Serving: 2 | Prep: | Cook: 10mins | Ready in:

Ingredients

- 2 T. canola oil
- quarter of an onion, sliced
- equal amount of carrot, cut into coins and the quartered
- 1/2 cup celery, sliced
- handful of peapods, strings removed
- optionally, some zucchini, sliced
- 1 large shitake mushroom, sliced
- 1 skinless chicken breast, cut in 1 inch pieces
- all purpose salt-substitute, to taste
- 2 dashes worcestershire sauce
- 4 dashes Tabasco, or to taste
- 1/4 cup low-sugar orange marmalade
- 11 oz. can mandarin oranges, drained
- prepared rice, for two

Direction

- Prep ingredients and line up near cook surface in order of appearance...preview this to determine best order
- Heat oil in large pan over med. hi heat and add onions, carrots and celery, cooking about 3 min.

- [If using frozen zucchini, add after chicken is cooked, if fresh...cook with onions.]
- Next add chicken, mushroom and seasonings (salt sub & sauces), cooking till chicken is cooked through...about 5 min.
- If mixture is just too, too dry, add about 2 T. water.
- Add peapods, cooking another minute.
- Stir in marmalade.
- Add mandarin oranges...heating through.
- Serve over rice.

---

246. Mango Chicken Salad Recipe

Serving: 4 | Prep: | Cook: 10mins | Ready in:

Ingredients

- For the salad
- 1 medium or large cucumber, peeled, seeded and cut into 2-inch-long sticks
- 1 large red bell pepper, seeded and thinly sliced
- 1 large (about 3/4 pound) mango, peeled and cut into 2-inch-long strips*
- 3 scallions, white and green parts, thinly sliced
- 1 1/2 pounds boneless, skinless chicken breasts, sliced or pounded into thin cutlets
- salt
- Freshly ground black pepper
- 1 to 2 teaspoon olive oil, or as needed
- For the dressing
- 1 to 2 large (about 3/4 pound) mangoes, peeled, flesh cut away from the pit*
- 1 teaspoon honey
- 1/4 cup orange juice, or more as needed
- 2 tablespoons white wine vinegar
- 1 tablespoon olive oil
- salt
- Freshly ground black pepper

Direction

- For the salad: In a bowl large enough to hold all the ingredients, combine the cucumber, bell pepper and mango strips with all but a tablespoon of the sliced scallion. Reserve the remaining scallions for a garnish. Set aside.
- Season the chicken cutlets with salt and pepper to taste. In a large sauté pan, preferably non-stick, over medium-high heat, heat just enough oil to coat the bottom. Add the chicken cutlets; it may be necessary to do this in two batches. Sauté, turning once until the cutlets are cooked through and nicely browned. It should take about 3 to 4 minutes on each side, depending on the thickness of the cutlets.
- Remove the cutlets from the pan and slice into strips similar in size to the vegetables, about 2 inches long. Add to the vegetable mixture. Set aside.
- For the dressing: In a blender, combine the mango flesh, honey, orange juice, vinegar, oil and salt and pepper to taste. Blend until smooth. If the dressing is too thick, add more orange juice, one tablespoon at a time, until the dressing is the desired consistency. It should be thick but pourable.
- To assemble, add the dressing to the chicken and vegetables. Toss to coat. Garnish with the reserved scallions and freshly ground black pepper, if desired. Serve immediately.
- To prepare mango:
- *Note: To prepare the mango, spear the stem end with a fork. Lop off one end of the mango to steady it on the counter and hold it upright with the fork. Use a sharp paring knife to peel away the skin, then cut the flesh from the pit, stopping when the flesh gets too fibrous and hard. The fruit can then be cut into cubes.

---

247. Marinated Chicken Breasts Grilled Or Baked Recipe

Serving: 4 | Prep: | Cook: 25mins | Ready in:

Ingredients

- 4 to 8 Boneless skinless chicken breasts.
- 1/2 to 1 Cup of red wine vinegar.
- 1/2 to 1 Cup of balsamic vinegar.
- 1 to 2 Cups of Kikkoman Terrayki sauce NOT marinade.
- 1 to 2 Tablespoons of ground white pepper.
- 1 to 2 Tablespoons of fresh coarse ground black pepper.
- 2 to 3 Tablespoons of cajun seasoning.
- 1 to 2 Tablespoon of garlic powder. NOT salt.
- 1 to 2 Tablespoons of onion powder. NOT salt.
- 2 Teaspoons fresh ground sea salt (optional). I do not use any salt.
- 1 Gallon ziplock bag or smaller. Big enough to get all the breast in plus the marinade I use gallon.
- This looks like a lot of marinade and it is but it works. DO NOT REUSE THE marinade DISCARD AFTER YOU PUT THE chicken ON THE GRILL SAFETY FIRST. LOL

Direction

- Wash the chicken breast off under running water.
- Try to get as much water off the breast as you can before you put them into the bag.
- Then wash your hands can never be to sanitary. LOL
- Add all the dry spices it may look like a lot but believe me it isn't.
- Add all the liquids.
- Get as much air out of the bag as you can and seal tightly.
- Shake it really well to combine all the ingredients.
- Set the bag in a bowl big enough to hold it in case the bag leaks.
- I let mine marinade for 24 hours.
- During the 24 hour period I shake the bag to mix it well every 6 to 8 hours.
- Heat the coals to a white hot spread the coals out evenly and put the chicken breasts making sure not to touch each other.

- Watch them closely because the Teriyaki in the marinade will burn easily with hot coals.
- When they are done to your liking serve them with a baked potato and a salad with everything in it but the kitchen sink in it bake your potato on the grill if you don't want to heat the kitchen up.
- Then see if that doesn't make you want more.
- P.S. leftovers are just as good.

248. Mediterranean Broccolli Couscous Platter Recipe

Serving: 1 | Prep: | Cook: 30mins | Ready in:

Ingredients

- 1/4 cup sliced onion
- 1 1/4 cup broccoli florets
- 1/2 cup cooked whole-wheat couscous
- 3 ounces cooked boneless, skinless chicken breast, diced
- 1 tablespoon extra-virgin olive oil
- 1 teaspoon minced garlic

Direction

- On the stove top over low heat, warm the olive oil. Add the garlic, onions, and broccoli, and sauté until the onions are translucent. Spread couscous over a plate, and top with the chicken and then the sautéed vegetables.

249. Mediterranean Chicken And Pasta With Kalamata Olives Sun Dried Tomatoes And Pine Nuts Recipe

Serving: 6 | Prep: | Cook: 20mins | Ready in:

Ingredients

- Mediterranean chicken and pasta with kalamata olives, sun-dried tomatoes & pine nuts
- ½ - 1 cup sun-dried tomatoes, quartered with scissors
- ½ - 1 cup kalamata olives
- 2 boneless, skinless chicken breast halves, cut into bite sized chunks
- ¼ - ½ cup rosemary-Infused white wine vinegar
- ¼ c olive oil
- ½ small onion, chopped fine
- 2-3 cloves roasted garlic, mashed
- ½ t dried oregano or 1-2 t fresh oregano
- Coarsely cracked black pepper
- 1 green or red bell pepper, chopped
- 4 ounces crumbled feta cheese
- ½ - 1 cup pine nuts
- About 1 cup marinated artichoke hearts
- ½ - 1 cup fresh grated parmesan or asiago cheese
- 2-3 green onions, chopped
- 2 cups uncooked hearty pasta, like a gemelli or a penne

Direction

- First, soak the cut-up sun-dried tomatoes. Reserve all the soaking water. Set aside.
- For the marinade, combine the vinegar, 2 T of the tomato-soaking water, 2 T of Kalamata olive brine, 2T olive oil, the chopped onion, oregano, pepper, and one of the mashed roasted garlic cloves. Marinate the chicken for about thirty minutes.
- Cook the chicken in its marinade in a large heavy skillet. When the chicken is nearly cooked, toss in the bell pepper and garlic, continue cooking, turning frequently. Meanwhile combine the remaining tomato-soaking water with enough plain water to cook the pasta. Add a pinch of salt and bring to a boil in a large pan, add pasta. When pasta is al dente, drain and toss with a dash of olive oil. Add the chicken, peppers, and garlic and all remaining ingredients. Toss lightly and serve immediately with a salad of cucumbers and tomatoes. A Sauvignon Blanc is very nice with this.
- I change this recipe depending on my taste at the moment as well as what I have on hand. It's equally good with fresh tomatoes and "regular" black olive, but the taste is very different.

---

250. Mediterranean Puff Pastry Chicken Pies Recipe

Serving: 2 | Prep: | Cook: 40mins | Ready in:

Ingredients

- 25 g crushed garlic
- 1 egg yolk
- 60 g chopped fresh spinach
- 2 boneless skinless chicken breast halves
- 30 g basil pesto
- 20 g chopped sun-dried tomatoes
- 65 g crumbled herbed feta cheese
- 2 frozen puff pastry sheets, thawed

Direction

- Combine crushed garlic and egg yolk.
- Place chicken breasts in a shallow glass dish and spread both sides with egg mixture. Cover dish with plastic wrap and refrigerate 4 hours, or overnight (recommended).
- Preheat oven to 375 degrees F (190 degrees C). Grease a baking sheet.
- Working on a lightly floured surface, unroll one puff pastry sheet.
- Place 1/2 cup spinach in the centre of the pastry sheet.
- Remove one chicken breast from marinade, shaking off any excess, and place on top of spinach.
- Spread 1 tablespoon pesto over chicken, layer with half the sun-dried tomatoes, sprinkle with half the feta cheese, and top with 1/2 cup spinach.

- Fold pastry sheet around chicken, using fork to seal pastry seam.
- Place chicken seam side down on baking sheet.
- Repeat steps with the second puff pastry sheet and remaining chicken breast.
- Bake 35 to 40 minutes.

251. Melt In Your Mouth Chicken Recipe

Serving: 8 | Prep: | Cook: 60mins | Ready in:

Ingredients

- 8 boneless chicken breasts
- 2 cans cream of chicken soup
- 8 slices monterey jack cheese
- 1/2 cup sherry wine
- 2 cups herbed stuffing mix
- 1/2 teaspoon garlic powder
- 1/2 teaspoon salt
- 1 teaspoon freshly ground black pepper

Direction

- Arrange chicken breasts in a baking pan.
- Place cheese slices over chicken.
- Mix soup and wine together and pour over the chicken.
- Sprinkle top generously with stuffing mix then dot with butter.
- Bake at 350 uncovered for 60 minutes.

252. Mexican Chicken Casserole Recipe

Serving: 6 | Prep: | Cook: 45mins | Ready in:

Ingredients

- 1-whole chicken or 4 chicken breast
- 1-small onion
- 1-7oz can of chopped green chiles
- 1-10.5oz can of cream of mushroom & cream of chicken soup
- 2 tbsp of real butter
- 1/2 cup of chicken broth which can be canned or broth from the cooked chicken
- 4 cups of shredded mild cheddar or Mexican blend cheese
- 1-pkg of yellow corn tortillas (make sure there is more than 13 in a pkg)

Direction

- Boil whole chicken or chicken breast (cut chicken up in small pieces)
- Place the cans of mushroom & chicken soup in a bowl (set aside)
- Mix in 1/2 cup of chicken broth and cut up chicken in the soup mix
- Chop 1 small whole onion
- Add the can of green chilies & chopped onion into a pan with the 2 tbsp. of real butter to sauté (cook)
- Once the green chilies and onions are cooked, mix in with the soup mixture of mushroom, chicken and chicken broth
- Cut the corn tortillas into 4 quarters
- Set oven at 350 degrees
- Lightly grease the bottom of a deep casserole pan
- Place 1 layer of corn tortillas on the bottom of pan than add the soup mix with a layer of cheese
- Do the same process in layers until mixture is all gone
- I do about 2 layers
- Cook for 20-25 mins

253. Mexicana Chicken Recipe

Serving: 6 | Prep: | Cook: 20mins | Ready in:

Ingredients

- 4 eggs
- 1 bottle green chile salsa
- 2 c fine bread crumbs
- 1/4 tsp salt
- 2 tsp each chile powder and cumin
- 1-1/2 tsp garlic salt
- 1/2 tsp oregano
- 6 boneless,skinless chicken breasts
- 1/4 c olive oil
- 4 c shredded lettuce
- 2 bunches scallions,sliced
- 3 tomatoes,sliced
- 3 limes sliced
- 3 avocados,sliced

Direction

- Mix eggs and half of salsa in medium bowl. Mix bread crumbs and seasonings together in another bowl. Dip chicken in salsa mixture, then bread crumb mixture. Fry slowly till done.
- Create each serving by laying piece of chicken on a bed of lettuce. Then place a little salsa on chicken, followed by a dollop of sour cream on top of salsa. Sprinkle with scallions. Garnish with tomatoes, limes and avocados.

---

254. Mikes Chicken Fried Chicken Recipe

Serving: 4 | Prep: | Cook: 20mins | Ready in:

Ingredients

- 2 whole boneless skinless chicken breasts
- 2 eggs
- 1 cup milk
- 1 Bottle Italian salad dressing
- 1 can chicken broth
- garlice powder
- salt
- pepper
- Tony Chacereys cajun seasoning Optional
- Orrington farms chicken soup base
- Crisco Shorteningfor frying
- 2 cups flour
- 1\2 cup cracker meal

Direction

- Split the whole breasts and butterfly each half. I use whole breasts! Feel free to use individual ones. I use them for the size.
- Start by Marinating the Chicken Breast in the Italian Dressing for 3 Hours. I add Garlic to the dressing and salt, pepper.
- Prepare the eggs and Milk for dredging Also add Garlic, salt, pepper to your flour and cracker meal. If you do not have cracker meal just use flour.
- Heat your Crisco for frying I usually make it 1 inch deep and about 360 degrees
- Remove your chicken from the marinade and season with Tony Chachere's first we dust it with the flour mixture then we dunk it in the milk and egg wash. Back in the flour mixture it goes for a final coating. I like a nice even coating.
- Cook Chicken breasts approximately 5 minutes on each side. DONT OVERCOOK.
- Remove to a paper towel lined platter to drain and hold.
- Prepare to make some good gravy for these! Drain excess oil leaving 1\4 cup and the cracklings from your chicken breasts. Add 3 tablespoons flour and stir. I usually cook this on medium heat for 3-5 minutes.
- Next add The Chicken Broth and 1 tablespoon of the soup base. You may add water if necessary for the desired consistency. The Gravy will have a nice flavour. Add pepper to taste the salt is covered by the soup base. Serve over the chicken breast and YUMMY.
- ENJOY!!!!

255. Mild Chinese Curry Recipe

Serving: 4 | Prep: | Cook: 35mins | Ready in:

Ingredients

- 2 chicken breasts (diced) (Anu use of sharp utensils must be supervised by an adult)
- 2 Tbsp vegetable oil
- 3 Tbsp Wing Yip Chinese curry Concentrate
- 1 medium onion (small dice) (optional)
- 1 large potato (medium dice)
- 60g frozen peas
- water

Direction

- 1. Heat the vegetable oil in a pan (this must be supervised by an adult)
- 2. Add the diced onions and cook until they are soft and start to turn a little brown at the edges.
- 3. Add the diced chicken and the curry concentrate.
- 4. Mix well and after 2 minutes add 500ml of water.
- 5. The curry will start to thicken as it cooks and you might need to add more water as required.
- 6. Add the potatoes and cook the curry until the potatoes are soft.
- 7. Add peas at this stage.
- 8. Serve with rice or on jacket potatoes

256. Miso Chicken Recipe

Serving: 4 | Prep: | Cook: 10mins | Ready in:

Ingredients

- 4 boneless, skinless chicken breasts, about 4 oz each
- 1 teaspoon canola oil
- marinade
- 2 tablespoons miso paste
- 1 1/2 teaspoons light sesame oil
- 1 1/2 teaspoon chopped ginger
- 1 1/2 teaspoons chopped garlic
- 1/4 teaspoon red pepper flakes

Direction

- Place chicken in a shallow dish
- Combine marinade ingredients with 1 tablespoon water; pour over meat
- Chill, covered, 1 to 2 hours
- Remove chicken from marinade; drain excess
- Heat canola oil in a large skillet over medium-high heat
- Cook chicken until no longer pink in the center, about 4-5 minutes per side
- The skinny
- 155 calories per serving
- 3.7 g fat (0.6 g saturated)

257. Moo Goo Gai Pan Recipe

Serving: 4 | Prep: | Cook: 10mins | Ready in:

Ingredients

- 1 pound skinless, boneless chicken breast halves, sliced
- 2 tablespoons cornstarch
- 1 tablespoon chinese rice wine or dry sherry
- 1/4 teaspoon white pepper
- 1 pound button mushrooms
- 1 1/4 cup chicken broth
- 1 cup peanut oil
- 1/3 cup thinly sliced bamboo shoots
- 3/4 cup thinly sliced Chinese cabbage
- 1/2 teaspoon sugar
- 2 tablespoons water

Direction

- Sprinkle chicken with 2 teaspoons cornstarch, rice wine, and pepper. Mix well. Simmer mushrooms in chicken broth 5 minutes. Drain, reserving broth. Heat oil in a wok. Add chicken and cook, stirring, just until pieces separate and chicken is no longer pink. Drain into a sieve over a bowl. Return 1 tablespoon oil to the wok. Add mushrooms, bamboo shoots, and Chinese cabbage. Stir fry 2 minutes. Add chicken broth and sugar. Bring to a boil. Return chicken to the wok. Dissolve remaining cornstarch in water and add to the wok. Cook, stirring, until thickened.

---

258. Moroccan Chicken And Lentils Recipe

Serving: 12 | Prep: | Cook: 35mins | Ready in:

Ingredients

- 8 cups water
- 3 teaspoons salt, divided
- 1 pound dried brown lentils, rinsed, drained
- 1 cup plus 2 tablespoons olive oil
- 1/2 cup red wine vinegar
- 3 tablespoons ground cumin, divided
- 2 tablespoons plus 2 teaspoons chili powder
- 2 garlic cloves, minced
- 1 large onion, chopped
- 1 1/2 pounds skinless boneless chicken breast halves, thinly sliced
- 1/4 teaspoon ground cinnamon
- 1 cup chopped fresh parsley

Direction

- Combine 8 cups water and 1 teaspoon salt in heavy large saucepan over high heat. Add lentils; bring to boil. Cover, reduce heat to medium, and simmer until lentils are tender, about 20 minutes. Drain well; rinse with cold water and drain again. Place in large bowl.
- Whisk 1 cup olive oil, vinegar, 2 tablespoons cumin, 2 tablespoons chili powder, garlic, and 1 teaspoon salt in large measuring cup. Pour 1 cup dressing over warm lentils and toss. Cool.

- Heat 2 tablespoons olive oil in large skillet over high heat. Add onion; sauté until dark brown and soft, about 5 minutes. Add chicken; sauté 2 minutes. Add 1 teaspoon salt, 1 tablespoon cumin, 2 teaspoons chili powder, and cinnamon. Sauté until chicken is cooked through, about 3 minutes longer.
- Arrange lentils on large platter. Place sliced chicken atop lentils. Drizzle with remaining dressing and sprinkle with parsley. (Can be made 2 hours ahead. Let stand at room temperature.)

---

259. Nasi Goreng Recipe

Serving: 2 | Prep: | Cook: 20mins | Ready in:

Ingredients

- 5 Oz. rice
- 5 Oz. grilled Chicken breast cut in dices
- 2 Tbsp. of butter
- 1 Medium onion (diced)
- 2 Pinches of shrimp paste
- 2 - 3 bouillon cubes
- 3 - 4 cloves of garlic (mashed)
- Black or white pepper
- 5 - 6 Slices of ginger
- 6 Tbsp. of soy sauce
- 2 - 3 Twigs of celery Thinly cut

Direction

- 1. Cook the rice, stir to prevent lumps and let cool off. In a skillet, heat the butter and sauté the diced onions.
- 2. Add the grilled chicken, shrimp paste, the bouillon cubes, ginger, garlic and a dash of black/white pepper. Stir all the ingredients.
- 3. Add the rice, soy sauce, continue stirring until the rice turn light brown. Turn the stove off, add the celery and stir.

260. New England Maple Chicken Recipe

Serving: 4 | Prep: | Cook: 60mins | Ready in:

Ingredients

- •1/2 cup Pure New England maple syrup - Medium or Dark Amber
- •1 chicken, 2-1/2 to 3 pounds, cut-up or equivalent chicken breasts
- •1/4 cup butter, melted
- •1/2 teaspoon grated lemon rind
- •1 tespoon salt (optional)
- •Dash of pepper (optional)
- •1/4 cup sliced, chopped or slivered almonds
- •2 teaspoons lemon juice

Direction

- PREHEAT oven to 400 F. degrees.
- Place chicken pieces in a shallow buttered baking dish.
- Mix remaining ingredients and pour evenly over chicken.
- Bake uncovered 50 - 60 minutes. Baste occasionally.
- Yield: 4 to 6 servings

261. One Dish Chicken And Rice Bake Recipe

Serving: 4 | Prep: | Cook: 45mins | Ready in:

Ingredients

- 1 can Cream of mushroom or 1/2 fat cream of mushroom soup
- 1 cup water
- 3/4 cup rice
- 1/4 tsp each of paprika and pepper
- 4 boneless chicken breast halves

Direction

- Mix first four ingredients in baking dish
- Place chicken on top
- For creamier rice, increase water to 1 1/3 cup
- Bake at 375° for 45 min

262. Ooey Gooey Chicken Burritos Recipe

Serving: 4 | Prep: | Cook: 25mins | Ready in:

Ingredients

- 1 pound chicken breasts, cut into bite sized pieces
- 2 tbsp. oil
- 1 3 oz. Package cream cheese, softened
- 2 cups shredded colby/monterey jack cheese
- 1 packet hollandiase sauce, prepared, or homemade hollandaise sauce
- 4 burrito style tortilla shells

Direction

- Preheat oil in a skillet. Add the chicken and cook until no longer pink.
- Add cream cheese and Colby and Monterey jack cheeses to the skillet.
- Stir until cheeses are mixed well with the chicken.
- Leave uncovered and let simmer for 10 minutes or until all the cheese has melted.
- Meanwhile prepare the hollandaise sauce and heat tortillas.
- Spoon chicken mixture onto a tortilla, and Roll.
- Top with hollandaise sauce.
- Enjoy

263. Orange Curry Chicken Recipe

Serving: 4 | Prep: | Cook: 50mins | Ready in:

Ingredients

- 8 Boneless, Skinless, Half, chicken breast
- 1/2 can (6oz) frozen orange juice undiluted
- 1/2 can cream of chicken soup undiluted
- 2 Tbls butter
- 1 cup thinly sliced onion Rings
- black pepper and salt to taste
- glaze
- 1/4 cup orange marmalade
- 2 tsps curry powder
- 2 tsps Sweet, hot mustard
- 1 tsps Dijon mustard

Direction

- Set oven to 350 degrees.
- In a casserole dish large enough to hold chicken breast without crowding, place orange concentrate, soup and butter. No chicken yet. Place dish in the warm oven for 5 minutes to warm ingredients, then remove and stir to mix well.
- Place chicken breast in the dish with warmed mixed sauce. Sprinkle with black pepper and salt. Place onion rings over chicken. Bake for 25 minutes, basting with juice in dish.
- GLAZE
- Mix the glaze and spread evenly over chicken. Bake 25 minutes longer.
- Serve with fluffy, white rice and the following condiments.
- Mango Chutney
- Chopped Onions
- Crushed Cashews
- Coconut Flakes.
- I usually like to plan my meals ahead of time. This one happened one night when time was short and I happened to have all the ingredients on hand. So it was on the fly. When these are successful it makes my day. Wish I were a true Chef. I like the pressure.

264. Orange Cashew Chicken And Rice Recipe

Serving: 0 | Prep: | Cook: 15mins |Ready in:

Ingredients

- My cooking method is by "eye and known taste". So I do not have strict amounts in this part. The estimated amounts are listed below in this ingredient section. Feel free to adjust.
- -Boneless chicken, any amt.
- -cashews, roasted, salted or not, any amt. Buy from bulk what you need.
- -Fresh chili pepper, hot or mild, your choice, diced fine, any amt.
- -orange juice, enough to make a sauce.
- -mandarin oranges.
- -craisins.
- -S&P, I use Crazy Janes salt.
- -rice. Use the GR Sites No More Boring rice Recipe. Or cook regular rice, any method, stove, mic, etc. and add ground ginger and butter to taste.
- FEEL FREE TO LEAVE OUT THE pepper OR ANYTHING ELSE YOU DON'T CARE FOR, AND SUBSTITUTE SOMETHING ELSE. IT'S ALL ABOUT YOUR TASTE. BUT, SWEET, SPICY, TANGY AND saltY ARE GOOD!
- I made this w/ about 1lb of chicken breasts, boneless. I used about 1/2 Cup of cashews, about 1/2 tsp of finely chopped hot pepper, 1 small can of mandarin oranges, about 1/2 C orange juice, about 1/4 C of craisins. For time and ease I used a "rice cup", nuked for 1 min, and added ground ginger and butter. I would have preferred the real thing, "No more Boring rice".
- You can easily figure what you need for the servings you will make and adjust the amounts to your taste.

Direction

- -Place chicken in a hot pan, med heat. Put S&P on chicken.
- -Choose and cook rice recipe.

- -Add cashews, pepper.
- -Brown, turn meat and nuts after 10 min.
- -Add Juice. Cover.
- -Turn meat and nuts again after 15 min. Cover.
- - Remove Chicken and nuts from pan to another dish.
- -Add oranges and cranberries to the chicken dish. Cover, keep warm.
- -Reduce liquid to about 1/2. Add more juice if needed. Reduce again if needed.
- -Add Sauce to chicken dish.
- -Serve over Rice.

265.   Orange Sauced Chicken (myrecipes.com) Recipe

Serving: 2 | Prep: | Cook: 20mins |Ready in:

Ingredients

- 1 cup fresh orange juice (changed from 1/4 cup)
- ¼ low sodium chicken broth (i omitted the chicken broth)
- 4 teaspoons orange marmalade (changed from 3/4 teaspoon)
- 4 teaspoons fresh lemon juice (changed from 1 teaspoon)
- 4 teaspoons cornstarch (changed from 3/4 teaspoon)
- 1/2 teaspoon dried crushed rosemary, or 1 teaspoon fresh
- 1/4 teaspoon salt
- ¼ teaspoon fresh ground black pepper
- 4 (4oz) boneless, skinless chicken breast halves
- 1 cup tablespoon dried Italian seasoned breadcrumbs
- 2 tablespoons olive oil
- 1 tablespoon chopped fresh flat leaf (Italian) parlsey

Direction

- 1. Combine first 8 ingredients in a medium bowl, stirring with a whisk to combine.

- 2. Dredge chicken in breadcrumbs.
- 3. Heat oil in a large nonstick skillet coated with cooking spray over medium high heat. Add chicken and cook 3 to 4 minutes on each side or just until lightly browned on both sides. Add broth mixture; cover; reduce heat and simmer, stirring occasionally for 4 to 5 minutes or until chicken is done and the juices run clear. Sprinkle with parsley to serve.
- Notes: I omitted the broth by accident but because it turned out so well I won't be adding it back. I did use fresh squeezed orange juice because I had extra orange juice. I only had sugar free marmalade so added 1 teaspoon honey.

266.   Oven Crisped Chicken Recipe

Serving: 4 | Prep: | Cook: 45mins |Ready in:

Ingredients

- 4-6 chicken breasts or thighs, cleaned, and salted to taste.
- olive oil

Direction

- Preheat oven to 375*
- Clean and salt chicken well.
- Place chicken on shallow baking sheet and coat well with olive oil (add some herbs i.e.; garlic, parsley for added flavor)
- Place in oven and bake for about 45 minutes until chicken is well done!

267.   PARMESAN AND BASIL FILLING Recipe

Serving: 4 | Prep: | Cook: |Ready in:

Ingredients

- Makes enough to stuff 4 bone-in, skin-on split chicken breasts.
- INGREDIENTS
- 2 ounces parmesan cheese , grated (about 1 cup)
- 2 ounces cream cheese , softened (about 1/4 cup)
- 1/4 cup minced fresh basil leaves
- 2 tablespoons extra-virgin olive oil
- 1 small garlic clove , minced or pressed through a garlic press (about 1/2 teaspoon)
- 1/8 teaspoon salt
- 1/8 teaspoon ground black pepper

Direction

- Mix all the ingredients together until uniform and spread 1 1/2 tablespoons per chicken breast under the skin as directed in Easy Stuffed Chicken Breasts with Cheese Filling (related).

---

268.   Pan Fried Coconut Chicken Recipe

Serving: 4 | Prep: | Cook: 10mins | Ready in:

Ingredients

- 4 skinless/boneless chicken breast halves (2 whole breasts) pounded flat
- Your favorite Asian marinade OR Joan's marinade:
- 1 can coconut milk
- juice from one lime
- 2 Tbs soy sauce
- salt and pepper to taste
- Breading:
- 2 eggs fork beaten
- 1 cup flour
- 1 cup packaged sweetened shredded coconut
- oil to fry

Direction

- Marinade the chicken in the coconut milk, soy sauce and lime several hours or overnight.
- Drain chicken and salt and pepper.
- Dip chicken in eggs coating well and then in flour mixed with the coconut.
- Shake off excess.
- Heat adequate amount of oil in a skillet for proper frying and fry chicken cutlets on medium high heat, turning a few times until golden and done.
- Do not let coconut breading burn.
- Drain on absorbent paper.
- Serve with Asian style noodles and coconut pancakes if desired.

---

269.   Pancit Bihon Recipe

Serving: 6 | Prep: | Cook: 15mins | Ready in:

Ingredients

- 1 8-oz. pack of rice stick noodles (pancit bihon)
- 1 large chicken breast
- ¼ lb. boneless pork, julienne
- 1/2 lb. tiger shrimp, shelled and deveined
- 3 chinese sausage, sliced
- ½ cup vegetable oil
- 1 medium carrot, julienne
- 2 celery stalks, julienne
- ¼ lb. snow peas or green beans, thinly sliced
- 1-½ cups shredded cabbage
- 2 cloves garlic, thinly sliced
- 1 medium red onion, sliced
- 2 1/2 cups chicken stock, homemade or canned
- 2 tbsp. soy sauce
- 2 tbsp. oyster sauce
- 1 tbsp fish sauce, to taste
- salt and pepper, to taste
- 3 green onion stalks, sliced, bias-cut (garnish)
- 1 whole lemon, cut in wedges

Direction

- Boil chicken until tender, about 30 minutes. Reserve broth. Let meat chill then shred.
- In a heated wok, separately stir-fry: carrot, celery, snow peas or green beans and cabbage until crisp-tender. Remove and set aside.
- Sauté garlic in 2 tablespoons of oil until lightly browned. Add onion. Stir-fry until translucent. Remove and set aside.
- Stir-fry separately: sausage, chicken, pork, and shrimp last.
- Pour in chicken stock. Bring to boil for 2 minutes. Season with soy sauce, oyster sauce, fish sauce, salt, and black pepper.
- Add noodles. You may need to add more stock if noodles seem dry. Stir constantly, scooping from bottom to top and until liquid has been absorbed. Drizzle remaining oil to prevent noodles from clumping. Stir with scooping method.
- Add vegetable mixture. Sprinkle garlic/onion mixture. Turn heat off and cover with lid for a few minutes, about 5 minutes until noodles are cooked thru.
- Garnish with green onions and lemon wedges.

270. Panko Crusted Chicken With Rum Raisin Sauce Recipe

Serving: 4 | Prep: | Cook: 30mins | Ready in:

Ingredients

- 1 egg white, lightly beaten
- 1/2 cup panko crumbs
- 1/3 cup shredded sweetened coconut (optional)
- 1 tablespoon canola oil
- 4 (4- to 6-ounce) boneless, skinless chicken breast halves
- 1/4 cup raisins
- 1 tablespoon unsalted butter
- 2 tablespoons dark brown sugar

- 2 tablespoons water
- 1 teaspoon dark rum or 1/4 teaspoon rum extract

Direction

- Place egg white in shallow pie plate. Combine panko crumbs and coconut, if desired, in another pie plate.
- Heat oil in nonstick skillet that has been sprayed with nonstick vegetable cooking spray over medium-high heat.
- Dip chicken in egg white, then in crumb mixture, coating evenly.
- Place in hot skillet and sauté until golden brown; turn and brown the other side until fully cooked and meat thermometer registers 170 degrees.
- Place chicken on platter and keep warm in oven.
- Meanwhile, prepare sauce.
- Pour boiling water over raisins and allow them to plump10 minutes; drain thoroughly and set aside.
- Melt butter in small saucepan. Stir in sugar and water.
- Cook until mixture thickens and begins to resemble syrup.
- Add drained raisins to sauce, along with rum.
- Heat through and ladle over chicken to serve.

271. Parmesan Chicken Recipe

Serving: 4 | Prep: | Cook: | Ready in:

Ingredients

- 1 lar 4 chicken breast halves
- ge egg, lightly beaten
- 1/2 cup Italian-seasoned breadcrumbs
- 2 tablespoons butter or margarine, melted
- 1 3/4 cups spaghetti sauce
- 1/2 cup mozzarella cheese
- 1 tablespoon Grated Parmesan cheese

- 1/4 cup Chopped fresh parsley

Direction

- 4 chicken breast halves
- 1 large egg, lightly beaten
- 1/2 cup Italian-seasoned breadcrumbs
- 2 tablespoons butter or margarine, melted
- 1 3/4 cups spaghetti sauce
- 1/2 cup mozzarella cheese
- 1 tablespoon Grated Parmesan cheese
- 1/4 cup Chopped fresh parsley
- Preparation
- Place chicken between 2 sheets of heavy-duty plastic wrap; flatten to 1/4-inch thickness, using a meat mallet or rolling pin. Dip chicken in egg, and dredge in breadcrumbs.
- Cook chicken in butter in a large skillet over medium-high heat until browned on both sides. Spoon spaghetti sauce over chicken; bring to a boil. Cover, reduce heat, and simmer 10 minutes.
- Sprinkle with cheeses and parsley; cover and simmer 5 minutes, or until cheeses melt.

---

272. Parmesan Garlic Chicken Recipe

Serving: 0 | Prep: | Cook: 30mins | Ready in:

Ingredients

- 1/2 cup grated Parmesan cheese
- 1/2 packet of Italian dressing mix
- 1/2 tsp. of garlic powder
- 3 boneless skinless chicken breast halves

Direction

- Preheat oven to 400°F
- Mix together cheese, dressing mix, and garlic powder
- Wet chicken breasts with water and cover in cheese mix
- Place chicken in a shallow baking dish

- Cook chicken for 20-25 minutes until chicken is no longer pink in the center

---

273. Parmesan Sherry Chicken Recipe

Serving: 4 | Prep: | Cook: 40mins | Ready in:

Ingredients

- 4 chicken breasts, boneless and skinless
- 1/2 cup half and half
- 2 cloves minced garlic
- 1 cup all purpose flour
- 1 cup plain bread crumbs
- 1/2 cup grated parmesan cheese
- 1 teaspoon kosher salt
- 1 teaspoon dried thyme leaves
- 1/2 teaspoon ground black pepper
- 4 T. butter
- 2 T. olive oil
- 1/2 cup dry sherry (such as Dry Sack), divided

Direction

- Between two pieces of plastic wrap, pound each chicken breast evenly, until approximately 1/4 inch thick. If you don't have a poultry mallet, use the bottom of a small skillet - works great!
- In a baking dish or similar wide, flat container, pour in half and half, add minced garlic, and then place chicken pieces in dish, turning to coat evenly. Let sit while you prepare the breading.
- In a large food storage bag, place flour, breadcrumbs, parmesan cheese, salt, thyme leaves, and black pepper. Shake well to combine.
- Bread each chicken breast by putting in plastic bag and shaking to coat completely. Remove to a separate plate to "stand by."
- In very large, non-stick skillet, heat butter and olive oil over medium-high heat, until very hot. Add chicken breasts to pan, and allow to

cook for approximately 3 minutes on one side. REMOVE PAN FROM HEAT, then add 1/4 cup Dry Sherry, then PUT BACK ON HEAT. Turn chicken breasts to other side, cook for approximately 3-4 more minutes. Again, REMOVE PAN FROM HEAT, then add remaining 1/4 cup Sherry, PUT BACK ON HEAT, and allow Sherry to "burn off" while chicken finishes cooking.

- Serve with classic fettuccini Alfredo and a green salad.

274. Party Chicken For A Crowd Recipe

Serving: 12 | Prep: | Cook: 35mins | Ready in:

Ingredients

- 1/2 boneless skinless chicken breast per person (12)
- 2 packages of cream cheese, (8 ounce each)
- 3 tbsp of green peppercorns crushed
- 1 1/2 tbsp of dried parsley
- 1 1/2 tbsp of tarragon
- 2 teaspoon of salt
- 1 tsp of grated lemon zest
- 3 eggs
- 3 tbsp of water
- seasoned bread crumbs (mom used Italian blend crumbs)
- 3/4 cup of melted butter

Direction

- Flatten each chicken breast with the flat side of a mallet until it is equally thin and malleable.
- Mix the cream cheese with the slightly crushed green peppercorns, parsley, tarragon, salt and lemon zest. Mix well and divide into 12 equal portions.
- (I roll it into a cylinder on wax paper, chill and then cut in equal pieces)
- Put a piece of chilled cream cheese in the center of a chicken breast half, roll the

flattened chicken breast around the cheese tucking in the sides to form a neat little bundles. It should stick together because of the cheese.

- Now dip it in the eggs mixed with the water, then into the seasoned bread crumbs.
- Now you must refrigerate this covered for at least 30 minutes.
- It will cook better if it starts out good and cold.
- Preheat oven to 350 degrees.
- Place chicken bundles in an oiled baking dish, pour melted butter over all and back uncovered for 35 minutes. Do not turn.

275. Pattis Easy Chicken Recipe

Serving: 4 | Prep: | Cook: 60mins | Ready in:

Ingredients

- 4-6 Boneless skinless chicken breasts
- 2 cans Golden mushroom soup
- 1 envelope of onion soup mix
- 1/2 cup of EITHER dry sherry or white wine OR milk
- 1 pkg of sliced mushrooms

Direction

- Preheat oven to 350
- Mix the soups, wine and mushrooms together
- Add some black pepper to your taste
- Spread some of the soup mix at the bottom of a casserole dish
- Lay the chicken out in the pan and cover with the remaining soup mixture
- Bake 350 for an hour
- *I have made this in the microwave and the crockpot and never changed the ingredients. I also have served as an appetizer and just cut the chicken into bite size pieces.

276. Paula Deens Baked Ham And Cheese Chicken Recipe

Serving: 4 | Prep: | Cook: 15mins |Ready in:

Ingredients

- 4 chicken breasts
- 1 cup all-purpose flour
- 2 teaspoons House seasoning, recipe follows
- 2 eggs, beaten
- hot sauce
- 1 cup bread crumbs
- 2 teaspoons Greek seasoning, recipe follows
- 1 cup grated Parmesan
- olive oil
- 4 slices ham
- 4 teaspoons chopped fresh parsley leaves
- 4 slices mozzarella cheese
- House Seasoning:
- 1 cup salt
- 1/4 cup black pepper
- 1/4 cup garlic powder
- Greek Seasoning:
- 2 teaspoons dried oregano
- 1 teaspoon salt
- 2 teaspoons onion powder
- 2 teaspoons garlic powder

Direction

- Dredge the chicken breasts in flour seasoned with House Seasoning, then dip in egg wash with hot sauce, to taste, then dredge in a mixture of bread crumbs, Greek Seasoning, and Parmesan.
- Brown the chicken on each side in a skillet with olive oil on medium-high heat.
- After frying, transfer chicken to a sheet pan.
- Top with 1 slice of ham, 1 teaspoon chopped parsley and 1 slice of mozzarella cheese.
- Place in oven for 8 minutes, just until cheese melts and starts to get bubbly.
- House Seasoning:
- Mix ingredients together and store in an airtight container for up to 6 months.
- Greek Seasoning:
- Mix ingredients together and store in an airtight container for up to 6 months.

277. Penne Di Funghi Con Pollo E Salsiccia Recipe

Serving: 4 | Prep: | Cook: 30mins |Ready in:

Ingredients

- ¾ Pound penne pasta
- 2 Links Spicy italian sausage, casings removed
- 1 Boneless chicken breast, sliced
- 2 Cups Loosely Packed arugula
- 2 Cups Crimini mushrooms, sliced
- ½ Ounce dried porcini mushrooms
- 1 Cup hot water
- 1 Cup white wine
- ¼ Cup heavy cream
- 3 Tablespoons shallots, chopped finely
- 3 Whole garlic cloves, diced finely
- ¼ Teaspoon Dried chili flakes
- 2 Tablespoon olive oil
- Kosher salt and black pepper

Direction

- Bring a large pot of water to boil. Add salt and cook the penne pasta just shy of al dente.
- Place the dried Porcini in a bowl with the hot water. Allow the mushrooms to reconstitute — about 10 minutes. Squeeze out extra liquid from the Porcinis (saving the liquid) and roughly chop them.
- Heat olive oil in a very large heavy pan (or pot) over medium-high heat. Season chicken with salt and pepper. Add Italian sausage to the pot and use a wooden spoon to crumble the meat and break into small pieces. Once the sausage is barely pink, add the chicken. Continue cooking until both are done. Use a slotted spoon and transfer it to a plate covered with paper towels.
- Using the same pan, lower the heat to medium and sauté the shallots until translucent. Add

garlic, chili flakes, and both mushrooms. Cook until the mushrooms are tender. Stir in wine and liquid that the porcini was reconstituted in–being careful not to add in the mushroom grit/sand. Raise the heat to medium-high and cook the liquids until it is reduced by half. Stir in the cream and cook for an additional 1-2 minutes. Return the sausage and chicken to the pot and add the cooked penne. Stir until all the penne has been coated. Season with salt and pepper to taste. Remove pan from the heat and toss in the arugula leaves. Toss until the leaves are just wilted. Serve and Enjoy!

278. Pesto Italian Pasta With Chicken Recipe

Serving: 4 | Prep: | Cook: |Ready in:

Ingredients

- 1 tab olive oil
- 4 boneless skinless chicken breast sliced into 1 in. strips (not the frozen one in a bag)
- 2 to 4 cloves garlic minced
- 1 red pepper cut into 1/4 in strips
- 1/2 cup fresh homemade pesto (buy it premade in a jar if nessary)
- 1 lemon quartered
- 1 cup Italian cheese I use several types what ever I have on hand and fresh grade you can buy pre-graded
- 2 to 3 cups cooked angel hair pasta (how hungry are you)

Direction

- Heat oil in large heavy bottom pan, add chicken and garlic, cook and stir until chicken changes color, or evenly browned. Add in peppers and cook for a few more mi. until chicken is cooked done.
- Add in your pesto and the juice of the lemon.
- Sprinkle with the cheese turn off the heat cover and make a salad.

- Plate the pasta and add the Italian cheese and chicken sauce.

279. Pesto Mozzarella Stuffed Chicken Breasts Recipe

Serving: 4 | Prep: | Cook: 25mins |Ready in:

Ingredients

- 4 Organics Boneless & skinless chicken Breasts (halves; about 1 2/3 lbs. total), rinsed and patted dry
- 1/2 tsp. freshly ground black pepper
- 1/2 cup Pesto pasta sauce
- 1/2 cup Perlini fresh mozzarella balls (or use larger balls cut into small pieces)
- 1/2 cup sliced Fire roasted red peppers

Direction

- Prepare a charcoal or gas grill for direct, high heat (you can hold your hand 1 to 2 in. above the cooking grate only 2 to 3 seconds; visit our Grilling Essential section for complete instructions).
- While grill heats, with a sharp knife, cut a pocket lengthwise in the edge of each chicken breast half, taking care to avoid cutting through to the other side. Season chicken pieces on both sides with pepper. Spread about 1 tbsp. pesto inside each pocket, then fill each with 1/4 of the mozzarella balls and 1/4 of the roasted red pepper slices. Rub remaining pesto over exterior of chicken to coat lightly.
- Place chicken on oiled cooking grate; cover gas grill. Cook, turning once with a wide spatula, until meat is browned and no longer pink in center (cut to test, but do not disturb filling)

280. Picture Perfect Grilled Chicken Recipe

Serving: 4 | Prep: | Cook: 35mins | Ready in:

Ingredients

- marinade
- 2/3 c extra virgin olive oil
- 1/4 c fresh squeezed lemon juice
- 3 T reduced sodium soy sauce
- 1/4 c white wine Worcestershire (or lea & perrins chicken marinade)
- 2 T spicy mustard
- 2 t fresh ground black pepper
- 2 T chopped garlic
- 1 t liquid smoke
- 1 t dried parsley
- 4 boneless skinless chicken breasts, or your fave pieces

Direction

- Mix all ingredients for marinade
- Put chicken in large Ziploc baggie
- Pour marinade over and massage until chicken is coated
- Place in fridge up to 4 hours, turning every so often
- Bring chicken to room temp just before grilling
- Grill on medium low heat until reaches internal temp of 165/170
- Turn only once

281. Pineapple Chicken Stir Fry Recipe

Serving: 6 | Prep: | Cook: 15mins | Ready in:

Ingredients

- 1 (20 oz) can unsweetened pineapple tidbits
- 2 Tablespoons cornstarch
- 1/4 cup cider vinegar
- 1/4 c ketchup
- 2 Tablespoons brown sugar
- 2 Tablespoons soy sauce
- 1/4 teaspoon ground ginger
- 1 1/2 lb boneless, skinless chicken breasts, cubed
- 3 Tablespoons vegetable or canola oil, divided
- 1/2 teaspoons garlic salt
- 2 medium carrots, sliced
- 1 medium grren pepper, julienned
- 1 medium tomato, cut into wedges
- Hot cooked rice

Direction

- Drain pineapple, reserving the juice; set pineapple aside. In a small bowl, combine the cornstarch and reserved juice until smooth. Stir in the vinegar, ketchup, brown sugar and ginger; set aside.
- In a wok or large skillet, stir fry the chicken in 2 Tablespoons oil for 5-6 minutes or until juices run clear; sprinkle with garlic salt. Remove and keep warm. Stir fry the carrots in the remaining 1 Tablespoon of oil for 4 minutes. Add the green pepper; cook and stir until vegetables are crisp-tender. Add the chicken and pineapple.
- Stir pineapple juice mixture and pour into pan with other ingredients. Bring to a boil; cook and stir for 1-2 minutes or until thickened. Add tomato wedges. Serve over hot rice.

282. Pineapple Glazed Chicken With Jalapeno Salsa Recipe

Serving: 4 | Prep: | Cook: 30mins | Ready in:

Ingredients

- 1/2 c pineapple juice
- 2 Tbs brown sugar
- 1 Tbs yellow mustard
- 3/4 c 1/4" cubes fresh pineapple

- 3 Tbs finely diced red bell pepper
- 1-1/2 Tbs finely chopped red onion
- 3 Tbs chopped fresh cilantro
- 1-1/2 Tbs canned,sliced jalapeno chilies,drained,coarsely chopped
- 4 boneless chicken breast halves with skin (1-3/4 lbs total)

Direction

- Preheat oven to 400 degrees. Bring pineapple juice, brown sugar and mustard to boil in small saucepan, stirring to dissolve sugar. Boil until glaze has thickened slightly, about 1 min. Season with salt and pepper.
- Mix pineapple, red pepper, cilantro, onion, and chilies in medium bowl. Season with salt and pepper.
- Line baking sheet with foil. Place chicken breasts on sheet and brush with glaze. Bake 15 mins. Brush again with glaze, then broil until cooked through and golden, watching closely to avoid burning, about 5 mins. longer. Let rest 5 mins.
- Spoon salsa over chicken and serve.

283. Pistachio Crusted Chicken With Coconut Chili Ginger Sauce Recipe

Serving: 8 | Prep: | Cook: 45mins |Ready in:

Ingredients

- BRINE FOR chicken
- Makes 1 1/4 cups (may need to double this recipe)
- 1 cup kosher salt
- 1/4 cup sugar
- 5 cloves garlic
- 2 bay leaves
- 1 Tbsp. black peppercorns
- pistachio CRUSTED chicken

- 4 brined, boneless chicken breasts (see brine recipe below)
- 1 quart buttermilk
- 1 pound salted pistachios, shelled and toasted
- 1 cup grated parmesan cheese
- 1/4 cup fresh thyme
- 1/3 cup chopped fresh rosemary
- 1/4 cup chopped fresh parsley
- 2 cups all-purpose flour
- salt and freshly ground black pepper to taste
- grape seed oil to taste
- coconut ginger SAUCE
- 1 Tbsp. unsalted butter
- 2 shallots, minced
- 2 blades lemongrass, chopped
- 3 (1/2-inch) piece, fresh ginger, thinly sliced
- 1 cup sweet white wine
- 2 cups chicken broth
- 2 Tbsp. Thai red curry paste
- 2 Tbsp. Chinese black bean chili sauce
- 1 (8-ounce) can coconut milk
- 1/2 cup (1stick) unsalted butter, softened and cut into pieces
- salt and freshly ground black pepper to taste

Direction

- BRINE:
- Place the salt, sugar, garlic, bay leaves, peppercorns and 2 cups cold water into a saucepan over medium-high heat.
- Stir constantly until the sugar and salt dissolve.
- Remove from the heat and cool to room temperature.
- When brining chicken use a nonreactive pot or plastic container. Completely submerge the poultry in cold water and weigh it down with a plate. Add the brine and cover.
- Let the chicken sit in the brine for at least two hours, preferably overnight.
- CHICKEN:
- Remove the chicken from the brine and cut in half.
- With a meat mallet, pound until 1/4-inch thick and place in a nonreactive bowl.

- Pour the buttermilk over the chicken, cover, and let sit for at least 1 hour in the refrigerator.
- In a food processor, place half of the pistachios, half of the parmesan cheese, and half of the herbs.
- Pulse 5 or 6 times until the mixture is finely chopped.
- Transfer to a bowl. Repeat this step with the rest of the pistachios and combine with the other pistachio mixture.
- Preheat the oven to 250°.
- Place the flour in another bowl and season it with salt and pepper. Remove the chicken from the refrigerator and prepare it for assembly.
- Preheat a large nonstick sauté pan over medium-low heat with a thin coating of grape seed oil.
- Remove one breast, shake off any excess buttermilk and dust the breast with flour on each side.
- Dip only one side of the chicken back in the buttermilk and press pistachios onto that side.
- Repeat that step with all the chicken.
- Place the chicken in the sauté pan, pistachio side down, and cook for 2–3 minutes.
- Turn and cook the other side for 2 to 3 minutes.
- Place in the oven to finish cooking for 8 to 10 minutes.
- Remove, let rest for 5 minutes and then slice to serve with the Coconut Chile Ginger Sauce.
- SAUCE:
- In a medium saucepan over medium-high heat, add the tablespoon of butter, the shallots, lemongrass, ginger slices and wine.
- Reduce to half.
- Add the broth, red curry paste and Chinese black bean chili sauce and reduce to half again.
- Add the coconut milk and reduce to half a third time.
- Remove from the heat and whisk the bits of butter into the sauce until all the butter has been incorporated.
- Season with salt and pepper.

- If you reheat, do not allow the sauce to boil or the butter will separate.

284.   Polynesian Chicken Recipe

Serving: 4 | Prep: | Cook: 35mins | Ready in:

Ingredients

- 4 boneless skinless chicken breasts or 8 chicken tenderloins
- 1/2 cup low sodium soy sauce (regular soy sauce would make it way too salty!)
- 1/3 cup honey
- 1 tablespoon hoisin sauce
- 2 star anise (i have used extract when i could not find the spice)
- 2 tablespoon grated ginger

Direction

- Combine all ingredient except chicken.
- I like to put the mixture in a big ziplock bag and then add the chicken and let it marinate for a few minutes.
- Place in baking dish, bake for 35 minutes @ 375 degrees or till chicken is done.

285.   Polynesian Style Chicken Recipe

Serving: 4 | Prep: | Cook: 45mins | Ready in:

Ingredients

- 2 Tbsp. Olive Oil
- 1c. Fresh Mushrooms, Sliced
- 1c. Green bell pepper, chopped in 1" pieces
- 1c. Red bell pepper, chopped in 1" pieces
- 1c. Yellow or Orange bell pepper, chopped in 1" pieces

- 1c. Onion, chopped in 1" pieces
- 1lb. chicken breasts, chopped 1" pieces
- 1/4 tsp. Salt. (optional)
- 3/4 c. Teriyaki Sauce (Easy Homemade Teriyaki Sauce)
- 1 lg. can Pineapple Chunks (drained and juice reserved)
- 1 tsp. Garlic Powder
- 1/4 tsp. Ground black pepper
- 1 Tbsp. Corn Starch
- 1 Tbsp. Water
- 6c - 8c Steamed Rice

Direction

- Heat olive oil in a large skillet or wok. Add mushrooms and sauté for 5 min. Add peppers and onions and continue to cook until vegetables start to soften. Approx. 8 - 10 min. Remove from skillet.
- Using the same skillet, add chicken and more olive oil if desired. Cook until chicken is almost done, seasoning with the salt (optional). Add teriyaki sauce, 1/2c. pineapple juice, garlic powder, and black pepper. Stir until mixed together. Add peppers/onions/mushrooms. Continue cooking until sauce starts to boil.
- In a small cup, mix corn starch and cold water. Stir until starch is dissolved. Pour over chicken and stir. Cook a few more minutes until sauce thickens.
- Add pineapple to chicken, cooking until pineapple is just heated through. Serve over rice.

286.   Poppy Seed Chicken Recipe

Serving: 4 | Prep: | Cook: 30mins | Ready in:

Ingredients

- 4 boneless, skinless chicken breasts
- 1/2 cup . margarine or butter
- 1 tube of round butter crackers such as Ritz
- 2 Tbs. poppy seeds

Direction

- Preheat oven to 375 degrees.
- Melt butter in 9x13 baking dish.
- Slice across raw chicken breasts to make 4 or 5 strips from each breast and set aside.
- In a large plastic bag, crush the crackers and add poppy seeds to bag.
- Roll each chicken strip in the cracker mixture to coat well and lay side by side in buttery casserole.
- Repeat with all strips and then shake excess crumbs and seeds over the top of the strips.
- Bake for 20 minutes.
- Carefully turn the strips over and bake for another 10 minutes.
- Turn the oven up to 450 degrees they need to brown a little more.

287.   Pork Chop And Potato Casserole Recipe

Serving: 4 | Prep: | Cook: 90mins | Ready in:

Ingredients

- 6 large pork chops OR boneless, skinless chicken breasts
- 6 potatoes, sliced
- 2-3 medium onions, sliced 1/2" thickness
- 1 can Cream Style corn OR cream of mushroom soup
- 1/4 cup water
- salt and pepper
- 1 green bell pepper, sliced or chopped
- Note: I like to add minced garlic or garlic powder to this and top the casserole with crushed potato chips mixed with 1/4 cup parmesan cheese. I only use the crushed potato chips when I bake this casserole in the oven.

Direction

- Brown pork chops OR boneless, skinless chicken breasts in a skillet.
- Place alternating layers of pork chops/chicken breasts, potatoes, onions and green peppers in a baking dish.
- Season.
- After first layer of pork chops, potatoes, onions and green peppers is in place, pour half the Creamed Corn OR Cream of Mushroom soup over the top.
- Layer again.
- Season to taste.
- Pour the remaining Creamed Corn OR Cream of Mushroom soup that has been mixed with water, over the top.
- Season and top with crushed potato chips.
- Bake at 350 or 375 F in a covered, casserole dish for 1 to 1-1/2 hours.
- Crockpot or Slow cooker method:
- Layer the same way in a crockpot.
- Cook on low heat for 6-8 hours or on high heat for 4-5 hours.

288.   Pretzel Crusted Chicken With Cheesy Mustard Sauce Recipe

Serving: 4 | Prep: | Cook: 15mins | Ready in:

Ingredients

- 1 zip lock type plastic food storage bag
- 4 small, boneless, skinless chicken breasts
- 1 5-ounce bag of salted pretzels, any shape
- 1 tablespoon thyme
- salt and pepper
- 2 eggs
- vegetable oil, for frying
- 2 tablespoons butter
- 2 tablespoons flour
- 2 cups milk

- 3/4 pound/ 2 1/2 cups, cheddar cheese, grated
- 2 heaping tablespoons spicy brown mustard

Direction

- Pre heat oil in a pan to a medium heat (1/4 inch deep).
- Place 1 chicken breast (and a little water) in the bag and seal it up, pushing out excess air. Use the bottom of a heavy pot or pan and pound each breast until flat, just shy of busting out of the bag. Repeat with the other 3 chicken breasts.
- Blend pretzels in a food processer until fine.
- Mix ground pretzels, thyme and some salt and pepper in a shallow dish (like a dinner plate)
- Beat eggs and pour into a second dinner plate with a splash of water added.
- One at a time coat each fillet in egg and then ground pretzels.
- Add chicken to pan (do 2 batches if necessary - about 4 minutes on each side or until cooked through).
- To make cheesy mustard sauce
- Heat butter in a pan over medium heat.
- Add flour and cook for 1 minute.
- Whisk in milk and when it starts to thicken add cheese and mustard and stir (figure of 8s!)
- When it has melted completely its ready - drizzle over chicken and serve with lots of veg or salad.

289.   Quick And Easy Stuffed Chicken Recipe

Serving: 4 | Prep: | Cook: 30mins | Ready in:

Ingredients

- 4 boneless skinless chicken breasts
- 1/2 cup spinach dip (I used spinach-dip.html">Baked spinach Dip unbaked)
- sea salt & black pepper, freshly ground - to taste

- olive oil spray or nonstick cooking spray (canola oil)

Direction

- Preheat oven to 350F. Prepare baking dish with cooking spray.
- Split each chicken breast, leaving about 1/2 inch attached, careful not to cut all the way through. Season inside with salt & pepper. Spoon 2 tbsp. of spinach dip into each breast. Secure breasts with toothpicks if needed. Place in baking dish. Spray lightly with cooking spray and season tops with salt and pepper. Bake for about 30 minutes or until juices run clear.

290.   Quick Easy N Fast Chicken Strips Recipe

Serving: 4 | Prep: | Cook: 10mins | Ready in:

Ingredients

- 4 skinless boneless chicken breasts
- 1 beaten egg
- 1 T. Dijon mustard
- 1 T. water
- 1/4 C. flour
- 3/4 C. dry seasoned bread crumbs
- 2 T. vegetable oil
- 2 T. butter
- 1/2 t. lemon pepper seasoning
- salt to taste

Direction

- Cut each chicken breast in 6 pieces.
- In a small bowl, mix together egg, mustard and water.
- Add the flour and lemon pepper together on a plate.
- Place the breadcrumbs on another plate or wax paper.

- Dip the strips in the flour, then the egg and the breadcrumbs. Repeat until you have coated all the chicken.
- In a 12 inch skillet add the oil and butter.
- Add the chicken and brown on all sides.
- It should take about 6 minutes.
- Season with salt.

291.   RED COOKED CHICKEN Recipe

Serving: 6 | Prep: | Cook: 50mins | Ready in:

Ingredients

- dark soy sauce, available at Asian markets, gives this dish its characteristic red color and deep, fruity flavor; you can substitute regular soy sauce, but the color will not be very dark, and the flavor will be blander. Sichuan peppercorns are available at Asian markets. If using both chicken breasts and thighs/drumsticks, we recommend cutting the breast pieces in half so that each serving can include both white and dark meat. The breasts and thighs/drumsticks do not cook at the same rate; if using both, note that the breast pieces are added partway through the cooking time. Serve with white rice.
- 4 pounds bone-in, skin-on chicken pieces (split breasts cut in half, drumsticks, and/or thighs), trimmed
- 2 tablespoons vegetable oil , plus more as needed
- 6 medium garlic cloves , minced or pressed through a garlic press (about 2 tablespoons)
- 2 tablespoons minced or grated fresh ginger
- 1 teaspoon Sichuan peppercorns (see note)
- 3 star anise
- 1/2 cup dark soy sauce (see note)
- 1/3 cup low-sodium chicken broth
- 1/4 cup Chinese rice cooking wine or dry sherry
- 3 tablespoons toasted sesame oil

- 3 tablespoons light brown sugar
- 4 hard-cooked eggs , peeled

Direction

- 1. Pat the chicken dry with paper towels. Heat the oil in a large Dutch oven over medium-high heat until just smoking. Brown half of the chicken on both sides, 5 to 8 minutes per side, reducing the heat if the pan begins to scorch. Transfer the chicken to a plate, leaving the fat in the pot. Return the pot to medium-high heat and repeat with the remaining chicken; transfer the chicken to the plate.
- 2. Pour off all but 1 tablespoon fat from the pot. (Add additional oil to equal 1 tablespoon, if needed.) Add the garlic, ginger, Sichuan peppercorns, and star anise to the pot and cook over medium heat until fragrant, about 30 seconds. Stir in the soy sauce, chicken broth, rice wine, sesame oil, and brown sugar, scraping up any browned bits.
- 3. Nestle the hard-cooked eggs and chicken, along with any accumulated juices, into the pot and bring to a simmer. Cover, turn the heat to medium-low, and simmer until the chicken is fully cooked and tender, about 20 minutes for the breasts (160 to 165 degrees on an instant-read thermometer) or 1 hour for the thighs and drumsticks (170 to 175 degrees on an instant-read thermometer), turning over the chicken and eggs halfway through cooking to ensure even coloring from the sauce. (If using both types of chicken, simmer the thighs and drumsticks for 40 minutes before adding the breasts.)
- 4. Transfer the chicken and eggs to a serving dish, tent loosely with foil, and let rest while finishing the sauce. Remove and discard the star anise. Skim as much fat as possible off the surface of the sauce. Pour the sauce over the chicken and eggs and serve.

292. Red Curry Chicken Recipe

Serving: 4 | Prep: | Cook: 10mins |Ready in:

Ingredients

- 4 boneless, skinless chicken breasts
- 1 T vegetable oil
- red curry paste
- 4 oz. coconut milk

Direction

- Cut chicken into 1 inch cubes.
- Sauté in oil until white.
- Mix in red curry paste until it coats the chicken evenly.
- Add coconut milk.
- Let simmer 5 min.
- Serve with rice.

293. Reuben Chicken Recipe

Serving: 0 | Prep: | Cook: 35mins |Ready in:

Ingredients

- 4 boneless chicken breasts (I used a 2 1/2 lb package of chicken breast tenders, which worked great)
- 6 oz Swiss cheese, sliced (shredded would also work just fine - I have a guy who doesn't love Swiss, so I used 4 oz sliced Mozzarella and 4 oz of sliced Swiss - it was delicious, but I would love only Swiss too)
- 1 16 oz can/jar sauerkraut, drained
- 8 - 10 oz thousand island dressing

Direction

- Preheat oven to 400 degrees (F).
- Rinse chicken and pat dry.
- Arrange chicken in baking dish sprayed with nonstick cooking spray.

- Layer the Swiss cheese and the sauerkraut over the chicken and cover with the Thousand Island dressing.
- Bake 25-30 minutes or until cooked through.
- Enjoy with hot buttered rice or smashed potatoes.

294. Roasted Chicken And Penne Recipe

Serving: 0 | Prep: | Cook: 2hours | Ready in:

Ingredients

- 8oz whole wheat penne pasta
- 2-4 cups shredded roasted chicken breasts sans skin (pre-purchased)
- 2 tablespoons of olive oil
- 5 large garlic cloves, chopped
- 3 12oz bags cherry tomatoes
- 3/4 teaspoon dried crushed red pepper
- 1/2 cup feta cheese
- 4-6 cups arugula

Direction

- Preheat oven to 475°F.
- Mix cherry tomatoes, garlic, crushed red pepper, and olive oil on rimmed baking sheet. Add a dash of salt and pepper.
- Bake 'till the tomatoes are soft and beginning to brown, stirring occasionally. Takes about 20 minutes.
- Move everything (juices too) from the baking sheet, to large skillet. Add pre-cooked chicken to the skillet and simmer for 5 minutes.
- Cook the penne until just tender but still firm to bite (8-10 minutes).
- Ladle out 1/4 cup of water from the penne pot and keep to the side.
- Drain the pasta and put back into pot.
- Add the tomato mixture, arugula, and 1/4 cup cooking water to the penne.
- Toss over medium heat just until arugula begins to wilt (~30 seconds).

- Season with salt and pepper.
- Transfer pasta to bowl.
- Sprinkle with feta cheese.
- Serve.

295. Roasted Red Pepper And Lemon Chicken With Shallots And Cannellini Beans Recipe

Serving: 4 | Prep: | Cook: 20mins | Ready in:

Ingredients

- 2T. olive oil
- 4 bonless skinless chicken breasts
- 1 med, onion finely minced
- 4 large cloves garlic
- 1c chicken stock
- 1 jar roasted red peppers
- 2 cans cannellini beans (drained and rinsed)
- salt and pepper to taste
- juice and zest of one large lemon
- 2t. hot pepper sauce
- 1/4c. parmesan cheese (grated) more if you like

Direction

- Preheat oven to 350
- Heat olive oil in a large oven proof skillet (not nonstick)
- Salt and pepper chicken
- Brown chicken on both sides
- Add onion to pan cook till translucent
- Add garlic cook 2min.
- Add chicken stock, roasted peppers, beans, salt, pepper, hot pepper sauce
- Bring to a boil
- Place in oven for 15-20 min.
- Remove from oven and add lemon juice and zest
- Sprinkle with parmesan cheese
- Serve with a nice crusty bread to soak up the juices

296. Rosemary, Black Pear Tomato Slices And Chicken Recipe

Serving: 4 | Prep: | Cook: 30mins | Ready in:

Ingredients

- 4 skinless chicken breasts (or precooked chicken breasts)
- 2 Black pear tomato
- 2 tbsp FRESH chopped garlic
- 2 sprigs of fresh rosemary
- Mozerella (or I use Bel Gioioso four cheese shred)
- 2 tbsp extra virgin olive oil or garlic basil olive oil

Direction

- Bake the chicken (I like to keep them plain, or add a little garlic)
- Add oil into an 8x16 pan/ casserole dish
- Slice tomatoes into 1/4" thick slices and place into the pan
- Flip the tomatoes to make sure both sides get some oil on them
- Place about a pinch of fresh garlic on each slice
- On top of that place a small pinch of rosemary from the sprigs
- Bake on 325 for about 10 mins
- After the 10 mins are up add a 1 tbsp. of cheese on each of the slices
- Then bake for another 2 mins (or until the cheese is melted)
- Place chicken on the plate and top with the tomato slices and ENJOY :)

297. SIMPLE CHICKEN CORDON BLEU Recipe

Serving: 4 | Prep: | Cook: 40mins | Ready in:

Ingredients

- 4 skinless, boneless chicken breast
- 4 slices Swiss or provolone cheese
- 4 thin sliced smoked ham
- ¼ cup all-purpose flour
- 1 egg; beaten
- 1 cup italian seasoned bread crumbs
- 4 tablespoons butter
- ½ cup chicken broth
- 1 cup whipping cream
- toothpicks

Direction

- Pound chicken breast to ¼-inch thickness.
- Sprinkle each piece on both sides with salt and pepper.
- Place 1 cheese slice and 1 ham slice on each breast.
- Roll up each breast using toothpicks to secure if necessary.
- Dredge each in flour, shake off excess, then in egg and finally in bread crumbs.
- Place seam side down in baking dish that has been sprayed with Pam.
- Place 1 tablespoon butter on each piece of chicken.
- Bake at 350° for 35 minutes until juices run clear.
- Meanwhile, in a saucepan, combine broth and whipping cream;
- Season to taste (salt, pepper, garlic, oregano).
- Simmer on low stirring until thickened;
- Pour over chicken.

298. SPECTACULAR BROCCOLI LEMON CHICKEN Recipe

Serving: 4 | Prep: | Cook: 10mins | Ready in:

Ingredients

- 1 lemon
- 1 Tbs.. vegetable oil
- 4 boneless chicken breast halves
- 1 can broccoli Soup
- 1/2 C. milk
- 1/8 tsp. pepper
- 4 C. cooked rice

Direction

- Cut 4 thin slices of lemon.
- Squeeze 2 tsp. juice from remaining lemon.
- Heat oil in skillet.
- Add chicken and cook until browned.
- Add soup, milk, lemon juice and pepper.
- Top chicken with lemon slices.
- Heat to a boil.
- Cover and cook over low heat 5 min. or until done.
- Serve over rice.

299. SUNDAY FRIED CHICKEN Recipe

Serving: 4 | Prep: | Cook: 25mins | Ready in:

Ingredients

- 4 chicken breast halves (boneless, skinless)
- 2-1/2 C. finely crushed cornflakes
- 1/2 tsp salt
- 1/4 tsp paprika
- 2 large egg whites

Direction

- In a plastic Ziploc bag place cornflakes, salt, pepper and paprika. Shake to mix well.
- In a shallow bowl beat egg white until slightly frothy.
- Coat chicken pieces in egg white and drop into bag of cornflake mixture.
- Shake to coat well.
- Arrange pieces on a non-stick baking pan and lightly mist with cooking oil spray.
- Bake at 425 degrees for about 25 minutes.

300. Santa Fe Stuffed Chicken Recipe

Serving: 4 | Prep: | Cook: 70mins | Ready in:

Ingredients

- 3/4 tsp chili powder
- 3/4 tsp cumin
- 1/2 tsp salt
- 1/4 tsp paprika
- 1/2 c unseasoned dry bread crumbs
- 2 TB butter
- 1/4 c chopped celery
- 1/4 c chopped onion
- 1/2 c corn
- 1 oz. shredded monterey jack cheese
- 2 TB chopped fresh cilantro
- 4 chicken breast halves,bone-in,skin on

Direction

- 1. Spray 12x8" baking dish with non-stick cooking spray. In small bowl, combine chili powder, cumin, salt and paprika; mix well. Reserve 1 tsp. seasoning mixture; set aside. To remaining seasoning mixture, add bread crumbs; mix well
- 2. In med skillet, melt butter over med heat. Add celery and onion; cook 5 to 7 mins or till veggies are tender. Add corn, cheese, cilantro and bread crumb mixture; mix well.
- 3. Loosen skin from each chicken breast to form pocket between skin and meat. Fill each

pocket with about 1/2 c corn mixture; secure opening with toothpick. Place skin side up in baking dish. Sprinkle chicken with reserved seasoning mixture.

- 4. Broil 4 to 6' from heat for 5-7 mins or till skin is brown.
- 5. Remove baking dish from oven; cover with foil. Bake in 350' oven for 35-40 mins or till juices run clear

---

301.   Saucy Chicken Balls Recipe

Serving: 8 | Prep: | Cook: 60mins | Ready in:

Ingredients

- 3 - 4 chicken breasts
- 1 cup flour
- 1 and 1/2 tsp salt
- 1/8 tsp. pepper
- 1 and 1//2 tsp. garlic powder
- 1 and 1/2 tsp.. onion powder
- 2 eggs, slightly beaten

Direction

- Combine flour with the spices (add other spices if you wish).
- Lightly beat eggs
- Cut chicken into strips long enough to roll into a ball
- Roll chicken balls into beaten egg mixture then
- Dip into flour mixture
- Fry in oil until lightly brown
- Drain on a paper towel.
- SAUCE:
- In a sauce pan, mix 1/2 cup sugar, 1/2 cup vinegar, 1 Tbsp. Soya sauce
- Add 1 can of pineapple chunks and liquid
- 1/4 cup catsup
- 2 Tbsp. cornstarch or a bit more depending on desired thickness of the sauce
- Bake at 275 for an hour
- Serve on egg noodles or rice.

302.   Saucy Chicken Burritos Recipe

Serving: 3 | Prep: | Cook: 120mins | Ready in:

Ingredients

- chicken breasts... as much as you want or need...
- 1 tin of tomatoe soup
- 1 jar of dolmios tomatoe, tomate paste
- 1/2 can of water
- 5 or more cloves of crushed garlic
- 6 burrito wraps or more
- grated cheese

Direction

- Cut the chicken breast into small pieces and place into a large pot.
- Add sauce, soup, garlic and water
- Simmer on a low heat for 2 hours...
- When the chicken is ready, you should be able to touch it lightly with a fork until it falls apart.
- Drain chicken and crush into thin flakes.
- Fill burrito wraps and place them neatly into a cooking/baking tray.
- Use leftover sauce to cover the burritos
- Add grated cheese, and put in oven till cheese is melted.
- Add sour cream and salad if desired.

303.   Saucy Chicken Recipe

Serving: 8 | Prep: | Cook: 60mins | Ready in:

Ingredients

- 6 to 8 boneless chicken breasts
- 1C mayonaise

- 1/2 C chili sauce
- 1/2 C orange marmalade or apricot jam
- 1 envelope of Lipton's onion soup

Direction

- Remove skin and all fat from chicken.
- Place remaining ingredients in a bowl and beat by hand one minute
- Place chicken in oblong baking dish, spoon sauce over chicken and cover with foil
- Bake at 375 for 30 minutes
- Remove from oven and turn chicken over, basting with sauce.
- Return to oven
- Keep chicken covered with foil
- Reduce heat to 350 and bake for another 30 minutes
- Do not overcook.
- Serve with rice or pasta

304. Sesame Chicken Nuggets Recipe

Serving: 4 | Prep: | Cook: 15mins | Ready in:

Ingredients

- 1/3 cup coarse-grained mustard
- 1/3 cup honey
- 2 tablespoons lime juice
- 1/4 teaspoon salt
- 1/8 teaspoon pepper
- 1 pound skinned boned chicken breasts, cut into 1 inch pieces
- 2 egg whites
- 1/2 cup sesame seeds, toasted
- 1/2 cup dry breadcrumbs

Direction

- Preheat oven to 350 degrees.
- Combine first 3 ingredients in a shallow bowl; stir well and set aside.

- Sprinkle salt and pepper over chicken, and set aside.
- Place egg whites in a bowl, and stir well.
- Combine toasted sesame seeds and breadcrumbs into a shallow dish, and stir well.
- Dip chicken in egg whites; dredge in sesame seed mixture.
- Arrange chicken in a single layer on a baking sheet coated with cooking spray.
- Bake at 350 degrees for 15 minutes, turning once.
- Serve chicken with mustard mixture.

305. Sesame Chicken Recipe

Serving: 4 | Prep: | Cook: 25mins | Ready in:

Ingredients

- 4 seven-eight ounce chicken breasts, lightly pounded
- 1 1/2 cups + 1 tablespoon soy sauce
- 1 1/4 teaspoons ground ginger
- 2 1/4 teaspoons fresh minced garlic
- 1/2 cup + 3 1/2 teaspoons white wine
- 1 cup + 3 tablespoons sugar
- toasted sesame seeds for garnish (see note above)
- green onions cut on the bias for garnish

Direction

- Combine soy sauce, ginger, garlic, wine and sugar in a mixing bowl and blend thoroughly
- Place the lightly pounded chicken breasts and the mixture (the marinade) in a large resealable plastic bag or a low baking dish (make certain all the chicken is covered or surrounded with the marinade)
- Place in the refrigerator and marinade for 4 hours before using
- Remove chicken from the marinade and (1) place on your grill - medium heat or (2) 5-6 inches under your broiler on a sheet pan or in a shallow baking dish or (3) oven bake the

chicken at 350 degrees F (be careful NOT to have the heat turned up too high or the sugar may burn)

- Remove the chicken from the heat and thin slice on the bias
- Arrange the chicken on a serving platter, pour the juices over the chicken and sprinkle with sesame seeds and green onions (or top a salad with the sliced chicken after topping with juices and seeds)

306.   Shortcut Chicken Manicotti Recipe

Serving: 4 | Prep: | Cook: 45mins | Ready in:

Ingredients

- 1 can (10-3/4 oz.) condensed cream of chicken soup
- 1-1/2 cups water
- 1/4 lb. (4 oz.) VELVEETA Pasteurized Prepared cheese Product, cut up
- 2 cups frozen broccoli florets
- 12 manicotti pasta, uncooked
- 1 lb. boneless skinless chicken breasts, cut into 1/2-inch strips
- 1/4 cup KRAFT 100% Grated parmesan cheese

Direction

- PREHEAT oven to 400°F. Mix soup, water and VELVEETA in microwaveable bowl. Microwave on HIGH 3 min. or until VELVEETA is melted and mixture is well blended, stirring after 2 min. Pour one-third of the soup mixture onto bottom of 13x9-inch baking dish; set aside. Add broccoli to remaining soup mixture.
- STUFF pasta with chicken strips; place in baking dish. Cover completely with remaining soup mixture. Sprinkle with Parmesan cheese. Cover with foil.
- BAKE 45 to 50 min. or until pasta is tender and chicken is cooked through.

307.   Simple Chicken Parmesan Companys Coming Recipe

Serving: 8 | Prep: | Cook: 20mins | Ready in:

Ingredients

- 8 medium chicken breasts or cut chicken pieces, about 1/2 inch thick
- 2 eggs, beaten
- 8 ounces shaved/grated parmesan cheese (can use Romano blend)
- 1 cup panko bread crumbs (optional)
- 2-4 T oil
- 16 ounces red pasta sauce (jarred is fine)
- salt, pepper, seasoning salt to taste

Direction

- Pat chicken dry and season w/ spices
- Place beaten eggs in shallow dish
- Place 1/3 of Parmesan and crumbs if using in a separate dish (add the rest as it is used up)
- Add oil to pan and heat over medium-high heat
- Dip the chicken in the egg, shake off excess and then dip in parmesan
- Fry chicken about 5 minutes each side in the oil
- Adjust heat if necessary
- Remove chicken from pan, may have to fry in batches
- Add red sauce to pan
- Place chicken back in pan and cook over medium-high heat for about 5 minutes
- Serve over whole pasta and enjoy!

308. Simple Curry Chicken And Rice Recipe

Serving: 1 | Prep: | Cook: 10mins | Ready in:

Ingredients

- 1/2 Cup of rice
- 1 Tablespoon of vegetable oil
- 1/2 a yellow onion
- 1 skinless chicken Breast
- 2 white mushrooms
- 1 Tablespoon of curry paste

Direction

- Fill pot with enough water to boil the rice, depending on the type of rice you use. I usually use Instant Rice because I'm a student in a hurry, so that ends up being the same amount of water than of rice. Bring this to a boil.
- In a pan, heat vegetable oil (canola, olive, whatever you want. I often like to cook it in chili oil) over medium heat.
- Dice yellow onions and throw in the pan.
- Sauté onions for a minute or so.
- While onions are sautéing, chop chicken breast into chunks. Throw them in the pan as well.
- Sauté chicken until it seems almost cooked, and the onions begin to brown.
- A bit before the chicken seems almost cooked, chop white mushrooms and throw them in.
- Add curry paste and cook for a few more minutes.
- Serve and enjoy!

309. Simple Lemon Chicken Recipe

Serving: 6 | Prep: | Cook: 12mins | Ready in:

Ingredients

- 6 medium chicken breast halves

- ¼ C flour
- ¼ tsp salt
- ¼ tsp pepper
- 1 Tbl butter
- 1Tbl EVOO
- 1 Cup chicken broth
- 3 Tbl flour
- ¼ C lemon juice
- 1 tsp sugar
- 2 Tbl chopped chives

Direction

- Rinse chicken and pat dry
- Combine ¼ c flour, salt and pepper in a plastic bag
- Add chicken pieces a couple at a time and shake to coat
- Cook chicken in butter and EVOO in large skillet over medium about 8 to 10 minutes, turning once
- Remove chicken, keep warm and reserve any drippings in skillet
- Whisk together broth and 3 Tbsp. flour until smooth; add to skillet
- Cook, stirring until thick and bubbly
- Cook one minute longer. Add lemon juice and sugar; heat through and serve over chicken

310. Singapore Chow Mein Recipe

Serving: 1 | Prep: | Cook: 10mins | Ready in:

Ingredients

- Thin noodles 136g
- Beansprouts 80g
- Diced onion 35g
- green pepper sliced 35g
- carrot sliced 35g
- Fresh chilli sliced 15g
- Small prawns 50g
- sliced chicken breast 50g (cooked)

- sliced pork 50g (cooked)
- Half medium sized egg beaten
- 1 teaspoon of hot curry paste, see link
- http://www.spicesofindia.co.uk/acatalog/indian-food-ferns-hot-curry-paste.html
- 1 teaspoon of salt and msg
- 1 tablespoon dark soy sauce
- 1 teaspoon white pepper

Direction

- Boiled the meats separately in water and drain.
- Heat wok to high.
- Add the egg in hot wok and all the vegetables and noodles.
- Stir fry for couple of minutes.
- Add the meats in wok.
- Stir fry again for about one minute.
- Add salt, msg, dark soy sauce and white pepper and stir fry for 2 minutes
- Add curry paste and stir fry in high heat until all ingredients are mixed evenly for another 2 minutes.
- Serve.

311. Singapore Noodles Recipe

Serving: 4 | Prep: | Cook: 30mins | Ready in:

Ingredients

- 250g pkg rice vermicelli
- 2 skinless boneless chicken breast
- 2 green onions
- 2 carrot
- 1 red pepper
- 2 tbsp of lime juice
- 1 tbsp soya sauce
- 1 tbsp water
- 2 tbsp veg oil
- 1 tsp bottled chopped garlic or 1 minced clove
- 1 tsp bottled chopped ginger or finely grated fresh
- 2 tsp yellow curry powder
- 1/2 tsp salt
- 1/2 tsp chopped fresh coriander (optional)

Direction

- Cook noodles and set them aside
- Cut chicken in half lengthwise and slice them into thin strips
- Slice onions into 1 inch pieces
- Slice carrots into thin julienne strips
- In a small bowl stir lime juice, soya sauce, water, and oil. Set aside
- Heat 1 tbsp. oil in wok over medium heat add chicken and stir fry until cooked
- Add carrot, pepper, onions garlic and ginger
- Sprinkle with curry powder and salt
- Add noodles then pour in lime mixture
- Stir often until noodles turn yellow
- Remove from heat and stir in coriander

312. Slow Cooker Cheater Chicken Cacciatore Recipe

Serving: 0 | Prep: | Cook: 8hours | Ready in:

Ingredients

- * 4-6 chicken breasts
- * 1-2 Cups hot salsa (or mild/medium if you want)
- * 1 taco seasoning package
- * 2-3 tbsp sour cream (added during the last hour)
- * 2 tsp corn starch (added to the sauce at the end to thicken)

Direction

- Add chicken breasts salsa and taco seasoning to slow cooker. Cook on low for 8 hours.

- During the last hour of cooking add sour cream and just before serving add cornstarch to thicken sauce

---

313.   Slow Cooker Chicken And Noodles Recipe

Serving: 6 | Prep: | Cook: 6mins | Ready in:

Ingredients

- 2 skinless, boneless chicken breast
- 4 cups water
- 1 onion, chopped
- 1 large carrot, chopped
- 2 stalks celery, chopped (optional)
- salt and pepper to taste
- 1 (12 ounce) package frozen egg noodles
- 1 tsp. thyme
- 1 tsp. dill weed

Direction

- Place chicken, water, onion, carrot, salt, pepper, thyme, and dill weed into a slow cooker. Add celery if desired.
- Set temperature to low and cook for 6 to 8 hours.
- When chicken is tender, remove from the slow cooker and tear or chop into bite-sized pieces. Set aside in a small casserole dish to keep warm.
- Turn the slow cooker up to high heat and stir in the frozen egg noodles.
- Cook until noodles are tender then return the chicken pieces to the broth.
- Adjust seasonings to taste.

---

314.   Sour Cream Baked Chicken Recipe

Serving: 4 | Prep: | Cook: | Ready in:

Ingredients

- 6 chicken breasts, split and boned
- 2 c. sour cream
- 1/4 c. lemon juice
- 2 tsp. salt
- 4 tsp. worcestershire sauce
- 3 tsp. garlic salt
- 1/2 tsp. paprika
- 1/2 tsp. pepper
- 1 c. bread crumbs
- 1/2 c. margarine, melted
- 1/2 c. butter, melted

Direction

- Rinse chicken breasts and pat dry. In bowl, combine sour cream, lemon juice and seasonings. Roll chicken breasts in sour cream mixture, place in bowl and top with any remaining sour cream. Cover; refrigerate overnight. Remove chicken breasts, taking up as much of sour cream mixture as possible. Roll chicken in bread crumbs to coat well. Place in baking dish.
- Mix margarine and butter; pour half the melted butter and margarine over chicken and bake at 350 degrees for 45 minutes. Pour remaining butter sauce over chicken and bake 5 minutes more.

---

315.   South Of The Border Chicken Sub Recipe

Serving: 6 | Prep: | Cook: 1hours | Ready in:

Ingredients

- 2lbs chicken tenders or chicken breasts, pounded out to fit sandwich rolls
- about 2T ancho or chipotle chili powder
- 1T ground cumin
- 1T ground coriander
- 2 limes
- about 1 cup salsa

- 1/2 cup guacamole
- 1/4 cup sour cream
- 1/4 cup mayo
- 8oz pepper jack cheese, sliced
- fresh cilantro
- kosher or sea salt and fresh ground pepper
- 6 sub style sandwich rolls(or similar)

Direction

- In small bowl, combine chili powder, cumin, coriander, a little salt and pepper.
- Sprinkle over one side of the chicken and the drizzle with the juice from the limes. Set aside for 30 minutes or refrigerate up to 8 hours.
- In medium bowl, combine salsa, guacamole, sour cream and mayo. Mix well and set aside.
- Grill chicken over medium high heat until done (165)
- Place a couple slices of cheese on the top side of each roll, then add the chicken.
- Build sammiches with the chicken, cheese, cilantro and the salsa mixture.
- You can also toss 'em back on the grill for a few seconds, to get all melty, if desired. :)

---

316.   Southern Smothered Chicken Recipe

Serving: 5 | Prep: | Cook: 270mins | Ready in:

Ingredients

- 5 boneless, skinless chicken breast halves (about 1 1/2 pounds)
- 1 package (8-oz.) pre-sliced fresh mushrooms
- 1 can (16-oz.) baby corn, drained (or frozen, thawed)
- 1 large vidalia onion, cut into 1/4-inch-think slices
- 2 cans condensed Creamy chicken Verde (Campbell's Southwest-style*)
- Fresh thyme
- cracked black pepper (optional)

Direction

- Trim fat from chicken; set aside.
- In a 4 to 5-quart slow cooker, combine mushrooms, corn, and onion and about a teaspoon of thyme. Place chicken on top of vegetables. Spoon soup over all.
- Cover and cook on LOW heat setting for 4 to 5 hours.
- Plate chicken breasts and spoon remaining gravy mixture on top of the chicken.
- Serve with thyme and cracked pepper. A nostalgic taste of the southern past!

---

317.   Southwest Chicken Stew Recipe

Serving: 8 | Prep: | Cook: 80mins | Ready in:

Ingredients

- 2 lbs boneless,skinless chicken(breast or thigh or both)
- 1 TB canola oil
- 2 c chopped onions
- 1 c chopped green pepper or red bell pepper
- 2 cloves garlic,minced
- 1 TB chili powder
- 1/2 tsp dried oregano
- 3 c cubed potatoes
- 14.5 oz can chicken broth
- 14.5 oz can diced tomatoes
- 15 oz can yellow corn,drained
- 1/4 c fresh cilantro or parsley

Direction

- Cut chicken into bite-size pieces. Heat oil in a Dutch oven and brown chicken over med-high heat.
- Add onions, green pepper and garlic and sauté 3 mins.
- Add chili powder, oregano, potatoes and chicken broth. Cover and cook over med-low heat for 45 mins or till potatoes are tender.

- Add tomatoes, corn and cilantro. Cover and cook 10 mins till heated through.

318. Southwestern Chicken Recipe

Serving: 8 | Prep: | Cook: 10mins | Ready in:

Ingredients

- for the marinade:
- 1/2 C fresh lime juice
- 6 Tbsp. soy sauce
- 1/4 C. vegetable oil
- 2 Tbsp. sugar
- 2 Tbsp. chopped fresh oregano
- 1 Tbsp. chopped fresh rosemary
- 1 Tbsp. minced garlic
- 1 1/2 tsp. chili powder
- 1/2 tsp. cayenne pepper
- 8 skinless boneless chicken breast halves
- for the ancho chili sauce:
- 3 dried ancho chilies, stemmed, seeded, torn into pieces
- 2 Tbsp. fresh lime juice
- 1/2 C. mayonnaise
- 2 Tbsp. brown sugar
- 1 Tbsp. chopped fresh oregano
- 1 tsp. chopped fresh rosemary
- 1/2 tsp. ground cumin

Direction

- Marinate the chicken:
- Combine all the marinade ingredients (except the chicken) in a clean empty jar. Put the lid on, and shake vigorously to mix.
- Trim the chicken breasts and remove the tenders. If desired, pound flat with a meat tenderizer.
- Place the chicken in 1 layer in a casserole dish. (Use 2 if necessary.)

- Pour the marinade over to cover. Turn the chicken to make sure all surfaces are coated with sauce.
- Cover with plastic, and marinate at room temperature for 4 hours or in the refrigerator overnight.
- Refrigerate any remaining marinade for another use.
- If the chicken has been refrigerated, bring it to room temperature about 1 hour before cooking.
- Make the Ancho chili sauce:
- Cover the chilies with hot water. Soak for 30 minutes, or until soft. The chilies should be dark red. Drain, reserving approximately 3 Tbsp. of soaking water.
- Puree chilies, soaking water, and lime juice in a blender until smooth. Scrape into a small bowl.
- Whisk in mayonnaise, brown sugar, oregano, rosemary, and cumin.
- Cover and refrigerate, if desired. The sauce can be made a day ahead.
- Grill the chicken:
- Over medium-high heat, grill the chicken until done, approximately 10 minutes.
- If no grill is available, the chicken breasts can be sautéed in a skillet with a tablespoon of oil.
- Serve the chicken with the Ancho chili sauce spooned over.

319. Southwestern Shells With Chicken And Corn Recipe

Serving: 6 | Prep: | Cook: 25mins | Ready in:

Ingredients

- 12 oz. Sea Shells pasta
- 1 tbsp. olive oil
- 1/2 lb. boneless skinless chicken breasts, cut into half-inch
- strips
- 1 tbsp. flour

- 1 1/2 c. whole milk
- 2 c. (8 oz.) shredded monterey jack cheese, divided
- 1 1/2 c. frozen corn, thawed and drained
- 1/2 c. thick and chunky salsa
- 1 can (4 oz.) chopped green chilies (opt.)

Direction

- Preheat oven to 350 degrees.
- Cook and drain pasta according to package directions.
- Heat olive oil in a large skillet over medium high heat.
- Cook chicken until lightly browned.
- Sprinkle with flour and stir while cooking for 1 more minute.
- Reduce the heat, slowly add the milk and cook for about 5 minutes or until milk is slightly thickened.
- Remove from heat; add 1 c. cheese, corn, salsa, and green chilies.
- Add in hot pasta and mix well.
- Place in lightly greased baking dish.
- Sprinkle with remaining cheese on top and bake for 20 to 25 minutes.

320.   Spaghetti Squash And Chicken Skillet Casserole Recipe

Serving: 4 | Prep: | Cook: 35mins | Ready in:

Ingredients

- 3 Tb butter
- 1 c Sliced fresh mushrooms
- 1/3 c Chopped leeks
- 1/4 c Chopped celery
- 3 Tb Chopped sweet red pepper
- 3 Tb Finely chopped fresh parsley
- 2 c cooked spaghetti squash
- 4 Boneless chicken breasts, cooked and cut into thin strips

- 1/4 c Crushed seasoned croutons
- 1/4 tsp salt
- 1/4 tsp seasoned pepper
- 1/8 tsp garlic powder
- Pinch of dried summer savory
- 1/2 c sour cream
- 2 oz Shredded swiss cheese (1/2 cup)

Direction

- Melt butter in a large skillet over medium heat. Add mushrooms and next 4 ingredients. Cook, stirring constantly for 5 minutes or until tender.
- Add spaghetti squash and next 6 ingredients, cook 4 minutes, stirring constantly.
- Stir in sour cream, cook, stirring constantly, just until thoroughly heated. Remove from heat.
- Sprinkle with cheese. Cover and let stand for 1 minute.
- To bake, prepare mixture according to directions and spoon into a lightly greased 1.5 quart casserole dish. Cover and bake at 350 for 20-25 minutes.

321.   Spicey Garlic Lime Chicken Recipe

Serving: 4 | Prep: | Cook: 20mins | Ready in:

Ingredients

- 3/4 teaspoon salt
- 1/4 teaspoon black pepper
- 1/4 teaspoon cayenne pepper
- 1/8 teaspoon paprika
- 1/4 teaspoon garlic powder
- 1/8 teaspoon onion powder
- 1/4 teaspoon dried thyme
- 1/4 teaspoon dried parsley
- 4 boneless, skinless chicken breast halves
- 2 tablespoons butter
- 1 tablespoon olive oil

- 2 teaspoons garlic powder
- the juice of one lime

Direction

- In a small bowl, mix together salt, black pepper, cayenne, paprika, 1/4 teaspoon garlic powder, onion powder, thyme and parsley.
- Sprinkle spice mixture generously on both sides of chicken breasts.
- Heat butter and olive oil in a large heavy skillet over medium heat. Sauté chicken until golden brown, about 6 minutes on each side. Sprinkle with 2 teaspoons garlic powder and lime juice.
- Cook 5 minutes, stirring frequently to coat evenly with sauce.

322.   Spinach Fettuccine Primavera Rachel Ray Recipe Recipe

Serving: 6 | Prep: | Cook: 15mins | Ready in:

Ingredients

- 1 lb spinach fettuccine
- 2 peeled carrots
- 2 Medium zucchini
- 2 tbsp extra virgin olive oil
- 2 tbsp butter
- 2 Scallots, thinly sliced (or 1 medium onion)
- 2 gloves garlic, minced
- 1 c frozen peas
- 1/2 c dry white wine
- 1 c vegetable or chicken stock
- Freshly ground pepper
- salt
- 1/2 c grated parmigiano Reggiano cheese
- 1/4 c chopped flat-leaf parsley
- 1 cooked chicken breast, shredded (optional)

Direction

- Bring water for pasta to a boil

- Salt water and add pasta, cook al dente (firm but not hard), about 7 to 8 minutes
- Use vegetable peeler to make ribbons of carrot and zucchini (do not remove skin from zucchini, just top and bottom cut off) Kepp teggies flat on counter and run the peeler the length of the veggie
- Drop ribbons into pasta water for the last 4 minutes.
- Heat large skillet over medium heat with oil and butter
- Sauté shallots and garlic (3-4 mins) then add peas and heat through (2 mins)
- Stir in wine and reduce for 1/2 a min
- Add stock
- Toss in Chicken Breast (optional)
- Toss drained pasta and veggies with sauce, season with salt and pepper and combine with cheese and parsley

323.   Spinach Fettuccine With Chicken And Pesto Recipe

Serving: 6 | Prep: | Cook: 15mins | Ready in:

Ingredients

- 3/4 lb. spinach fettuccine, hot cooked
- 1 cup heavy cream
- 1 cup unsalted butter, cut into pieces
- 3/4 cup grated parmesan cheese
- 2-3 Tbsp. cooking oil
- 4 boneless, skinless chicken breast halves, cut into bite-size pieces
- 4 Tbsp. pesto
- salt and pepper, to taste

Direction

- In a medium heavy saucepan, heat cream over medium heat. Add butter and stir until melted. Gradually add Parmesan cheese and stir until melted. Reduce heat to low and keep sauce warm.

- Heat oil in a large skillet over medium heat. Add chicken and stir until chicken is completely cooked, about 3-4 minutes. Transfer to a bowl, using a slotted spoon. Mix in 1 Tbsp. pesto.
- Toss hot cooked fettuccine with remaining pesto and cheese sauce. Arrange pasta on a platter. Spoon chicken over and season with salt and pepper. Serve immediately. Pass additional grated Parmesan cheese.

324. Spinach Stuffed Chicken Breasts For Two Recipe

Serving: 2 | Prep: | Cook: 1hours |Ready in:

Ingredients

- 1/4 cup water
- 2 Tbsp. roasted red pepper Italian with Parmesan Dressing, divided
- 1 cup chopped frozen spinach thawed and squeeze out excess water
- 1/2 cup onion and garlic crutons crushed
- 2 Tbsp. coarsely chopped red peppers
- 1 Tablespoon finely chopped onion
- 2 slices bacon fried crisp and crumbled
- 2 small boneless skinless chicken breast halves (1/2 lb.), pounded to 1/4-inch thickness
- 1/4 cup Shredded mozzarella cheese or feta cheese

Direction

- HEAT oven to 350°F.
- BRING water and 1 Tbsp. dressing to boil in large skillet on medium-high heat.
- Stir in spinach, stuffing mix, onion and peppers; cover.
- Remove from heat. Let stand 5 min.
- Then add bacon.
- PLACE chicken, top-sides down, on cutting board; spread with stuffing mixture.
- Roll up, starting at one short end of each breast.

- Place, seam-sides down, in 8-inch square baking dish; brush with remaining dressing.
- BAKE 35 min. or until chicken is done (165ºF).
- Top with cheese; bake 5 min. or until melted.

325. Squash Stuffed Chicken Breast Recipe

Serving: 4 | Prep: | Cook: 30mins |Ready in:

Ingredients

- 1 tablespoon butter
- 1/2 cup finely diced acorn squash
- 1 green bell pepper, diced
- 1 small onion, finely diced
- 1 stalk celery, chopped
- salt and pepper to taste
- 4 skinless, boneless chicken breasts
- 2 ounces shredded cheddar cheese
- 2 cups all-purpose flour for coating

Direction

- Preheat oven to 350 degrees F.
- Lightly grease a 9x13 inch baking dish.
- In a medium skillet, melt butter or margarine.
- Add the squash, green bell pepper, onion and celery.
- Sauté until slightly tender.
- Season to taste with salt and pepper.
- Remove from heat, add cheese and mix together.
- Slice chicken breasts on the side about 3/4 of the way through.
- Stuff mixture evenly into each slit chicken breast until full.
- Dredge each breast in flour to coat completely, and brown coated chicken in skillet.
- Place browned chicken breasts in the prepared baking dish, cover and bake in the preheated oven for about 30 minutes or until chicken is cooked through and juices run clear.

326. Stove Top Easy Chicken Bake Recipe

Serving: 4 | Prep: | Cook: 40mins | Ready in:

Ingredients

- 1 cup hot water
- 1 pkg. STOVE TOP Lower Sodium Stuffing Mix for chicken
- 1 lb. (450 g) boneless skinless chicken breasts, cut into bite-size pieces
- 1 can condensed cream of chicken soup
- 1/3 cup sour cream
- 3 cups frozen mixed vegetables, thawed, drained

Direction

- Heat oven to 400°F.
- Add hot water to stuffing mix; stir just until moistened. Set aside.
- Mix chicken, soup, sour cream and vegetables in 13x9-inch baking dish; top with stuffing.
- Bake 30 min. or until chicken is cooked through.

327. Stovetop Barbecued Chicken Recipe

Serving: 4 | Prep: | Cook: 20mins | Ready in:

Ingredients

- 4 boneless, skinless chicken breast halves
- cooking spray
- 1 small onion
- 1 can chicken broth
- 1 1/2 cups instant (5-minute) rice, uncooked
- 1/4 cup ketchup
- 1 T light or dark brown sugar, firmly packed
- 1 T lemon juice
- 1 T white vinegar (or cider vinegar)

- 1 tsp worcestershire sauce
- 1 tsp garlic powder
- 1/2 tsp onion powder
- 1/2 tsp dry mustard powder (or 1 tsp prepared mustard)
- black pepper to taste
- 1 cup frozen green peas

Direction

- Spray a large nonstick skillet with cooking spray, and heat over medium heat.
- Peel and coarsely chop the onion, adding it to the pan as you chop. Let cook, stirring frequently.
- Slice each breast into strips 3/4 inch wide. Add to the skillet as you slice.
- Raise the heat to high and add the broth and rice (doesn't matter if the chicken hasn't browned.)
- Stir well and bring to a boil, meanwhile adding the barbeque seasonings (ketchup, brown sugar, lemon juice, vinegar, Worcestershire, garlic & onion powders, mustard, and pepper.). Stir well, and cover.
- When the broth boils, reduce heat to medium-high and cook for 4 minutes.
- Uncover and stir in the peas, then re-cover and continue to cook until almost all the broth is absorbed and the rice is tender, about 3 minutes more.

328. Straw Hats Recipe

Serving: 10 | Prep: | Cook: 30mins | Ready in:

Ingredients

- 1 pound chicken breasts, boneless and skinless
- 1 pound lean ground beef, I use 97 percent lean ground beef
- ½ cup chopped onion, perhaps omit the onions if only kids are being served
- 1 pound cooked pulled pork, homemade is best and it shouldn't be spicy *

162

- 1 package of taco seasoning, divided
- 15 ounce can of black beans
- 2 cups shredded cheddar cheese
- Fritos Scoops® corn chips, a large bag
- tomatoes, diced
- black olives, sliced
- avocados, sliced
- lettuce, shredded, I use hearts of romaine lettuce
- salsa
- sour cream
- Catalina dressing

Direction

- Preheat an oven to 200°F.
- Cut the chicken into strips then sauté them in a little olive oil till almost done. Add ½ of the taco seasoning, some water and simmer for 5 minutes. Remove from the skillet and place it on a warm plate, shred the chicken and cover with foil. Place it in the oven to hold warm.
- Using the same skillet, sauté the ground beef and the onions over med-low heat till there's only a bit of pink in the meat. Crumble the meat with a spatula as it cooks. Add the remaining ½ of the taco seasoning, some water and simmer for 5 minutes. Remove from the skillet and place it on a warm plate, cover with foil and place it in the oven to hold warm.
- Warm up the pulled pork in a small pot over the stovetop. At the same time warm up the black beans in another small pot over the stovetop and hold warm.
- Set up a taco bar type of arrangement with all of the meats in separate containers, the beans left in the pot and the rest of the 'add on' ingredients in their separate containers.
- *See my recipe for pulled pork on this website. It's called "Dale's Pulled Pork".

---

329.   Stuffed Chicken Chop Recipe

Serving: 4 | Prep: | Cook: 20mins |Ready in:

Ingredients

- 1 beaten egg
- 1/2 cup milk
- 4 boneless skinless chicken breasts
- 1 1-2 cups seasoned bread crumbs
- 2/3 cups grated parmesan cheese
- 1 tsp. seasoned salt
- 1/2 cup seasoned flour
- 1 1/2 cups sliced fresh mushrooms or 1 can sliced, drained mushrooms
- 4 slices of bacon, diced
- 1/4 cup chopped onions
- 1/2 tsp. minced garlic
- 1 pkg. softened cream cheese
- 1 tsp. minced, fresh dill
- 1/2 tsp. dried rosemary
- 1/2 tsp. dried oregano
- 1/4 tsp. coarse salt
- 1/8 tsp. fresh cracked black pepper
- bacon drippings

Direction

- *Preheat oven to 450 degrees F.
- *Flatten chicken breasts and lightly pound to an equal consistency. Cover and set aside.
- *Mix milk and eggs together, set aside.
- *Fry bacon pieces until just crisp and remove from the pan. Add the onion, garlic and mushroom to the pan and heat until browned. Set aside.
- *Put fresh herbs into food processor, chop finely. Change to dough blade and add softened cream cheese. Mix together. Remove mixture to a bowl and add bacon, onion, garlic, mushrooms, pepper and parmesan cheese. Mix until blended and creamy, set aside.
- *Put approximately 1 tsp. cheese mixture on the chicken breast and fold lengthwise.

- *Dip in milk and egg mixture, flour and bread crumbs.
- *Place in bacon drippings in the frying pan for approximately 4 minutes per side.
- *Move to vented oven rack and bake 20 minutes or until cooked throughout.

330.   Stuffing Stuffed Chicken Recipe

Serving: 4 | Prep: | Cook: 1hours30mins | Ready in:

Ingredients

- 1box stove top stuffing (i used the apple flavored one)
- 4 boneless chicken breasts
- seasoning salt
- 1 can cream of chicken soup
- 1/2c white cooking wine

Direction

- Preheat oven to 350
- Prepare stuffing according to package directions
- Spoon stuffing out into four separate mounds on a baking dish
- Place a chicken breast on each mound, making sure the breast is pulled out across the mound
- Sprinkle with some seasoning salt
- Bake for 45 min
- Mix soup and wine in a bowl
- Spread over top of chicken breasts
- Bake an additional 30 to 45 mins

331.   Summer Sandwich Recipe

Serving: 4 | Prep: | Cook: 20mins | Ready in:

Ingredients

- 1/4 cup mayonnaise or salad dressing
- 2 tablespoons pesto
- 1 loaf (12 oz.) focaccia bread, split
- 2 small boneless skinless chicken breast halves (1/2 lb.), grilled, sliced
- 4 Provolone cheese slices
- 3/4 cup roasted red peppers
- 1 jar (6 oz.) artichoke hearts, drained, thinly sliced
- 1 cup mesclun salad greens

Direction

- Mix mayo and pesto until well blended; spread evenly onto cut sides of bread. Cover bottom half of bread with remaining ingredients and top half of bread. Cut into four wedges to serve. Makes 4 servings, one wedge each grilled chicken breasts sliced
- Mesclun greens are a unique combination of salad greens consisting of mild leaf lettuce, bitter radicchio, escarole and curly endive, with hints of peppery arugula or watercress.

332.   Super Easy Stove Top Chicken Rice Casserole Recipe

Serving: 4 | Prep: | Cook: 40mins | Ready in:

Ingredients

- 2 cups water
- 1 cup rice
- 1 pound ground chicken breast or thigh
- 1 can cream of chicken soup (or cream of mushroom, etc.)
- 1 packet Lipton onion soup

Direction

- In a pot, bring two cups of water to a boil
- Add chicken, break apart with a fork, and cook thoroughly until water is boiling again
- Mix the cream of chicken soup and Lipton onion soup, add to boiling water and chicken

- Add rice to the boiling soup and chicken
- Stir all ingredients thoroughly, cover, and simmer for 20 minutes (or until rice is soft)
- Remove from heat and serve

minute). Add peppers and carrots. Stir 2-3 minutes. Add peas and sauce. Cook until it comes to a boil. Add cashews and serve immediately.

333. Sweet Spicy Cashew Chicken Recipe

Serving: 6 | Prep: | Cook: 3mins | Ready in:

Ingredients

- Sauce:
- 1/2 c ketchup
- 4 T soya sauce
- 1/2 tsp. salt
- 2 T worstershire sauce
- 3 T sugar
- 1 1/2 tsp. sesame oil
- 1/4 tsp cayenne
- 1/2 c chicken broth
- The Rest:
- 2 T cornstarch
- 1/2 tsp. sugar
- 1/4 tsp salt
- 3 whole boneless chicken breasts, skinned & cut into 3/4" pieces
- 1/4 c oil
- 2-3 T minced fresh gingeroot
- 1 T minced garlic
- 1 sm. onion chopped
- 2 red bell peppers - cut into 1" triangles
- 2 carrots, sliced diagonally and thinly
- 2 c snow peas
- 1 1/2 c cashews

Direction

- Combine sauce ingredients and set aside. In a bowl, combine cornstarch, sugar and salt. Add chicken and toss. Heat wok or frying pan to highest heat. Add oil. Heat to hot, not smoking. Add chicken, ginger, garlic and onion. Stir until chicken is opaque (about 1

334. Sweet N Sour Chicken Recipe

Serving: 4 | Prep: | Cook: 10mins | Ready in:

Ingredients

- 2 ea 8 oz cans pineapple chunks, juice drained and reserved
- 2 tb cooking oil
- 1 ea green pepper, cut into 1 inch squares
- 1 ea onion, cut into thin wedges
- 1 clove garlic, minced
- 1 lb boneless chicken breast, cubed
- 2 tb cornstarch
- 1/2 c Karo light corn syrup
- 1/4 c cider vinegar
- 3 tb soy sauce
- 2 tb catsup

Direction

- Drain the pineapple, reserving the juice. In a large skillet, heat the oil over a medium high heat. Add the green pepper, onion, and garlic. Stir fry for 2 minutes. Remove.
- Stir fry the chicken and lightly cook until it is white through and through.
- Return the pineapple, green pepper, onion and garlic to skillet.
- Add the cornstarch to the reserved pineapple juice. Add to skillet. Add corn syrup, cider vinegar, soy sauce, and catsup. Bring to a boil and cook for 2 minutes.
- Serve over cooked white rice.

335. Sweet Amp Tangy Chicken Strips Recipe

Serving: 4 | Prep: | Cook: 20mins | Ready in:

Ingredients

- 4 skinless boneless chicken breasts
- 1/2 Cup of Kellog's frosted Flakes - Crushed
- 1/4 Cup of VH plum sauce
- Pinch of salt & pepper

Direction

- Turn on oven to 450 degrees.
- Cut Chicken into Strips.
- Put Strips into Lg zip lock bag or med size plastic container.
- Pour 1/4 cup of Plum Sauce in covering all chicken with sauce.
- Crush 1/2 Cup of Frosted Flakes and put in a separate container.
- Add a pinch each of Salt & Pepper to the Frosted Flakes.
- Place each Strip into the Flakes mixture, turning over to ensure all sides are covered in flakes.
- Place on a (tin foiled & sprayed) Baking sheet
- Bake on 2nd highest shelf in oven for 15-20 mins

336. Swiss Chicken Casserole In The Crock Pot Recipe

Serving: 6 | Prep: | Cook: 3mins | Ready in:

Ingredients

- 6 boneless skinless chicken breasts
- 6 slices swiss cheese
- 1 can cream of mushroom soup
- 1/4 cup milk
- 2 cups stuffing mix
- 1/2 cup butter melted

Direction

- Lightly grease slow cooker or spray with cooking spray.
- Place chicken breasts cooker then top with cheese.
- Combine soup and milk stirring well.
- Spoon over cheese then sprinkle with stuffing mix.
- Drizzle melted butter over stuffing mix then cook on low for 10 hours.

337. Swiss Chicken Divan Recipe

Serving: 8 | Prep: | Cook: 45mins | Ready in:

Ingredients

- 1 (16 ounce) and 1 (10 ounce) packages frozen broccoli florets, thawed
- 8 boneless skinless chicken breast halves
- 8 slices swiss cheese
- 8 slices boiled ham
- 2 cans cream of chicken soup
- 1 1/2 cups sour cream
- 3/4 cup white wine
- 1/2 teaspoon salt, or to taste
- 1/4 teaspoon ground black pepper
- 1/2 teaspoon garlic powder
- seasoned stuffing mix

Direction

- In greased 13x9 inch baking pan, layer with thawed broccoli.
- Arrange chicken breasts on top of broccoli.
- Top each chicken breast with a slice of cheese followed by a slice of ham.
- Whisk together soup, sour cream, wine, salt, pepper and garlic powder.
- Spoon over chicken.
- Cover with foil and bake at 400 degrees for 25 to 30 minutes.
- Uncover and sprinkle with stuffing mix.

- Return, uncovered, to oven and bake 15 minutes or until chicken juices run clear and crumbs are lightly browned.

338. Szechuan Orange Ginger Chicken Recipe

Serving: 4 | Prep: | Cook: 10mins | Ready in:

Ingredients

- 4 boneless, skinless chicken breasts, in chunks
- 1 green pepper, in chunks
- 1 red pepper, in chunks
- 1/2 cooking onion, in chunks
- 1 orange
- 1 tsp. bottled chili paste
- 2 tbsp. sherry or mirin
- 1 tsp. granulated sugar
- 1 tsp. cornstarch
- 2 tbsp. peanut or sesame oil
- 1 tsp. minced garlic
- 1 tbsp. minced ginger

Direction

- Cut chicken, onion and peppers into one inch squares. Using a vegetable peeler, removed the peel from the orange, including the white. Cut rind into thin julienne strips about 1 1/2 inches long; set aside. Squeeze orange and reserve 1/4 cup juice.
- In small bowl combine reserved orange juice, chili paste, sherry or mirin, sugar and cornstarch; stir until smooth.
- In wok, heat oil over high heat, add chicken and onions and stir-fry for 2 minutes or until chicken is no longer pink. Remove. Add orange rind, garlic and ginger; stir-fry for 10 seconds. Add pepper and stir-fry for 1 minute. Add chili paste mixture and bring to a boil. Return chicken and onion to wok and stir until heated through.

339. Tandoori Chicken With Yogurt Sauce Recipe

Serving: 4 | Prep: | Cook: 30mins | Ready in:

Ingredients

- 1 1/2 cups plain low-fat yogurt, DIVIDED (I use Greek yogurt)
- 4 garlic cloves, minced
- 2 teaspoon ground turmeric
- 2 teaspoon ground ginger
- coarse salt and ground pepper
- 4 bone-in, skinless chicken breasts halves (10 to 12 ounces each) **(I used 8 boneless, skinless thighs)
- 2 granny smith apples
- 1 tablespoon chopped fresh cilantro

Direction

- Preheat oven to 475° (I cooked the thighs at 425 for 30 minutes).
- In a bowl or large zip top bag, mix 1 cup yogurt, the garlic, turmeric, ginger and 3 tsp. salt and 1/2 tsp. pepper. Add the chicken, making sure to coat it all evenly. Marinate for a couple hours or overnight.
- Transfer chicken to a rimmed baking sheet.
- Bake until 160 degrees or the juices are no longer pink, about 30 minutes.
- Peel and coarsely grate the apple into a bowl.
- Add the remaining 1/2 cup yogurt and cilantro, mix well, and serve with the chicken.

340. Teriyaki Chicken Burgers With Swiss, Bacon & Pineapple Recipe

Serving: 4 | Prep: | Cook: 30mins | Ready in:

Ingredients

- 4 regular sized brioche buns, toasted (click on recipe link) buns-for-sliders.html">Miniature Brioche buns For Sliders
- ~
- 4 organic chicken breast halves, boneless and skinless
- 1 clove garlic
- fresh ginger, peeled, 1 inch piece
- 1/2 cup soy sauce
- splash of mirin
- granulated sugar, to taste
- splash of water
- splash of canola oil
- ~
- honey-Dijon Mayo:
- 1/4 cup best foods mayo
- 1 tablespoon Dijon mustard
- organic honey, to taste
- ~
- 6 pieces cooked applewood smoked bacon, cut in half
- 4 slices swiss cheese
- 4 lettuce leaves
- 1 large avocado, thinly sliced
- fresh pineapple, slice into thin spears (2-3 per burger)

Direction

- Mix all ingredients for honey-Dijon mayo and keep in fridge until ready to use.
- Slightly pound each chicken breast to thin them out, if needed. Place chicken in plastic bag along with all teriyaki marinade ingredients. Close bag and shake well. Let marinate in fridge for at least one hour.
- Heat oven to broil. Broil chicken for about 5 minutes on each side. Place hot broiled chicken on plate, covering each breast with a slice of cheese cover with foil to rest (make sure foil does not touch the cheese). Place pineapple on same pan used to broil chicken and broil for about 5 minutes, or until caramelized. Add bacon strips to pan and broil just enough to reheat.
- To Assemble:

- Spread honey-Dijon mayo on both sides of toasted bun. Place chicken topped with cheese on bottom half of bun. Top with bacon, pineapple, and lettuce leaf. Press avocado slices onto top half of bun and close the burger. Slice in half and serve.

---

341.   Teriyaki Chicken Recipe

Serving: 4 | Prep: | Cook: 15mins | Ready in:

Ingredients

- 1/4 c sesame seeds
- 6 tsp salt reduced soy sauce
- 6 tsp honey
- 1 tsp sesame oil(optional)
- 1 tsp ginger
- 1 clove garlic crushed
- 1/4 tsp ground pepper
- 4 skinless chicken breast fillets, cut into small chunks
- spring onions for garnish

Direction

- In a medium bowl, combine the sesame seeds, soy sauce, honey, sesame oil, ginger and pepper. Mix well and set aside 2 Tbsps. of marinade
- Add chicken to the remaining marinade in the bowl and stir to coat.
- Cover bowl with clear plastic wrap and refrigerate for 30 mins or overnight.
- Preheat the grill to hot
- Remove the chicken from the marinade and place on the rack of the grill pan (or just in a dish)
- Grill chicken until no longer pink in the middle or until juices run clear roughly about 12-15 mins (baste chicken with reserved marinade and turn only once)
- Garnish with spring onions and serve immediately

342. Thai Chicken Curry With Sweet Potato And Spinach Recipe

Serving: 4 | Prep: | Cook: 10mins | Ready in:

Ingredients

- 1 tablespoon neutral vegetable oil (I use grapeseed oil)
- 1 medium yellow onion, diced
- 1 cup low-sodium or homemade chicken broth
- 1 (14-ounce) can light coconut milk
- 2 tablespoons fish sauce
- 1 tablespoon brown sugar
- 2 teaspoons (or to taste) red curry paste
- 1 teaspoon Sriracha hot chili sauce, or to taste
- 1 large sweet potato, peeled and diced into 1/2 inch cubes
- 12 ounces boneless skinless chicken breasts, sliced about 1/4 inch thick
- 5 ounces fresh baby spinach leaves

Direction

- Heat the oil in a skillet. Add the onion and sauté until tender. Add the stock, coconut milk, fish sauce and brown sugar. Bring to a simmer, add the curry paste and stir until it dissolves.
- Add the sweet potato and simmer for 10 minutes, or until almost tender. Add the chicken, cook 3 - 4 minutes. Stir in the spinach and cook until it just wilts.
- Per Serving: 260 Calories; 12g Fat; 26g Protein; 18g Carbohydrate; 2g Dietary Fiber; 50mg Cholesterol; 125mg Sodium.

343. Thai Peanut Chicken Salad Recipe

Serving: 6 | Prep: | Cook: 15mins | Ready in:

Ingredients

- With so many ways to kick up the flavor of chicken salad, why do so many recipes still produce a sloppy, stodgy mess of mayo and underseasoned chicken? Here's what we discovered:
- Test Kitchen Discoveries
- A whole roasted chicken produced better flavor than the poached chicken most recipes require, but the lengthy cooking time was a turn-off. We found sautéed boneless, skinless chicken breasts to be every bit as tasty as the roasted chicken—and required just a few minutes of cooking time.
- To create four distinctly flavored salads, we replaced some of the mayonnaise with a more flavorful and equally creamy ingredient, such as blue cheese dressing, peanut butter, or sour cream.
- To lighten the texture of the dressings, we added a potent liquid, such as hot sauce or soy sauce. Our revamped dressings were less thick—and didn't weigh the chicken down.

Direction

- Serve wrapped in lavash bread or a tortilla. Use more or less jalapeno as desired.
- 1/2 cup mayonnaise
- 1/4 cup chopped fresh cilantro leaves
- 2 tablespoons peanut butter
- 1 tablespoon soy sauce
- 1 tablespoon lime juice
- 2 teaspoons grated fresh ginger
- 1 red bell pepper, seeded and sliced thin
- 1 - 2 jalapeño chilies, seeded and minced
- 5 cups cooked boneless, skinless chicken breast
- Salt and pepper
- Combine mayonnaise, cilantro, peanut butter, soy sauce, lime juice, ginger, bell pepper, and jalapeno in large bowl. Add chicken and toss until coated. Season with salt and pepper. Serve or cover and refrigerate for up to 2 days.

344. Thai Style Stir Fried Chicken Recipe

Serving: 4 | Prep: | Cook: 10mins | Ready in:

Ingredients

- 1/4 cup rice vinegar
- 2 tablespoons brown sugar
- 2 tablespoons fresh lime juice
- 2 teaspoons red curry paste
- 1/8 teaspoon crushed red pepper
- 1 pound skinless, boneless chicken breast, cut into bite-sized pieces
- 1 1/2 tablespoons vegetable oil, divided
- 1 cup chopped onion
- 1 cup chopped carrot
- 1 (8-ounce) package presliced mushrooms
- 1/2 cup light coconut milk
- 1 tablespoon fish sauce
- 1/2 teaspoon salt
- 1 cup fresh bean sprouts
- 1/4 cup chopped fresh cilantro

Direction

- Combine rice vinegar, brown sugar, lime juice, red curry paste, and crushed red pepper in a large zip-top plastic bag. Add chicken; seal and marinate in refrigerator 15 minutes, turning once.
- Remove chicken from the bag, reserving marinade. Heat 1 tablespoon oil in a large non-stick skillet or wok over medium-high heat. Add chicken; stir-fry 4 minutes. Remove chicken from pan; keep warm. Add remaining 1 1/2 teaspoons oil to pan. Add onion and carrot; stir-fry 2 minutes. Add mushrooms; stir-fry 3 minutes. Add reserved marinade, scraping pan to loosen browned bits. Add coconut milk and fish sauce; bring to a boil. Reduce heat, and simmer 1 minute. Stir in chicken and salt; cook 1 minute. Top with sprouts and cilantro.

345. The New Chicken Le Cordon Bleu Recipe

Serving: 4 | Prep: | Cook: 20mins | Ready in:

Ingredients

- 4 boneless, skinless chicken breasts
- 4 thin slices Black Forest or Westphalian ham or other smoky dry ham, cut into 2-inch x 4-inch pieces
- 4 slices gruyere cheese, cut into 2-inch x 4-inch pieces
- 1 dash salt
- 1 dash pepper
- 1/2 cup chopped fresh parsley
- 1/2 cup chopped fresh rosemary
- 1/2 cup chopped fresh sage
- 2 tablespoons olive oil

Direction

- Gently pound chicken breasts, one at a time, between sheets of waxed paper or parchment paper with a rubber or wood mallet or the side of an empty wine bottle until they are very thin 1/4-inch thick and about 5 inches wide and 7 inches long.
- Season the top of each piece of chicken with salt and pepper.
- Lay a slice of ham and a slice of cheese horizontally along the bottom half of each breast, fold a 1/2-inch strip of each side inward and then fold the top over to enclose the filling completely.
- Mix the parsley, rosemary and sage together in a wide shallow bowl or pie plate.
- One at a time, put a filled chicken breast in the herb mixture, press to adhere as many herbs as you can, then turn and coat the other side with herbs.
- Coat all the breasts with herbs and set them on a plate until ready to cook.
- At this point they can be covered with plastic wrap and stored in the refrigerator for up to 24 hours.

- Heat oil in a large skillet or sauté pan over medium-high heat. Season the herbed, stuffed breasts with salt and pepper.
- When oil is hot, carefully lower chicken into pan, reduce heat to medium and cook, uncovered, until the underside is a deep brown color, about 5 to 6 minutes. Turn the chicken over and cook on the other side until well browned and the chicken is cooked through, another 5 to 6 minutes.
- Transfer the chicken to a warm platter and serve hot.

346. Thick And Hearty Chicken And Chorizo Chili Recipe

Serving: 10 | Prep: | Cook: 40mins | Ready in:

Ingredients

- 1/2 cup corn or veg. oil
- 1 very large or 2 med. white or yellow onion, diced
- 1 red bell pepper, diced
- 1 yellow bell pepper, diced
- 1 green bell pepper, diced
- 1/3 cup parsely, chopped
- 2 pounds boneless,skinless chicken breasts, cut into1/2" pieces
- 1/8 cup of chili powder
- 1/2 Tablespoon of salt
- 1 Tablespoon black pepper
- 1/2 Tablespoon ground cumin
- 1 Tablespoon brown sugar
- 10-12 cloves fo fresh garlic, curshed
- 12 oz pork chorizo
- 2(15.8 oz)cans chili beans, drained
- 2(15.8 oz) cans black beans, drained
- 1 (28 oz) can whole tomatoes
- 1 (29 oz) can tomato sauce
- 1 (14.5 oz) can stewed tomatoes
- 1 package of flour tortillas(optional)
- shredded cheader cheese (optional)

- sour cream (optional)

Direction

- **All ingredients should be cut and ready before cooking***
- In a large pot on med. heat add the first 12 items
- Stir and let mixture cook for about 10 minutes, continuing to stir occasionally.
- Add garlic, chorizo, chili beans, and black beans
- Continue to cook and stir
- Add whole tomatoes, tomato sauce, and stewed tomatoes
- Continue to cook on med. heat, stirring for about 30 min. or so until whole tomatoes get soggy.
- Serve in bowls with sour cream and cheese, or on warmed tortillas
- Enjoy!!!!!

347. Toasted Orzo Chicken Soup Recipe

Serving: 4 | Prep: | Cook: 30mins | Ready in:

Ingredients

- One 32 oz. container chicken stock
- 1 lb boneless skinless chicken breasts,or tenders
- 2 Tbs butter
- 3/4 c orzo pasta
- 2 Tbs EVOO
- 1 small zucchini,finely chopped
- 1 carrot,finely chopped
- 1/2 small red bell pepper,finely chopped
- 2 shallots or 1 small onion,finely chopped
- salt and pepper
- 1 c frozen green peas
- 1/4 c fine chopped flat leaf parsley
- 2 tsp grated lemon peel

Direction

- In med. pot, bring chicken stock and chicken to a simmer. Lower the heat and poach chicken about 12 mins.
- Heat Dutch oven or soup pot over med. heat. Add the butter to melt. Add the orzo and cook, stirring, until deeply toasted, 3 to 5 mins. Transfer to a plate.
- Add the EVOO, 2 turns of the pan, to Dutch oven. Add the zucchini, carrot, bell pepper, shallots and garlic; season with salt and pepper. Cook, stirring occasionally, until the vegetables are softened, 7 to 8 mins. Return orzo to pot.
- Remove chicken from stock. Skim and discard the fat from the stock; transfer the stock to the Dutch oven. Chop, dice or shred the chicken and add to the soup with 2 c water. Bring soup to a boil and cook until the orzo is just tender, about 5 mins. Add the peas during the last min. of cooking.
- Turn off heat; stir in parsley and lemon peel. Serve immediately.

---

348.   Too Simple Crock Pot Chicken Recipe

Serving: 4 | Prep: | Cook: 3mins |Ready in:

Ingredients

- 4 chicken breasts; (with the bone)
- 1 package dry onion-flavored soup mix
- Squares of foil as a pocket for each breast

Direction

- Skin the chicken breasts. Cut in half if large so the recipe is now 8 servings).
- Place each breast in a square of foil and sprinkle some of the soup mix on it. (One packet of soup mix is enough for all four breasts; you can use any flavor dry soup you like, experiment! I like using onion mushroom or use a spicy mix).

- Wrap the foil tightly around each breast and place in a crockpot, seam-side up.
- Try to layer the chicken as best you can.
- Cook 8-10 hours on low.
- The chicken is super moist and flavorful and falls right off the bones.

---

349.   Tuxedo Chicken Recipe

Serving: 4 | Prep: | Cook: 20mins |Ready in:

Ingredients

- 6 cups (12 ounces) bow tie pasta (farfalle)
- 4 skinless boneless chicken breasts (about 1 1/3 pounds)
- 1 tablespoon of butter
- 1/2 cup of chopped onion
- 2 cups frozen chopped broccoli
- 1 container (8 ounces) of reduced fat sour cream
- 1 cup half and half
- 1 tablespoon Dijon mustard
- 2 teaspoons of worcestershire sauce
- 1/4 teaspoon garlic powder
- We liked it topped with romano/parm grated cheese

Direction

- Cook pasta according to directions
- Melt butter on medium low in a 12 inch skillet
- Add chopped onion and cook until soft about 3 minutes
- Slice the chicken into 1/2 inch strips
- Raise heat to medium high and add chicken cook until no longer pink in the center.
- Meanwhile, place broccoli in a microwave safe dish and microwave 3-4 minutes until warm
- Remove the chicken from the skillet with a slotted spoon and set aside
- Reduce the heat to medium low & stir in sour cream and half and half into the chicken juices to blend well

- Add mustard, Worcestershire, and garlic powder.
- Stir well and continue to cook until the sauce is slightly thick about 2 minutes (do not boil)
- Return the chicken to the skillet and add the broccoli then raise the heat to medium high and bring the sauce almost to a boil
- Reduce heat to low and simmer to blend the flavors 1-2 minutes
- Drain the bowties and place on a serving plate and top with the chicken mixture
- Serve

350. Very Easy Chicken Parisienne Recipe

Serving: 4 | Prep: | Cook: 45mins | Ready in:

Ingredients

- 6 five ounce chicken breasts, skinned and boned
- 1-10 ounce can cream of mushroom soup
- 1 cup fresh sauteed mushrooms
- 1 cup sour cream
- 1/2 cup sherry
- paprika

Direction

- In pan with butter, sauté' mushrooms, sprinkling a little black pepper and white pepper
- Place chicken in shallow, baking casserole dish
- In medium bowl, combine remaining ingredients, except paprika
- Pour over chicken
- Sprinkle generously with paprika
- Bake at 350 degrees for about 45 minutes, or until tender

351. West Coast Chicken Breasts Recipe

Serving: 4 | Prep: | Cook: 30mins | Ready in:

Ingredients

- 4 large boneless skinless chicken breast halves
- 1/4 cup chopped sun dried tomatoes packed in oil well drained
- 1/4 cup packed chopped fresh basil leaves
- 1 clove garlic minced
- 1 tablespoon olive oil
- 1/4 teaspoon freshly ground pepper
- 1/4 teaspoon paprika
- 1 slice whole wheat bread crumbled to make soft crumbs

Direction

- Preheat oven to 425 then prepare shallow baking dish with olive oil flavored cooking spray.
- Pound chicken breasts to 1/4" thickness then combine tomatoes, basil and garlic in a small bowl.
- Spread tomato mixture evenly over chicken breasts and roll up and place seam side down in dish.
- Combine oil, pepper and paprika in a small bowl then brush evenly over chicken rolls.
- Sprinkle with bread crumbs then press crumbs onto chicken rolls so they adhere.
- Bake 15 minutes or until the chicken is tender and the crumbs are browned.

352. White Bean And Chicken Chili Recipe

Serving: 4 | Prep: | Cook: 45mins | Ready in:

Ingredients

- 1 tablespoon olive oil
- 4 skinless, boneless chicken breasts, cubed

- 1 onion, chopped
- 1-1/4 cups chicken broth
- 1-4 ounce can diced green chiles
- 1 teaspoon garlic powder, more to taste
- 1 teaspoon ground cumin, more to taste
- 1/2 teaspoon oregano
- 1/4 teaspoon cayenne pepper
- 1-15 ounce can cannellini beans, drained and rinsed
- chives for garnish
- sour cream for garnish
- Shredded Monterey Jack chees for garnish
- cooked rice or baked potato for serving

Direction

- In a large saucepan, heat oil over medium-high heat.
- Cook chicken and onions in oil for 5 minutes, until onion is tender.
- Stir in chicken broth, chilies, garlic, cumin, oregano and cayenne pepper.
- Reduce heat and simmer 15 minutes.
- Stir in beans and simmer an additional 20 minutes, or until chicken is thoroughly cooked.
- Serve over rice or potato and garnish with Monterey jack cheese, sour cream and chopped chives.

---

353. White Chicken Enchiladas Recipe

Serving: 0 | Prep: | Cook: 1hours |Ready in:

Ingredients

- Makes: 1- 9X13 pan, 6-8 servings Prep: 1hour Cooking Time: 30 minutes
- Ingredients:
- 4 chicken thighs or 2 Split chicken breasts
- 2 cups of chicken stock(from boiled chicken breasts)
- 1/4 cup butter

- 1/4 cup flour
- 1 can green chiles
- 1 1/2 cups sour cream
- 1 bunch of fresh cilantro chopped(split in half)
- 1 small onion
- 3 cloves of garlic
- 4 tsp chipotle peppers in adobo sauce, just the sauce(add more if you want it spicy)
- kosher salt to taste
- 16 oz of colby jack shredded(split in half)
- 1 pkg of flour tortillas
- 1 bag of tortilla chips

Direction

- Put chicken in a large pot, cover with water and a 1tsp of kosher salt. Bring to boil. Turn down to simmer for about 20 minutes or until chicken is done. Pull chicken out, cover with foil and let rest. Once chicken is cool to handle, pull skin and fat off. Shred or break up remaining chicken in a large bowl. Dice onion. Add to bowl. Add 1/2 of chopped cilantro. 1/2 cup sour cream, 1/2 can green chilies, 8oz of shredded cheese. Toss until combined.
- Take a 9X13 casserole pan and spray with cooking spray. Now, roll enchiladas. Take one flour tortilla at a time add filling and roll tightly. Put rolled tortilla seam side down in prepared pan, and repeat until pan is full or filling is gone.
- Make enchilada sauce. In large saucepan melt butter, add flour to make a rue stir and cook for one minute until bubbly. Add 2 cups of chicken stock slowly and cook until bubbly and thickened. Add remaining green chilies, adobo sauce, and sour cream. Heat thoroughly but do not boil again. Remove from heat. Pour over enchiladas. Bake a 350 for 30 minutes. Once bubbly, add remaining shredded cheese and return to oven for 5-10 minutes. Sprinkle with remaining chopped cilantro and serve with a side of tortilla chips. Enjoy!!
- Quick tips: You can use already prepared chicken, a rotisserie from the grocery store or any chicken you already have cooked from a previous meal. You can use bottom chicken

stock and use the 2 cups of it that the recipe calls for. This eliminates a lot of time preparing the chicken and stock. Also, this recipe should give you extra chicken stock to freeze for another meal as well!

354. White Chili Recipe

Serving: 8 | Prep: | Cook: 60mins | Ready in:

Ingredients

- 3 cups onion, chopped
- 4 cloves garlic, minced
- 2 tablespoons olive oil
- 2 jalapeno peppers, minced
- 8 ounces chopped green chiles, 2 cans
- 2 tablespoons cumin, or more to taste
- 1 teaspoon oregano
- 1/2 teaspoon ancho chile powder
- 1/2 teaspoon salt
- 2 cups chicken broth, canned
- 40 ounces cannelini beans, drained
- 4 cups cooked chicken breast halves, shredded
- 1 can corn, DelMonte Summer Fresh - keeps the crunch!

Direction

- In a soup pot over medium-high heat, sauté onions and garlic in oil until onion is soft.
- Add jalapenos, chilies, cumin, oregano, Ancho chili powder and salt. Cook 1 minute.
- Stir in chicken broth, beans and chicken. Bring to boil
- Reduce heat and simmer, uncovered, for 20-25 minutes or until slightly thickened.
- Stir in corn and continue heating another 15 minutes.
- To serve, ladle into bowls and top with a dollop of sour cream and shredded cheddar.
- NOTE: You can use leftover turkey for this...yum!

355. White Wine Marined Grilled Chicken With Tomatoes And Basil Recipe

Serving: 4 | Prep: | Cook: 20mins | Ready in:

Ingredients

- 1 small white onion sliced
- 3 cloves garlic crushed
- 2-1/2 cups dry white wine
- 4 boneless skinless chicken breasts
- 3 cups chicken broth
- 1/2 teaspoon salt
- 1 teaspoon freshly ground black pepper
- 2 cups peeled seeded and chopped fresh tomatoes
- 1/4 cup butter
- 2 tablespoons extra virgin olive oil
- 1/3 cup thinly sliced basil leaves

Direction

- Combine onion, garlic and wine then bring to simmer.
- Carefully ignite fumes of wine.
- When flame subsides pour into container large enough to contain breasts without overlapping.
- Chill then add breasts to cold marinade making sure they are completely covered.
- Cover and refrigerate 24 to 36 hours.
- Remove chicken breasts from marinade and set aside then strain liquid into small saucepan.
- Bring gently to simmer but do not allow mixture to boil.
- Skim surface of anything that floats to top.
- Continue simmering and skimming until wine is clear about 20 minutes.
- Add chicken broth to wine and skimming as it cooks reduce gently to 1/2 cup.
- This will take about 45 minutes.
- Remove chicken breasts from liquid and season with salt and pepper.

- Grill over medium high heat until cooked through but still moist about 6 minutes per side.
- Add tomatoes to reduced wine and broth then bring to simmer.
- Stir in butter by the tablespoon until incorporated then add oil and basil leaves.
- Divide sauce among 4 plates and top with grilled chicken breast.

356. White Wine Sauced Chicken With Dried Apricots & Cranberries Recipe

Serving: 0 | Prep: | Cook: 50mins | Ready in:

Ingredients

- 3-4 boneless, skinless chicken breasts
- 1 medium onion, diced
- ~~~~~~~~~~~~~~~~~~~
- spice rub:
- 1/2 tsp ground coriander
- 1/2 tsp ground cumin
- 1/2 tsp Spanish paprika
- 1/4 tsp dry mustard
- 1/8 tsp cinnamon
- salt and pepper to taste
- ~~~~~~~~~~~~~~~~~~
- 3/4 cup dry white wine
- 1/2 cup dried apricots
- 1/4 cup dried cranberries
- 1/2 cup chicken broth

Direction

- Preheat oven to 350.
- Sprinkle chicken with the spice rub on both sides and allow to "marinate" at room temperature while preparing the dried fruit.
- Heat wine to just boiling. Remove from heat - add apricots and cranberries and soak, covered, for at least 10 minutes to plump.

- Brown the chicken in olive oil. (Skin side down first- that is, if there would be skin!) When you turn the chicken to brown the other side, add the onions. Push chicken to the outside of the skillet and sauté the onions until slightly soft.
- Arrange chicken and onions in a baking dish (with cover). Mix chicken broth into the wine/fruit mixture and pour over the top of the chicken and onions.
- Cover and bake 30-35 minutes.
- Serve with rice pilaf or couscous.

357. Zesty Chorizo Chicken And Rice Recipe

Serving: 4 | Prep: | Cook: 40mins | Ready in:

Ingredients

- 1 to 2 chopped chicken breast
- 1 pkg. ground chorizo sausage
- 1 medium onion, chopped
- 2 cloves garlic, minced
- 3/4 cup uncooked rice (I used brown instant, but use what works for you)
- 1 3/4 cup chicken broth
- 1/2 cup salsa (for a milder version, use just stewed tomatoes or some tomato sauce)
- 1/2 cup whole kernal corn (or peas, or carrots--your choice)
- 1 tbsp oil

Direction

- Heat oil in skillet. Add chicken and brown lightly. Add chorizo sausage, onion and garlic. Use fork and stir sausage while it's cooking so that it will brown in small bits. Cook until all meat is done and veggies are tender.
- Add rice, broth and salsa or tomatoes. Heat to a boil. Cover and cook over low heat for 15 minutes, or until rice is tender.
- Stir in corn or peas and cook, covered about 5 more minutes.

- You may want to top it with cheese, some broken tortilla chips, sour cream, cilantro, or any other of your favorite toppings. Enjoy!

358. A Tu Fae Recipe

Serving: 6 | Prep: | Cook: 35mins | Ready in:

Ingredients

- 1 pound of thawed chicken breast or subsitute with Polish sausage
- 1 can of rotel (hot or mild) do not drain.
- 1 can cream of chicken soup
- 1 can cream of mushroom soup
- 1 cup of milk
- served on top of rice

Direction

- Thaw chicken breast in microwave until it turns white
- Cut the chicken breast into smaller bite size pieces
- Pour the cream of chicken, cream of mushroom soup, rotel, and chicken pieces into a large sauce pan.
- Heat to boiling and then turn down to med heat and simmer for 25-30 minutes.
- You can add salt and/or pepper for flavor.
- Tips:
- Depending on the rice you use try and time it to be finished about the same.
- When you refrigerate leftovers keep in mind that it does tend to become spicier the next day.

359. Baked Chicken Breasts To Perfection Recipe

Serving: 4 | Prep: | Cook: 35mins | Ready in:

Ingredients

- 2 1 1/2# whole chicken breasts with skin,rinced and dried
- 2 Tbs. soft butter
- 1/2 tsp. salt
- pepper as needed
- 3 Tbs. vegetable oil

Direction

- Preheat oven to 450F.
- Line bottom of broiler pan with heavy foil
- Place broiler rack on top
- In a small bowl mix salt and butter
- Gently free skin an both sides of breasts and with a small spoon insert 1/4 of the mixture to the center of each breast and smooth it around, coating the breasts under the skin
- Oil outside of breasts with 1 1/2 tsp. oil each
- Salt and pepper underside of chicken
- Use only pepper on top
- Spread ribs apart so breast rests on the ribs and they don't fold under.
- Bake 35-40 minutes till done
- The following is why this is a veritable recipe:
- Add 1 Tbs. chopped kalamata olives-2 tsp. chopped parsley and 1 tsp. lemon zest to butter-follow above recipe
- Add: 2 tsp. chopped chipotle in adobe sauce, 1 tsp. ground cumin and 2 tsp. chopped cilantro to butter mix
- Add: 2 cloves of minced garlic, 2 tsp. fresh rosemary, minced and 1 tsp. lemon zest etc.
- Add: 2 Tbs. dried porcini mushrooms, reconstrued with boiling water, drained and chopped finely and 1 tsp. each fresh thyme and rosemary to butter etc.

360. Chinese Chicken And Shrimp Recipe

Serving: 4 | Prep: | Cook: 10mins | Ready in:

Ingredients

- 2 chicken breasts boned and cubed
- 21/2 tablespoons oil
- 4 teaspoons thinly sliced fresh ginger
- 1 onion thinly sliced
- 1/4 cup sliced celery
- 2 teaspoons cornstarch
- 1 cup (250)ml chicken stock
- 11/2 tablespoons sherry
- 11/2 tablespoons brown sugar
- 1 green pepper cut in squares
- 1/2lb(250)g shelled shrimp
- 21/2 tablespoons soy sauce

Direction

- 1. Quickly brown the chicken cubes in the oil until crisp on all sides in a frypan.
- 2. Add the ginger onion and celery and cook until soft.
- 3. Mix the cornstarch with the chicken stock.
- 4 Add to the chicken mixture and bring to a boil
- 5 Stir in the remaining ingredients and cook over a low heat for about ten minutes stirring constantly.

---

361.   Creamy Chicken Enchiladas Recipe

Serving: 510 | Prep: | Cook: 30mins | Ready in:

Ingredients

- 3 cooked chicken breasts cut into bite size pieces or shredded
- 1 can of refried beans (regular can, not large)
- 1 small can chopped green chillies with their juice
- 1 pkg cream cheese (fat free tastes just as good in this recipe)
- 1 pkg large flour tortillas (10 count)
- 1 large can red enchilada sauce 9 (can use green instead if you like)
- shredded cheese (I use Fiesta or Mexican blend, something with mozerella in it or just straight mozeralla is good too)

Direction

- In a skillet combine chicken, beans, green chilies, cream cheese and heat until all cream cheese is melted and everything is combined well.
- Place 2 Tbsp. or so of mixture in each tortilla and wrap up and place in lightly greased 9x13 baking dish (sometimes I use one 9x13 and one 9x9 because I run out of room).
- Continue until all mixture is used up.
- Pour enchilada sauce over the enchiladas and bake at 350 degrees F for 20 minutes.
- Add shredded cheese to top of enchiladas and place back in oven for 5 to 10 more minutes.
- Serve.

---

362.   Lemon Chicken Recipe

Serving: 2 | Prep: | Cook: 30mins | Ready in:

Ingredients

- 1 tablespoon butter
- 1 tablespoon olive oil
- 2 boneless chicken breast halves
- 4 garlic cloves, chopped
- 8 slices lemon
- 2 tablespoons fresh lemon juice
- Chopped fresh parsley

Direction

- Melt butter with olive oil in heavy medium skillet over high heat. Add chicken to skillet and sauté until brown, about 2 minutes per side. Overlap 4 lemon slices on each piece of chicken. Pour lemon juice around chicken. Simmer until chicken is cooked through, about 5 minutes

363. Potato Chip Chicken Recipe

Serving: 4 | Prep: | Cook: 30mins | Ready in:

Ingredients

- 4 skinless boneless chicken breasts
- 1/2 cup yogurt (or sour cream)
- potato chips (any flavor you want)

Direction

- Preheat oven to 350 degrees F.
- Put potato chips into ziplock bag and thoroughly crush them with a rolling pin
- Dredge chicken breasts in yogurt
- Roll in potato chips
- Place chicken breasts in greased baking dish
- Bake for 30 min., serve hot

364. Sour Cream And White Wine Chicken Recipe

Serving: 4 | Prep: | Cook: 60mins | Ready in:

Ingredients

- 1 cup low fat sour cream
- 1 can of condensed cream of chicken soup
- 1/3 cup dry white wine
- 4 boneless skinless chicken breasts
- 1 medium red onion chopped
- 2 cups small mushrooms quartered

Direction

- Preheat oven to 350 F
- Combine sour cream, soup and wine, mix well with a whisk. Add mushrooms and onion, stir.
- Put chicken in a 9X13 inch baking dish. Pour sour cream mix over the chicken. Bake in the preheated oven for an hour till chicken is cooked through.

365. Super Kraft Dinner Recipe

Serving: 4 | Prep: | Cook: 25mins | Ready in:

Ingredients

- 2 bxs. Kraft Dinner...macaroni and cheese
- 2 boneless skinless chicken breasts
- onion
- 2 cloves garlic
- 1/4 cup apple juice
- 2 -3 cups broccoli florets, cooked in salted water
- 1/2 tsp. dill weed
- salt -pepper

Direction

- Prepare Kraft Dinner as directed
- Meanwhile, cut up chicken in bite size pcs. and cook in some olive oil until completely done!
- Remove chicken from pan.
- Add more butter or oil if needed in pan and keep pan hot.
- Chop up onion and garlic.
- Put salt-pepper and dill over them and sauté in the hot oil for a few minutes.
- Pour apple juice in the pan and deglaze.
- Return chicken to pan and cover, simmer for a few mins.
- Then mix in the prepared Kraft Dinner.
- Add the cooked broccoli and mix gently.

Index

Conclusion

Thank you again for downloading this book!

I hope you enjoyed reading about my book!

If you enjoyed this book, please take the time to share your thoughts and post a review on Amazon. It'd be greatly appreciated!

Write me an honest review about the book – I truly value your opinion and thoughts and I will incorporate them into my next book, which is already underway.

Thank you!

If you have any questions, **feel free to contact at:** *author@friesrecipes.com*

Eva Rabe

friesrecipes.com

Printed in Great Britain
by Amazon